Report of the Bicentennial Commission on Education
for the Profession of Teaching of the
American Association of Colleges for Teacher Education

Educating a Profession

REPRINT WITH POSTSCRIPT 1985

Commission Members and Authors:
Robert B. Howsam
Chair
Dean C. Corrigan
George W. Denemark
Robert J. Nash

Postscript 1985
Robert B. Howsam
Dean C. Corrigan
George W. Denemark

ACKNOWLEDGMENTS AND DISCLAIMERS

American Association of Colleges for Teacher Education

This material does not necessarily reflect the viewpoints of the American Association of Colleges for Teacher Education (AACTE). AACTE is printing this position paper to stimulate discussion, study, and experimentation. AACTE expresses its heart-felt appreciation to those individuals, organizations, and agencies that contributed to the work of the AACTE Bicentennial Commission on Education for the Profession of Teaching (CEPT). AACTE acknowledges with appreciation the time, resources, competence, and commitment which the Commission members contributed. This report constitutes their collective wisdom. Their ideas and recommendations are a standing tribute to their professionalism and a valued contribution to the rethinking on the profession of teaching, on the threshold of the American Bicentennial.

To
George W. Denemark
1921-1985

Contents

FOREWORD
TO THE 1985 EDITION

A decade has passed since the Bicentennial Commission on Education for the Profession of Teaching (CEPT) initiated its work, which culminated in *Educating a Profession*. In the intervening years an enormous amount of effort has focused on reforming and revitalizing the education profession. The essential message of *Educating a Profession* was that the training arm of the profession offered a vital instrument for improving schools and teaching. The improvement of teacher education—both preservice and inservice—was and still is an essential corollary of reforms proposed and/or implemented elsewhere in the system.

With the publication of *A Nation At Risk*, the report of the National Commission on Excellence in Education, the efforts of the CEPT group found new meaning and importance. The national study panel amplified the earlier concerns and focused new attention on the nation's schools and upon those who staff them. Subsequent reports and books added to the attention given to schooling in America. In this climate a rereading of *Educating a Profession* prompts much introspection and analysis. If we had been serious in our efforts to implement the recommendations of the Bicentennial Commission on Education for the Profession of Teaching, would we be today a "nation at risk"? If we had paid heed to the importance of moving teaching from the ranks of a semi- or emerging profession to that of a genuine profession, would we have suffered the contemporary criticism of the teaching force? If we had sought to implement the proposals for transforming the governance of teacher education and renewing our programs, would we be the subject of the hundreds of task force reports, studies, analyses, and other efforts through which we have suffered?

In 1976, Drs. Howsam, Denemark, Corrigan, and Nash laid out an impressive agenda for transforming teacher education. Nine years later, little of that agenda has been achieved. Why? Three of the original authors have examined what they originally prepared, investigated events in the ensuing period, and now offer their analysis of ways to fulfill the original objective of fashioning an intervention that would dramatically move teaching to the status of a profession. They have worked for more than a year in preparing the analysis that follows.

The importance of their analysis, particularly in light of contemporary reform efforts, has created the need for AACTE to reissue *Educating a Profession*. The authors present a bold analysis of the constraints and limitations that have prevented major reform. We have included that material as a postscript. We are deeply appreciative of such efforts. All will not agree with the diagnosis—nor with the solutions; but whether we agree or disagree we must convey our appreciation to those who are willing to present new ideas, confront the challenges that greet such ideas, and provide leadership to the profession. The authors have our gratitude.

It is once again our responsibility to carefully consider the message of the revitalization of teacher education and the reform of the teaching profession. The message is very clear. Are we up to the challenge of accomplishing great change in the coming decade? I believe we are. I believe we must move forward.

David C. Smith
President
AACTE

January 1985

Foreword

In 1976 the American people celebrate 200 years of a unique experiment in the annals of human endeavor. The Bicentennial celebrations represent the triumph of an experiment in which rationality and equality were the guiding principles. Never before have so many people from such diverse backgrounds and experiences had the opportunity to fashion their own lives and the life of their society. Not without imperfections and often despite serious flaws, our nation has sought to weave a tapestry of different colors, beliefs, and ideas that is both resilient and brilliant. The experiment has succeeded because men and women have learned the value and importance of debate and discussion, of interaction and involvement.

As part of that celebration commemorating the American experiment, the Commission on Education for the Profession of Teaching (CEPT) has issued a clarion call on the importance of Educating a Profession. The call is not only for transformation and change in the governance of teacher education but also in the preparation and renewal of America's teachers.

The Commission was appointed by the Board of Directors of the AACTE to study and develop a report that would reveal the present structure, process, and governance of teacher education and chart a course for the future. Robert B. Howsam, as chairman of the Commission, Dean C. Corrigan, George W. Denemark, and Robert J. Nash worked for nearly two years to prepare this report and are to be commended for their diligence, industry, and scholarly study.

The ideas, recommendations, and strategies presented are those of the Commission and are an effort to encourage study and change in American teacher education. They are provided to fellow teacher educators first, and then to other members of the profession for the purpose of stimulating debate and discussion. It is anticipated that from such debate will evolve statements of consensus that can be carried into other forums and arenas. There, dialogue and discussion will promote still wider consensus and agreement. The ultimate purpose of this report, therefore, is to fashion an intervention from which will emerge a more dynamic, responsive, and proactive profession.

In the nearly 150 years since the development of the first normal schools in America, teacher education has undergone significant and far-reaching changes. Certainly no change has been more significant in the institutional transformation of American teacher education than its diminishing status and role. Today, if teaching is a major profession, it is the only major profession which does not depend almost entirely for the preparation of its practitioners upon a separately organized professional school. To reach the goal of professional attainment will, however, take more than one report or one association's efforts.

At 200 years in our nation's history, the profession of teaching is fragmented and divided. This report provides a strategy for putting it together.

Educating a Profession presents the challenge and course for action. Teacher educators must take the first step!

Professionals who possess the scholarship, dedication, and discipline to develop considered positions on fundamental issues and have the courage to submit those positions to the rigorous scrutiny of their peers deserve the highest possible praise. Whether we agree or disagree with the views expressed, we must respect, support, and encourage those who are willing to lead the dialogue. It is a risky business taking strong stands on controversial issues. The authors have had the courage to put their professional reputations on the line to aid not only the AACTE but the entire profession of teaching. On behalf of the Board of Directors I extend to them our deep appreciation and urge each of us to consider their positions with the careful thought that such a very significant document deserves.

John Dunworth
President
American Association of Colleges
for Teacher Education

January 1976

Acknowledgments

The Commission acknowledges the contributions made by some very special people.

The Board of Directors of AACTE who entrusted this important assignment to us and lent continuing support throughout.

David Imig, AACTE staff liaison to the Commission, who met with the Commission throughout its work and contributed immeasurably to all facets of the process of preparing the Report.

Edward Ducharme, professor, University of Vermont, for his written contributions and insightful critique at the August retreat and on many other occasions from the time the Commission was formed.

Michael Minor, assistant professor, University of Kentucky, for his involvement in discussion and clarification of the issues and reviews of the literature.

Joel L. Burdin, Annette MacKinnon, and Ruth Barker of AACTE for technical assistance in preparing the final copy for publication and getting the Report published.

Betty Triplett, University of Kentucky; Carol O'Connor, University of Houston; and Greg Voorheis, University of Vermont; graduate assistants, for their research and collation of materials.

Our secretaries and office staff who spent countless hours on manuscripts and correspondence on top of their regular duties. Jewel Harper and Diane Hilscher, University of Houston, Mildred O'Dell and Katherine Greene from the University of Kentucky. Barbara Matthews, University of Vermont, for her expert clerical assistance in typing the materials many, many times, including the final copy.

On October 2-3, 1975, a number of reactors were invited to a meeting in Kentucky to critique a draft copy of the Report from their personal perspective, with no consensus expected. Responses at this meeting were particularly helpful in identifying specific gaps in the Report and areas which needed further clarification. The people who so unselfishly gave their time to this task and to whom the Commission is indebted are as follows:

Robert D. Bhaerman, director of research, American Federation of Teachers (AFT)

Phyllis Black, teacher, Van Antwerp Middle School (N.Y.)

Dave Darland, associate director, Instruction and Professional Development, National Education Association (NEA)

William Drummond, professor, College of Education, University of Florida

Martin Haberman, dean, Division of Urban Outreach, University of Wisconsin-Milwaukee

Joseph Kerns, program specialist, Teacher Corps, United States Office of Education (USOE)

Myron Lieberman, professor, College of Education, University of Southern California

Margaret Lindsay, professor, Teachers College, Columbia University

Paul Olson, professor, Department of English, University of Nebraska

*Donald E. Orlosky, director, Leadership Training Institute (LTI), College of Education, University of South Florida

Edward Pomeroy, executive director, AACTE

Kevin Ryan, associate dean, College of Education, The Ohio State University

*Allen Schmieder, chief, Support Programs, USOE

B.O. Smith, professor emeritus, University of South Florida

*William L. Smith, director, Teacher Corps, USOE

A special note of thanks is extended to William L. Smith, director of Teacher Corps, and Allen Schmieder, chief, Support Programs, Division of Educational Systems Development, for making it possible to link the work of the Commission with Teacher Corps and educational personnel development (EPD) projects (USOE) and thereby provide some funds for staff assistance for Commission activities. The Report, published by AACTE, in turn will be utilized by Teacher Corps and the EPD project personnel.

The Commission expresses both appreciation and apologies to colleagues who responded to requests to submit papers and/or react to the Report. Because the Commission did not receive funds for staff assistance until late in the process, communication with the many people who offered help was not carried out as originally intended. As promised in earlier communications, all papers sent to the Commission have been forwarded for possible inclusion in the ERIC system and review by the *Journal of Teacher Education*. Our hope is that these persons and their associates will be central in the subsequent uses of the Report.

While highly appreciative of the many suggestions from colleagues, the Commission has maintained its independence throughout the preparation of this Report and is fully responsible for its contents.

---

*Unable to attend. Critique prepared and presented to Commission.

Bicentennial '76:
New Directions

Ours is a "lover's quarrel"
with our professional world.

The year is 1976.

Our nation is celebrating its Bicentennial anniversary and taking advantage of the opportunity to renew its commitments and revitalize its efforts.

As a part of its own Bicentennial activities, the American Association of Colleges for Teacher Education (AACTE) established a Commission on Education for the Profession of Teaching (CEPT). CEPT was charged with a comprehensive effort to examine all aspects of American education and the teaching profession which have relevance for teacher education institutions and the Association, to draft recommendations, and to report in time for the AACTE Annual Meeting of the Bicentennial year. It was the Association's intention to use the report in charting its directions as it entered the third century of this nation's history. What follows constitutes the report of the Commission.

Anniversaries customarily have two faces. One looks back from whence we have come; the other looks forward in anticipation of the future. The look back rarely yields full satisfaction, so *celebration* is accompanied by resolve to make further progress. This Commission was not permitted the luxury of celebrating past accomplishments. It was not asked to chronicle the history of the teaching profession and teacher education. It was not asked to highlight achievements to date. And it was not asked to seek agreements with and among the other parties involved in the profession and teacher education. Such interactions by design were left for the Association as a priority agenda for the immediate future.

In many ways, the Commission would have been more comfortable in beginning with a history of accomplishments of the teaching profession and in using such a chronicle as a prelude to challenges for

1

the future. Our awareness as a nation of two centuries of achievement helps us to have faith in our ability to meet our present social, economic, and political challenges, serious though they undoubtedly are. In the same way, realization of the contributions of schools and teachers to two centuries of progress helps keep in perspective problems facing educational institutions and those who serve within them. The absence of "celebration" in this report hopefully will not obscure the professional good will and dedication which underlie the descriptions, analyses, and recommendations which constitute the report of this Commission. To paraphrase Robert Frost, ours is a "lover's quarrel" with our professional world.

The American Association of Colleges for Teacher Education and this Commission are deeply and appreciatively aware of the contributions America's schools have made. Naturally, from a biased perspective, we attribute much of the success of the schools to teachers who have given dedicated service. Nothing in the body of this report can in any way detract from that. Nor is there anything in this report that needs to be viewed negatively either by teachers or by teacher educators. All of us have known for decades that teacher education has never been adequate. Equally, we have known that changing conditions have made teaching progressively more difficult. The gap between what we have needed to do and what we have been able to do has been no secret. For too long, teachers and teacher education have proclaimed their professional status, knowing that it was more aspiration than reality.

Elementary and secondary teachers in the United States are over 2.4 million strong. They are well organized, even though not unified. And they have developed power both in a political and an organizational bargaining sense. They are moving rapidly to improve working conditions and self-governance aspects of being a profession. These accomplishments, important as they are, cannot by themselves bring self-fulfillment as a profession, however. The essence of a profession is possession of competence—including knowledge, values, and skills—needed to deliver a professional level of service to society. That individual teachers often do display a high level of competence and significant success in teaching is evident, but the existence of these relatively few teachers does not in itself make a profession. Not until all teachers have an adequate level of competence, and not until the profession itself and its preparing institutions can demonstrate that the ability of teachers is due to the quality of their preparation, can we claim to have a genuine profession.

If the promise of the teaching profession is to be achieved, we must attend to the processes by which its knowledge base is developed and transmitted. Much of this present report addresses itself to problems in the areas of development of bases for professional competence and

2

teacher preparation. Another problem concerns disunity within professional ranks and lack of recognition of kinship between school-based and campus-based professional educators. This report describes the relationships which should exist between these two groups and suggests governance mechanisms to promote this relationship. Less well understood are the myriad of problems which exist within and among institutions which prepare teachers. At the recognized risk of producing some divisiveness within the membership of our own organization, the report probes this array of problems. Teacher education will have to put its own institutional and organizational houses in order if it is to survive, thrive, and make its potential contribution.

The design of the total study is foreshadowed by the name given to the Commission. Two concepts are key, namely *Profession* and *Education for*. By its very nature, many view teaching as belonging among the established professions. Its organizations and teachers themselves long have proclaimed that teaching is a profession. Despite this, professional status and circumstances have yet to be achieved. Somewhere within society, within the school as institution, within the organized profession, within preparation institutions, within the governance system, within the nature of the teaching act, and elsewhere exist forces which interact to inhibit what seems to be the destined thrust of teaching to mature professionally. Clearly there will be no simple solution. Neither will there be any single dominant factor. Instead a complex of forces must be expected.

The report concentrates first on what constitutes a profession.

Chapter One states a set of characteristics of professions and semi-professions. Chapter Two assesses the extent to which teaching presently meets the criteria of professions. The discrepancies are marked. Central is the relative absence of a validated body of knowledge and skills subscribed to by the profession, passed by means of preparation programs to the inductees, and used as the basis for determining entrance to and continuance in the profession. Also, governance practices are less well developed in the teaching profession. Chapter Two looks at societal factors, conditions in schools, and the nature of teaching.

Chapter Three examines the various elements involved in the governance of teacher education and explores collaborative relationships among participating partners. Chapter Four considers the array of questions embedded in preservice, inservice, and continuing teacher preparation. Chapter Four also highlights the concept of adequate "life space" within which teacher educators can conduct effective initial preparation and subsequent life-long efforts at professional proficiency. In addition, Chapter Four makes recommendations for the education of teacher educators.

Chapter Five considers the issues of individual and institutional

3

quality control and explores their implications for certification, program approval, recruitment and selection, and supply and demand. This chapter also addresses the problems of adequate resources and necessary funding. Chapters Four and Five develop the concept of human service educator and its far-reaching implications for the profession of teaching. The section on "Reflections" summarizes and clarifies some concepts and themes which have special meaning for the Commission.

What follows, then, is the work of a small group of people, drawn from AACTE institutions, who have striven—with the aid of a small group of reactors from other organizations—to identify the problems and challenges which face teacher education, to identify solutions, and to propose courses of action. The report is not a blueprint. Rather, it is an unfinished but forceful agenda. "The floor is open for discussion."

Though we view the courses of action to be taken as more or less open, the need for action is not. Events of tremendous importance for teacher education are taking place at an accelerating pace.[1] Only a determinedly proactive stance can insure that teacher education institutions as we know them will have a significant role in the emerging systems of teacher education.

FOOTNOTES

1. E.C. Pomeroy, "What's Going on in Teacher Education—The View from Washington," *Journal of Teacher Education* 26, no. 3 (Fall 1975): 196-201.

ONE

The Professions: A Conceptual Model

*Professionals have a strong service motivation
and lifetime commitment to competence.*

TOWARD A DEFINITION OF PROFESSION

Every society has certain functions to be performed if life within it is to be sustained and if the quality of life is to be maintained or improved. Societies differ, however, in the way they organize to provide for performance of these functions. Simple societies diffuse the functions over populations. Complex societies, on the other hand, create work specialization and invent institutions and organizations to facilitate delivery and improvement of services.

Over history, people have differentiated between the kinds of work to be performed on the basis of a task's importance and difficulties. In complex modern societies, the occupational categories include professional, semiprofessional, paraprofessional, skilled, and unskilled trades categories. Each of these represents *service to others*, made necessary by the reality that few if any people possess the knowledge and skills needed or the inclination to be self-sufficient in meeting their own needs. Thus, the difference between levels of occupations is not in the *element* of service, but in the *nature* of the service. Some needs are so fundamental that failure to meet them seriously interferes with the quality of life or with life itself. Professions customarily involve this kind of service.

People in their daily lives deal with problems such as health, security, and learning. In doing so, they draw on such knowledge as their own experience has given them. On the other hand, they are likely to confront circumstances where their own ability is inadequate to protect them. At these times, they seek expert assistance. In primitive societies, people seek the services of witch doctors, elders, or chiefs—"experts" into whose hands have passed such knowledge, skills, and rituals as the society has accrued. In modern societies, they seek the services of professionals who have been educated in the most valid knowledge and skills available from research and practice. In both primitive and modern cases, the individual is turning to the role or institution—not primarily to the individual practitioner as such—which is responsible for insuring that service to the client is competent within the limits of the existing art or science. Since most people alone are not competent to judge the level of expertise of the one who is to help, *they must trust.* The profession is the source of that confidence and assurance.

In the hierarchical structuring of occupations within our society, the professions occupy the top position. Quite naturally, occupations strive to as high a position within the hierarchy as they can possibly achieve. The word *profession* has been self-applied to many occupations, especially in modern times. Opting to use the name does not, however, insure that the status of profession will thereby be achieved. Also, occupations which are high in stature are not particularly eager to have their privileges shared more widely.

CHARACTERISTICS OF A PROFESSION

As is often the case in societal matters, criteria used by the society in determining occupational status tend to be obscure and imprecise. Students of occupations—notably sociologists—have devoted their attention to discerning and stating the criteria, however. The list of characteristics which follows is a composite drawn from a variety of authoritative sources. [1]

1. Professions are occupationally related social institutions established and maintained as a means of providing essential services to the individual and the society.
2. Each profession is concerned with an identified area of need or function (e.g., maintenance of physical and emotional health, preservation of rights and freedom, enhancing the opportunity to learn).
3. The profession collectively, and the professional individually, possesses a body of knowledge and a repertoire of behaviors and skills (professional culture) needed in the practice of the profession; such knowledge, behavior, and skills normally are not possessed by the nonprofessional.
4. The members of the profession are involved in decision making in the service of the client, the decisions being made in accordance with the most valid knowledge available, against a

background of principles and theories, and within the context of possible impact on other related conditions or decisions.

5. The profession is based on one or more undergirding disciplines from which it draws basic insights and upon which it builds its own applied knowledge and skills.
6. The profession is organized into one or more professional associations which, within broad limits of social accountability, are granted autonomy in control of the actual work of the profession and the conditions which surround it (admissions, educational standards, examination and licensing, career line, ethical and performance standards, professional discipline).
7. The profession has agreed-upon performance standards for admission to the profession and for continuance within it.
8. Preparation for and induction to the profession is provided through a protracted preparation program, usually in a professional school on a college or university campus.
9. There is a high level of public trust and confidence in the profession and in individual practitioners, based upon the profession's demonstrated capacity to provide service markedly beyond that which would otherwise be available.
10. Individual practitioners are characterized by a strong service motivation and lifetime commitment to competence.
11. Authority to practice in any individual case derives from the client or the employing organization; accountability for the competence of professional practice within the particular case is to the profession itself.
12. There is relative freedom from direct on-the-job supervision and from direct public evaluation of the individual practitioner. The professional accepts responsibility in the name of his or her profession and is accountable through his or her profession to the society.

CHARACTERISTICS OF SEMIPROFESSIONS

In addition to the classic professions of law, medicine, theology, and university teaching and to newer professions such as architecture, engineering, and optometry, there is a much longer list of occupations which aspire to professional status. Some of these can be dismissed as pretenders. Others are somewhere near the periphery of professional status on the basis of the criteria specified earlier. Because they are dynamically developing and approaching societal and professional acceptance, these may be described as *emergent professions*. (Figure 1 indicates the categories or levels of professions to which reference is made.) They are about to become professions. Goode identifies social work as a semiprofession that will become a profession in the foreseeable future.[2]

The semiprofessions are occupations which sociologists have chosen to define as meeting some of the criteria of professions, but not others. Etzioni notes that:

Their training is shorter, their status is less legitimated, their right to privileged communication less established, there is less of a specialized body of knowledge, and they have less autonomy from supervision or societal control than "the" professions.[3]

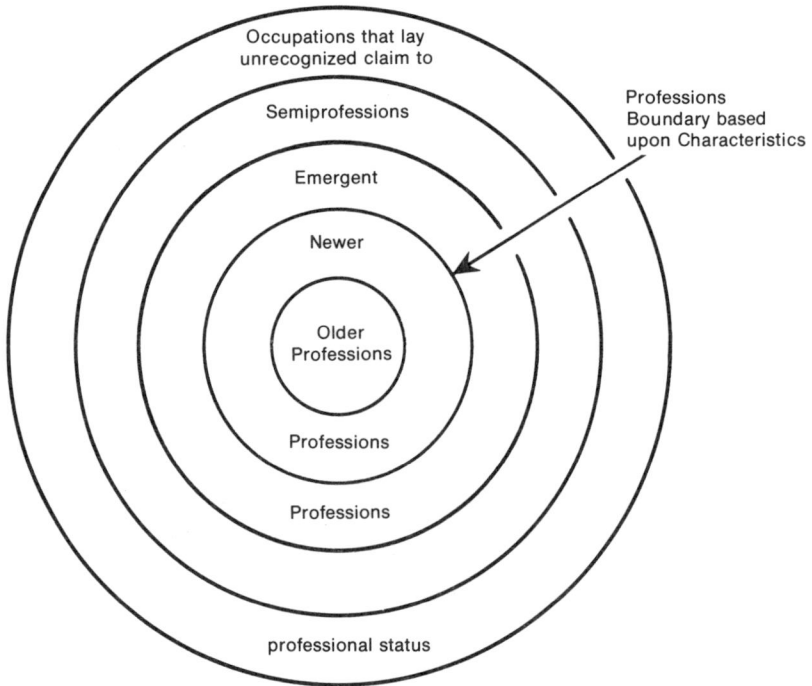

FIGURE 1. Levels of Professions

These characteristics, supplemented by others drawn from different sources, constitute a list of 12 characteristics of semiprofessions. In most cases, the characteristic is expressed in terms of the degree to which semiprofessions meet the criteria of mature professions as listed earlier.

1. Lower in occupational status.
2. Shorter training periods.

3. Lack of societal acceptance that the nature of the service and/or the level of expertise justifies the autonomy which is granted to the professions.
4. A less specialized and less highly developed body of knowledge and skills.
5. Markedly less emphasis on theoretical and conceptual bases for practice.
6. A tendency for the professional to identify with the employment institution more and with the profession less. (Note that it is not the condition of employment rather than private practice which makes the difference. Rather it is the identity relationship.)
7. More subject to administrative and supervisory surveillance and control.
8. Less autonomy in professional decision making with accountability to superiors rather than to the profession.
9. Management of organizations within which semiprofessionals are employed by persons who have themselves been prepared and served in that semiprofession.
10. A preponderance of women.
11. Absence of the right of privileged communication between client and professional.
12. Little or no involvement in matters of life and death.

It should be pointed out that the classification of professions into "full" and "semi" categories is primarily an analytic exercise which, however, does appear to represent reality rather closely. In this sense it has great utility. On the other hand, the distinctions do not appear as clearly in practice. The semiprofessions as categorized by sociologists often are recognized in state law as professions and granted licensure and even professional practices privileges. The privilege of refusing to reveal confidential client information before judicial and quasi-judicial bodies, on the other hand, remains unique to the older professions. Both the older professions and some emerging professions have been recognized in courts of law as competent to give expert professional testimony. Neither courts nor legislatures clearly differentiate between established and the semiprofessions as they deal with claims for professional status and other privileges.

FOOTNOTES

1. C. Argyris and D.A. Schon, *Theory in Practice* (San Francisco: Jossey-Bass, 1974); E.H. Schein, *Professional Education* (New York: McGraw-Hill, 1972).
2. W.J. Goode, "The Theoretical Limits of Professionalization," in *The Semi-Professions and Their Organization: Teachers, Nurses, Social Workers,* Amitai Etzioni, ed. (New York: The Free Press, 1969), p. 280.
3. Etzioni, ed., *The Semi-Professions,* ibid., p. v.

TWO

The Profession of Teaching

*To fail to develop principles, concepts, and theories,
and to validate practice is to restrict the
occupation (of teaching) to the level of a craft.*

*Teaching meets the basic criterion for
being considered a profession:
it is a matter of life and death.*

TEACHING AS A PROFESSION

Teachers have long proclaimed that teaching is a profession. They
have lamented the failure of the society in general, and political and
governmental agencies in particular, to grant teachers the conditions,
privileges, and responsibilities appropriate to a profession.

Whether or not teaching meets the full criteria for being a profession is an often debated issue. Actually, teaching meets some of
the criteria well and falls short on others. What follows is a brief
examination of teaching in terms of whether it meets the characteristics of a profession as outlined earlier.

Teaching is an occupationally related social institution established
as a means of providing essential instructional services in the schools.
This is well established both in practice and in law. Also, teaching
is concerned with one area of societal need or function—professional
intervention to enhance learning in a variety of instructional settings.

Though many teachers are recognized as individually competent
and skilled in their performance, the teaching profession is characterized by lack of a common body of knowledge and repertoire of
behaviors and skills needed in the practice of the profession. Lortie
variously refers to this agreed-upon body of knowledge and skills as
"technical" or "professional" and "subculture" or "culture."[1]

In this report, the term *professional culture* will be used in Lortie's
sense of the collective knowledge, skills, behaviors, attitudes, and
values that constitute the bases for professional expertise and decision
making. Lortie's research confirms what has been widely known:
teachers do not possess a common body of professionally validated
knowledge and skills which is transmitted in the process of professional socialization, held in common with other teachers thereafter,

10

and constantly increased through the career span of the teacher. Rather, each teacher develops personal strategies largely independent of others.

Indeed, there has been an almost romanticized courting of the "art of teaching" with the often-expressed assertion that teaching is not a science. Agreements on the issue within teacher education itself have been lacking. In recent years, however, there has been notable progress in developing the professional knowledge, behaviors, and skills necessary for a professional culture. There is widespread belief that there are no fundamental professional/technical barriers standing in the way of professionalization at this time. The problems lie elsewhere. Basic to the problem of developing a professional culture is the long held view that there is not much to teaching, and that most people with more knowledge than the learner can teach. Teaching has been based more upon conventional wisdom, folkways, and personal experience than upon solidly validated professional knowledge and skill. The tradition dies hard.

Though teachers often may not be as aware of their role and its significance as they might be, they are involved in continuous decision making. Every moment has its uniqueness; every situation is in some ways different from every other. There is no index of craft-like answers available in a professional cookbook or manual. Teachers must draw upon what they have in professional insights and intervention strategies in order to decide how to help children learn. There is a general lack of acceptance of the validated knowledge base that does exist on the part of practitioners, teacher educators included. What is known has not been adequately synthesized, taught, and learned. Lacking such an organized base, teachers turn to other rationalizations for their performance. Many deny the science of teaching and instead proclaim the art. Similarly, most teachers have a far from adequate knowledge of presently available principles, practices, and theories. Professions cannot exist without an undergirding science. *To fail to develop principles, concepts, and theories, and to validate practice is to restrict the occupation to the level of a craft.*

The undergirding disciplines of teaching are relatively easy to identify; psychology, sociology, anthropology, and philosophy are most central. For a considerable period, psychology and philosophy were emphasized; recently, anthropology and sociology have received increasing attention. However, most teachers have had little opportunity to study these disciplines in depth or to explore their significance for practice in the teaching profession. Probably relatively few make conscious and systematic use of insights from the disciplines.

Teachers are organized into one or more professional associations which, despite some gnawing jurisdictional disputes, are relatively effective in representing teacher interests. For a long time, the professional associations have striven to improve the conditions necessary for effective service (benefits, working conditions, teacher involvement) and the autonomy needed by a profession. There has been more evidence of effort and success in the former than in the latter. At the present time, professional control and autonomy are low. Long traditions supported by law and regulation have left the profession with little direct control, but with considerable influence in matters of teacher education, licensure, and performance standards. At this time, the stage seems set for dramatic change in the direction of greater professional responsibility and autonomy. In some states, professional practice legislation already has been passed and put into effect.

In the absence of agreement on the substance of the professional culture needed by the teaching profession, there can be no agreed-upon performance standards either for admission to, or continuance in, the profession. Preparation for and induction into the profession are tragically inadequate. The time and resources devoted to the professional aspects of teacher preparation are markedly lower than for any other profession or semiprofession.

The trust placed in the teaching profession by society is paradoxically both high and low. People generally think well of teachers. However, the feelings do not appear to be based on awareness of and trust in their professional expertise. Rather, confidence seems to be based in personal and surrogate parent considerations. Generally, people are aware that what is expected of teachers is beyond reasonable expectation. At the same time, the profession, given the actual level of professional culture available, has been in no position to inspire other kinds of expectations. In the meantime, changing social conditions press schools harder and harder to deliver expertise, and teachers become less and less confident of their ability to meet the challenges they face.

Probably most American teachers are highly service oriented and dedicated. Unfortunately, the dedication tends to be to teaching rather than to the professionalization of their teaching. Teaching has always been marked by ease of entry. Due to teacher shortages, there also has been ease of reentry. Thus, there has been high turnover and much transiency. Inadequate initial preparation, ease of entry, short-term career goals, and a high level of transiency combine to hamper the development of a professional culture of teaching. The process appears circular and self-reinforcing.

Most teachers are employed in public service; thus, authority to teach comes from a contract and an assignment. Customarily, teachers receive some form of tenure after a probationary period; this is withdrawn only after difficult due process. Customarily, administrators provide evidence in hearings, and administrators or the school board hear the cases. There are few instances of peer review or cases where the organized profession itself conducts the proceedings. Expert testimony from teachers has yet to become established practice. In effect, therefore, authority and accountability both are employment related.

Theoretically and legally, teachers are supervised and evaluated by administrators. In practice there is little supervision and rarely is their serious evaluation after the probationary period. Teachers have a great deal of autonomy within their classrooms. To date, the profession has shown little capacity to accept responsibility for insuring that individual teachers are competent and accountable. With the growing emphasis on collective bargaining, it is unlikely that teachers will increase their participation in policing their own ranks in matters of competence. They can, however, be expected to bargain for greater professional authority for the teacher.

TEACHING AS A SEMIPROFESSION

It is clear that teaching presently falls short of meeting the recognized criteria for a mature profession. Comparison with the criteria for subprofessions shows a much closer correspondence.

Teaching is markedly lower in occupational status than other professions such as medicine or law. The length of the training period is the lowest of all the professions when the *professional* component is separated from other elements of teacher preparation programs (13 percent of a bachelor's degree program is the national average for secondary teachers; elementary is only somewhat higher).

Though in practice teachers often are "left alone" by the public, the reason appears to be more of a general "back-the-teacher" phenomenon than a legitimation based on expertise. This support may be rooted in the long accepted "in loco parentis" concept. Recognition of teachers as professionals has yet to emerge in schools or in cases of law as a significant force. Indeed, the "prudent parent" has often been the criterion used in case law. Folkway validation and professional legitimacy are far apart as concepts of authority; teaching has a long way to go to achieve a full measure of professional autonomy.

Since so many aspects of professional realization depend upon the relative absence of a professional culture in teaching practice, it must be seen as the most critical factor in the professional status of teaching. Little progress will be made until educators develop and use a body of recognized professional expertise. Unfortunately, neither teachers in service nor teacher educators place strong faith in the importance of theory of conceptual systems or of research findings. Neither is there consensus on the development of appropriate technical skills which all teachers should master.

Teachers identify more closely with and accept the authority of the employing school or school system than the organized teaching profession. School systems are hierarchically organized and administered. Teachers have little opportunity to participate in administrative and supervisory functions or in personnel evaluation and decision-making processes. There is little teacher organization involvement even in the central functions of schools—the work itself. Probably this tendency is due to the controlling nature of educational organizations. Thus, professional autonomy and accountability are compromised in favor of institutionally delegated responsibilities. Administrators, however, are from the teaching profession. They "rise" from the ranks, take special preparation, are certified, and seek administrative posts. Customarily, both teaching experience and teaching certification are prerequisites to administrative certification. The designation *principal* is itself an abbreviation of the older term *principal teacher*.

Especially at the elementary school level there is a preponderance of female professionals. Etzioni considers that it is unlikely that any profession which is predominantly female will rise beyond the semiprofessional level. However, since Etzioni's work was published in 1969, it did not have the benefits of considering recent developments in equality for women and their growing presence in other professions. In an important sense, of all the criteria regarding semiprofessions, this one appears least defensible. The appearance of cause-effect may be entirely false. In the past, women were heavily involved in the semiprofessions. On the other hand, few women have been included in the mature professions. It is not self-evident nor plausible that the presence or predominance of women in a profession will automatically downgrade it. The study of other cultures where women have equality indicates that the existing situation in America is cultural rather than fundamental.

ON MATTERS OF LIFE AND DEATH

Etzioni presents a convincing case that teaching presently is a semiprofession—especially when assessed against a number of his criteria. However, he is less convincing when he measures teaching against two of his other characteristics—privileged information and matters of life and death. He associates the mature professions with access to privileged client information and with concern for matters of life and death. Of the semiprofessions, he says:

> Semi-professional organizations are more concerned with the communication and, to a lesser extent, the application of knowledge, their professionals are less likely to be guaranteed the right of privileged communications, and they are rarely directly concerned with matters of life and death.[2]

He indicates that the primary school and the social work agency are the two major institutions with staffing from semiprofessionals.

It is interesting to those who know schools and the lives of teachers, especially elementary teachers, that these two criteria of privileged communication and matters of life and death should be seen as primary reasons why teaching should be viewed as a semiprofession. The opposite interpretation could be used for both social work and primary teaching.

Both teachers and social workers encounter revelations of the intimacies of personal, marital, and family life through both formal and informal, intended and unintended activities. Children reveal the innermost secrets of families to teachers. In parent-teacher and/or parent-teacher-child interviews, parents share with teachers information relevant to learning and behavior problems. It is not so much access to privileged information that differentiates teachers from other professionals. Rather it is the legal privilege of refusing to disclose the information in various forms of judicial settings on the one hand, and the preparation—or lack thereof—for skillful and ethical performance in gathering and using such information on the other.

Even more significant, however, is the question of "matters of life and death." The issue must turn on what is life and what is death. Doctors, lawyers, and teachers all deal with critical areas of human existence; all deal with aspects of living and dying. The tragedy is that most people do not recognize the life and death nature of teaching. Yet some teachers succeed in opening children to their learning environments while others preside over processes that downgrade attitudes, lower the level of self-image and aspirations of children, and result in people being less than they might have become.

Every moment in the lives of teachers and pupils brings critical decisions of motivation, reinforcement, reward, ego enhancement, and goal direction. Proper professional decisions enhance learning and life; improper decisions send the learner towards incremental death in openness to experience and in ability to learn and contribute. Doctors and lawyers probably have neither more nor less to do with life, death, and freedom than do teachers. *To deny the child the skills and qualities of the fully professional teacher exacerbates the assaults on freedom which the custodial school involves, leaves untreated the injuries to attitude and ego which much of mass education renders inevitable, and leaves to chance the kinds of interventions by teachers that open minds and enhance self-images. Therefore, the teaching profession must continue its negotiations with society in behalf of more perfect education for its children. Teaching is definitely a matter of life and death.* It should be entrusted only to the most thoroughly prepared professionals.

IMPLICATIONS OF BEING A PROFESSION

There is almost unanimous agreement among teachers and other professional educators that teaching belongs in the company of the mature professions. A similar level of agreement could be anticipated on the issue of seeking the status of full-fledged profession. Whether the same high level of consensus would survive a careful examination of what status would mean—both individually and collectively—is less certain.

In some respects, teachers live in the best of all occupational worlds. Entry to the profession has been easy. A properly planned bachelor's degree has meant a liberal education, one or more academic specializations, the required professional preparation, and a certificate to teach, good for at least a reasonable period of years. Though remuneration has been skimpy, a number of conditions have been relatively favorable. The school day and the academic calendar have been convenient for personal and family schedules. Advanced study and part-time other work have been accommodated. Employment opportunities have been favorable; and after a probationary period positions have been secure. Demands that teachers pursue inservice or continuing education have been minimal. Teachers of reasonable competence have been relatively free of administrative supervision and permitted to preside over classrooms with a minimum of interference. None of this is to suggest that the job has been easy. Quite the opposite has been true. Nonetheless, many of the prerequisites of being professional have come to teachers despite the lack of critical elements of professionalism.

To press the claim to full professional status is to risk loss of some privileges or to pay a higher price for them:

1. Specific and much more rigorous criteria of professional competence will have to be met before teaching can become a full profession.

2. Preparation will require longer periods. Initially, a minimum of five years can be expected; later six or seven years may be required.

3. Continuing and inservice education will mark each teacher's lifelong career. Keeping up to date will not be optional, though individuals will determine how this is done.

4. Accountability for performance will become much more specific and demanding. Such clear criteria as there are will be applied. Conversely, there will be no accountability for what is unknown to the profession, or for outcomes beyond the control of the professional teacher.

5. Teachers may become subject to professional discipline and liable for suit on the grounds of either unethical or incompetent behavior in much the same way as other professions. Teachers and

16

other educators will give evidence in hearings and cases, drawing on the professionally agreed upon knowledge, behaviors, and skills of the professional culture.

6. There could be a loss of some of the personal respect and affection for teachers as a *professional* basis for respect is emphasized.

7. Teachers' associations will become much more significant in both the professional and conditions-of-work elements of the life of teachers. Relationships with administrators, supervisors, school boards, communities, and parents would be altered significantly.

Some of the above outcomes will happen whether or not teachers seriously commit themselves to professionalization. Teacher education will have to increase in the length and rigor of preparation. Inservice and continuing education will be emphasized. The accountability issue already is high on the agenda of teacher concerns. Clearly stated expectations and criteria, together with circumstances favorable to realizing educational goals, could improve rather than exacerbate the accountability problem.

Professional discipline and liability for suit are more perplexing than the problems just discussed. The increase in the incidence of malpractice suits in other professions is causing concern throughout the society. Litigation will come to teaching regardless of its degree of professionalization. In any case, possession of a professional culture and its use in practice seems the best way to avoid legal problems. Another view of malpractice suits is that they provide a means for society to make the established professions more responsive. Positive results of litigation will be a reexamination of professions and development of a more responsive posture and a more satisfactory level of accountability. Professional self-discipline should assist in this public process.

The potential impact which professionalization will have on the respect and affection given to teachers is uncertain. Indeed, the relationship between teachers, pupils, and parents presently is neither adequately described nor understood. It might be a persistent cultural carryover from earlier times; it may also be related to the prevalence of women as teachers over the last century. Clearly, teachers have been more directly involved over a protracted period in the lives of children than any adults other than parents. Teaching has been so close to parenthood that some of the most protected rights of parents, in the form of the doctrine of "in loco parentis," have been granted legally and practically to teachers. This has not happened in any other profession. Whether it will continue with or without professionalization is by no means clear. In any case, teachers have little choice but to improve their capacity to serve effectively.

Mixed into the surrogate-parent relationships are other elements such as love and self-sacrifice. Elementary teachers especially are perceived as loving children. In some sense, all teachers have been self-sacrificing; they have worked under difficult circumstances for little economic reward. The concept of professionalism bears very differently on each of these qualities, however. Professionals are persons who make objective decisions based on data. They love humankind and dedicate their lives to service; but they avoid openly declaring personal, loving relationships in order that their decisions and performance will be as objective and valid as possible. For this reason, doctors do not treat their own families, and lawyers avoid representing their own children. To do so would be to strain objectivity and engender guilt when professional efforts fail.

Teachers have been loath to move in the direction of a professional culture. Instead, they have relied on personal experience and conventional wisdom and have been wary of available professional expertise. Professional education has been derided and downgraded within the profession itself. To persist in this can only cut the professsion off from development and dissemination of the expertise which changing times demand. The relationship between teacher and child/parent has changed despite the desire to retain it. Most teachers no longer teach in villages or identifiable communities; indeed, it is hard to get teachers for such service. Realistically, the nature of teaching relationships already is becoming more professional, but it is hollow without an accompanying professional culture.

Nostalgia to the contrary, the teacher's role in the future will not be cast in the setting of a traditional classroom. Most futuristic educational projections have collaborative team behavior as a major element in their design. This emerging professional role modifies the traditional intimacy of the one-teacher, one-class situation. For the child, it becomes "my teachers;" for the parent, "the children's teachers;" for the teacher, "my colleagues and the children."

Such a change does not reduce the quality of human relationships in teaching. A continuing and essential characteristic will be a teacher's capacity to have warm, empathic relationships with a variety of children. However, the essence of this relationship is "helping." *This Commission holds that the interests of learners, parents, society, teachers, and the teaching profession are not served by clinging to past memories, by longing for the return of earlier conditions, or by resisting the kinds of change which logic demands and which opportunity presents. In reality there is no choice but change toward greater professionalization if schools are to meet their challenges.*

THE NATURE OF EDUCATION AND SCHOOLING IN OUR SOCIETY

A fundamental societal need is to socialize its citizens, particularly

18

its children and youth, in the ways of that society. In simpler societies, socialization goes hand in hand with living in the community; learning occurs naturally. As societies become more complex and as work becomes specialized, learning the behaviors of the adult world comes less naturally. Education becomes a conscious process, and the role of teacher comes into existence. Subsequently, schools develop as places within which both teachers and pupils play out their roles. Curricula are designed to accomplish the learning which society considers important. What was once so natural in simple societies becomes organized into a complex social system.

The learning process is a complicated and fragile phenomenon. It thrives best in natural and warm human settings. When it has to be institutionalized—as indeed it must in complex societies—it is most likely to suffer. That learning and teaching have sometimes suffered in the schools of America is a tragic reality. Our highly technological society has shown little sensitivity to the unique needs of the individual, to the complexity of the learning process, or to the life-long effects which accrue from schooling and which are far lower in quality than the nation could provide. Ivan Illich notes this destructive incompatibility between the child as person and learner on the one hand, and the school as a crude and inappropriate setting for learning on the other. He calls for deschooling America. While recognizing the essential truths in his descriptions, *this Commission does not agree with Illich's solution. Instead it advocates efforts at reschooling. Central to this process is a massive upgrading of the teaching profession through teacher education at all levels—preservice, inservice, and continuing.*

Persistence Rather Than Change

Students of educational history often observe that schools have changed little over long periods of time. Though the trappings are different, the form is substantially the same. What was once an isolated one-room structure is now a massive conglomerate of one-room structures strung out along corridors. The teacher who taught a number of grades in the one-room school now teaches a single grade. Instruction may be less formal, but it still follows the lesson-presentation-assignment mode. Discipline is still emphasized. Motivation is still extrinsic. Despite the marvels of the electronic age, schools make less use of technology than any other comparable enterprise. Schooling is still largely a mass process rather than an individualized and personalized one. What was done in schools in pioneer days as a matter of necessity persists long after the circumstances have changed and new options have become available.

In recent years, however, the public has begun to question many aspects of schooling. There is mounting interest in alternative schools, tuition vouchers, contract education, lower compulsory attendance, and accountability. Though nothing is likely to totally destroy or displace the public schools in the near future, their viability or continuance should not be taken for granted. Public schools were originally designed for a rural society and have persisted largely unchanged. As a society we should be able to construct an educational system that is capable of meeting the needs of our changing social order.

The School as a Primary Institution

The early school was established as one of the *primary institutions* which shared with home, church, and community the functions of preserving and passing on the community way of life. Working closely together, these four primary institutions served as custodians of community norms and mores. The roles of parent, teacher, and clergyman were endowed with both authority and respect. Together the institutions exercised a system of sanctions which kept the cherished ways intact. Heretics were not welcome within the village, and heresies were not tolerated within the school. The school, like other primary institutions, was culture preserving and highly responsive to the wishes of the community. The law endowed citizens with the right to run their own school within the limits of state law. Communities have always tried to do so by whatever processes they could despite growing difficulties, especially in larger cities. Their efforts have been based on the perspectives, values, and ways of the past. Change has not been prevalent.

In more or less stable times, the conservative tendencies of communities cause little or no apparent problem. The situation changes, however, as the pace of change quickens. The gap between what the younger generation needs and what the community offers widens. Disaffection and alienation result. Under such circumstances the opportunity to pass on the best from the past is lost. Both the community and its youth suffer.

Emergence of Secondary Institutions

The specialization which characterizes complex societies causes the establishment of a vast array of new institutions and organizations. What used to be done in family and local communities moves to businesses, industries, and organizations which are removed from community influence and control. These *secondary* institutions gradually take over more and more of the socialization processes; primary institutions find it harder and harder to preserve the ways of life which they value. Their influence is undermined without any deliberate intent to do so.

In our society the primary institutions, which used to be the institutions of socialization, no longer are able to control the learning or behavior of young or old citizens. The secondary institutions involved in mass media, recreation, transportation, production, and promotion have become the dominant forces in influencing people. They are not responsive to local communities and are protected by the Constitution from restraint of their activities. Their business is change rather than preservation. Everywhere they bring their persuasive messages. Young and old know instantly of happenings all over the world. All ideas—favorable and unfavorable—are presented to the public. The media reveal new ways of life for all to see, contemplate, and try if they wish. Marshall McLuhan's "global village" has become a reality.

The socializing of people has, in large part, been removed as a function of primary institutions; secondary institutions now mold people's values, thoughts, and behaviors to a degree never before possible. The primary institutions often fight futile rearguard actions of preservation and appear recalcitrant in the eyes of the young. Schools suffer severely under this condition.

Role Conflict for the Teaching Profession

The school is caught in the dilemma of its posture toward change and preservation. Its local and governmental charge causes it to be conservative and preservative. The teaching profession has also been past oriented, partly because of its own disposition, but also because it had to be if it was to have public support and acceptance. The profession rarely chooses to joust with citizens in favor of a more suitable school situation for their children.

Mead points out, however, that the role of teacher has long had elements of cultural subversion within it.[2] The American goals of opportunity for all and social mobility, both of which are change oriented, have made this possible by assisting the student toward the American goals of social mobility. The child was taught to go places and do things the parents had not experienced; one value—preservation—was constantly in conflict with another—change. The twin functions of assimilation into the dominant culture of immigrant minorities and upward mobility for all Americans won out. Advertently or inadvertently, the school has served as an agent of change.

Nonetheless the school remained a place for "safe" ideas. Adopted curricula backed by publicly screened textbooks and materials kept bounds on social thought. Controversial issues were deliberately proscribed; children were taught "what" to think but not "how." The system worked well enough for its purposes in the simpler days of towns and low-level technology. Its purposes are no longer served, however, since the socially protective environment has been breached by technology in the hands of secondary institutions. This has created the anomalous situation of what is probably one of the most open societies on earth having schools that are relatively closed institutions.

As Mead implies, it is not easy for a role to encompass both change and preservation in a given relationship. Yet both are needed in teachers and in schools. In some tasks, the schools probably should have the freedom of a secondary institution. (Trends in recent years seem to indicate that schools increasingly will be expected to diversify programs and provide more direct assistance in preparing students for adult and world-of-work roles. This is a move toward a secondary institution role for the school.) In other tasks, schools may expect to serve as the primary institution socialization agent. There remains, however, the task of developing a workable compromise.

Other conflicts of consequence also developed. The city's rise created great change in human relationships. The natural cross-age interaction of the extended family and the small community gave way to the impersonality of the city. Gradually, to fill the void, other relationships emerged. Clubs and organizations based on factors such as interest and status developed for both young and old. All ages of people, but teenage youth in particular, organized themselves by age-level stratifications. Communication, which had been from older to younger with selective monitoring, now was directly available to all through mass media. The young became increasingly mobile with their own vehicles. Opportunities for cross-age interaction were weakened; most disappeared. A "generation gap" of serious proportions, brought about by rapid change, was made more serious by lack of means for interaction and communication.

Children and youth had great difficulty communicating with parents. Many youths turned hopefully to the schools, but school professionals were of the older generation too. Also, they were charged with preserving the culture of the past. Teachers had never been taught to deal with controversy, to preside over open processes of exchange, to be the source of wisdom in the presence of immaturity. Hard social issues brought to school by well-informed young were strange, controversial, divisive, and proscribed. Teacher preparation, either in academic or professional studies, had not equipped school personnel for this new role. Those teachers who ventured into the realms of thought being explored by the young were discouraged by the public, school board, and administrators. Today, some teachers have learned to relate more effectively to the world of new ways and ideas in their classrooms and risk doing so. Still unresolved, however, are the professional dimension of this role and the teacher preparation needed for it.

At least some of the ambivalence over the nature of teaching derives directly from primary and secondary institution role conflict. The primary institution role derives from culture preservation. In it the teacher draws cues from the community and society. In the secondary role, the teacher intervenes directly to bring about change in the learner. The former emphasizes traditional values; the latter, emergent ones. The secondary role will require teachers who possess an extensive repertoire of professional behaviors and skills, and a broader, more open view. Teachers cannot master this role without well-developed professional skills.

Cultural Pluralism and Multicultural Education

Over the last two decades, our nation has painfully come to grips with the fact that our way of life has not succeeded in extending equal rights to all people. What the Constitution guarantees and what the courts have granted de jure is not what exists de facto. Much of the burden for correcting the situation has been placed on the schools. Since schools are agencies of goverment supported by public funds, they cannot confer benefits on one group while withholding them from another.

Often, with cataclysmic suddenness, the courts give schools mandates to drastically alter programs, administrative arrangements, teacher assignments, and resource allocation. Concomitantly, these mandates dramatically change the lives of teachers. Teachers are not prepared either personally or professionally for such service. Most have been reared in middle- or lower middle-class homes and communities, ensconced safely away from the concentrations of minority and lower socioeconomic groups. Many possess a conventional wisdom bias toward minorities. Probably few could look forward with anticipation to assignment to inner-city schools; fewer still know how to go about instructionally and socially redressing the injustices that have been done to minorities. All teachers need professional preparation for this role.

Adopting multicultural education is one of the official government responses to the challenge of equal access to educational opportunity. Multicultural education, as defined by the government, includes (a) knowledge of cultures and of subcultures, with special emphasis on those minority groups which are pervasively represented in American communities; (b) awareness of how specific cultures influence learners' responses to school and learning situations, and skill in sensitizing professional behavior to learners; (c) transformation of personal prejudices so that negative biases are minimized, and positive appreciation of minority children increased; and (d) adjustments in curricula to implement the transition from the concept of "melting pot" to "cultural pluralism."

Just as the public's esteem affects teachers' self-perceptions, so too does the dominant group's perception of minorities affect children's self-images. Consequently, the school has a legal, moral, and professional obligation to become the institution where opportunity to learn is enhanced for all. The school is not to be a place for discounting the worth of any individual. Furthermore, because of their charge to preserve diverse cultural elements in society, schools are to enhance the individual culture of each group. As a corollary, schools participate in the process of assisting all citizens—majority and minority—to understand and respect each other.

Multicultural education is a great challenge to the teaching profession. *It is not that the challenges themselves are new since championing the rights of children striving to achieve a pedagogy responsive to all children's learning needs and helping expand educational opportunities to include all social groups are inherent in the role of teacher.* What is new and significant is the commitment to preserve and enhance rather than melt away the uniqueness of cultural groups in the society. New also is the too seldom emphasized need for teachers to search for and emphasize the core values of American life which are the basis for unity amidst diversity.

The World of Work

The 1970s have seen a realization that the lives of children are lived largely in isolation from what has come to be referred to as the "world of work." Neither home, school, nor community have done much to provide either a variety of direct work experience or information about work. Once again society, through intervention of federal agencies, has turned to the schools for a solution to the problem.

Even a casual scrutiny of conditions within modern society reveals that children and youth have little direct contact with adults in their work roles. Many children have only the vaguest awareness of what their own parents do. Many have superficial or false notions, distorted by generalizations from what they see in television or movies. Some school textbooks—particularly readers—tend to have this effect. Rarely do working people appear in schools to tell of life in their occupations; rarely do students experience work places through field trips. Few students have the opportunity to combine vocational experience with schooling, though the number in cities is growing with the new emphasis on work.

Teachers have little experience with, or knowledge of, a variety of work settings. Little deliberate effort has been made to provide this. Most are poorly prepared for performing the "world of work" role in their teaching assignments or in curriculum building. If the school is to be effective in this new mission, teachers will have to be trained to teach about the work world in the curriculum, provide career education as preparation for vocational choice, and help students clarify personal values in terms of their implications for a lifetime of meaningful work. They also will need to learn to involve the adult society in the school and the child in the adult work world. Teacher education will need to include these aspects of the teacher's role in the preparation program.

Lifelong Education

The last two decades have seen a rapid development in the diffusion of aspects of formal education to many agencies and institutions. Social change brings with it a need for further education and reeducation for all citizens. New knowledge, new technologies, and new ways of thought and behavior flood all walks of life. The schools assume some of the responsibility for extending educational opportunity, but changing curricula is a slow process and schools have a limited capacity to respond. In response to unmet needs, other agencies have attempted to fill the gap.

On-the-job training has grown phenomenally as companies deal forcefully with the problem of people obsolescence. Most businesses and institutions have educational programs for their members. Adult education has burgeoned; one-half of the population is involved in it in one way or another. So pervasive is the need that corporations have entered into the *business* of education, often in direct competition with schools. A whole new education industry has emerged. In all of its forms, nonschool education already is estimated to exceed school education in extent.

Lifelong learning rapidly is becoming a reality. No longer is the individual's life necessarily split between the dependent learning period of school attendance and the independent living and working period of adulthood. Learning is a lifetime stream, and this development will affect schools and the teaching profession in significant ways. Schools can include learners of all ages throughout their lives. Teaching can be a profession needed everywhere. What is now schooling can be beneficially reinstitutionalized, and even to some extent deinstitutionalized.

None can know for sure what these changes portend for the future. What appears certain is that schools and the teaching profession will be involved in continuous change for the foreseeable future. Continuing education will become increasingly more important. Whether schools as we know them come or go, the need for skilled professional educators and teachers will persist. Whether the teaching function will be professionalized remains an open question to be answered in part at least by professional educators themselves.

SCHOOLS AND PROFESSIONALIZATION IN OUR SOCIETY

The development of a profession is strongly influenced by (a) its past from which it is hard to escape and (b) by the conditions under which it must work. The previous section dealt with societal conditions relevant to the teaching profession. Here we will take a brief look at the school.

Early Public Schools in America

Throughout history, in almost all civilizations, formal education has been the privilege of elites. The American experience has been different, at least outwardly. This society made an early commitment to provide free public education to all. That intent is undisputed. In truth, however, there was at that time no way quality education could have been provided, quality being understood as an effective system under which each student achieves success reasonably commensurate with personal needs and potential.

Given the dimensions of the problem and the resources available, communities did what made sense. They established a system where pupils were exposed to a teacher in large groups, getting what they could in the process. Some historians have seen the mass education system which resulted as comparable to the mass production systems which developed in factories. The teacher was comparable to the worker, while the pupils were raw materials to be processed into a finished product. Supervisors, at first in the form of a visiting committee, but later as principal teacher and principal, oversaw the work of the teacher and the quality of the product. Children were sent to school to learn what the teacher had to offer.

The facilities were built to accommodate the "scarce resource" which then was teacher time and talent. A dais at the front of the room made the teacher the center of attention and provided easy surveillance of all. Children sat at desks facing the teacher. Desks were fastened to the floor, in order to discourage student-distractive interactions and disorder. Rigid schedules, paced by ringing bells, conserved and directed teacher time. A severe disciplinary system with canes, corner stools, expulsion or suspension, homework and extra assignments, and detention assisted in achieving conformity and preventing disruption of teaching. Children sat in silence much of the time, often with arms folded. Parents backed the school by punishing the child at home if there was a school infraction. Reading, writing, and arithmetic—the tools of simple literacy—occupied most of the school's attention. Deeply embedded in instructional materials (*The McGuffy Readers*, for example) and in teacher behavior was a strong emphasis on morality, compliance, patriotism, self-denial, and hard work.

However, necessity was not the mother of all elements of the school invention. Many aspects of the school mirrored the values and beliefs of the time. Children were to be seen and not heard at home as well as at school. Punishment was pervasive and severe both at school and at home. Instructional strategies for the times were compatible with the community's religious and social beliefs and practices.

The Intervening Years

That many schools have changed so little in their fundamental characteristics since pioneer days is difficult to understand. A visit to a small restored schoolhouse evokes little surprise in many children. They find the situation quaint but not strange. Some older people nostalgically point out that their schools were just a small-scale version of the new open-concept school.

A few of the best schools today, particularly those which are effective and innovative, are markedly different from other schools in philosophy, in curriculum, in their approach to discipline, and in the roles of teacher and pupil. Learning in these schools is seen as an active process. The pupil is the worker while the teacher is a facilitator and helper. The learner is perceived as unique. Teachers emphasize individualization of instruction and encourage learners to avoid undue dependency. Thus, there is less teacher dominance and curriculum rigidity, and more purposeful individual and group activity. The lockstep system of grades with forced passing or failing dates is broken; now the system tolerates and encourages continuous progress. In its successful forms, such an approach to education changes the nature of a school. A smorgasbord of opportunity is available. Teams of teachers and learners work together to maximize learning.

Changing either a primary institution such as the school or the profession which serves within it is no simple task. At best it is likely to take a generation or longer. Thus the permanence of present-day innovations must remain in doubt. It does appear, however, that the newer approaches are pedagogically sound and consistent with our societal values and aspirations.

Persistent Elements of Schools Which Affect the Teaching Profession

Schools affect the teaching profession even as the teaching profession affects the schools. The following descriptions of conditions which exist in schools are in no way intended to excuse the profession and blame schools. Each is a cause of professional problems and a result of failure to improve the profession.

A CUSTODIAL INSTITUTION. The school is a custodial type of institution where individuals must come whether they want to or not, and where those who operate the institution must accept and retain individuals whether they want to or not. (There are few such institutions in society, prisons being the most conspicuous example.)

Compulsory attendance laws tended to turn schools into custodial institutions. Access to schooling can be a privilege, a right, or an obligation. In the first case, the school can decide whether to grant the privilege using such criteria as it wishes or is permitted. The school loses this discretion when the law requires continuous attendance through a given age.

Custodial institutions by their very nature tend to alienate the client. Alienated clients are not open to learning experiences. Prisons, despite massive efforts, have never had great success in reclaiming the aberrant individual. What successes they have probably are with the least recalcitrant of the inmates in the area of vocational and avocational skills.

It is undoubtedly an error to perceive the school as custodial for all children or as equally custodial at all age levels. Observably, many children enjoy school and are not conscious of its custodial features. Well known also is the fact that the behavior of administration and teachers can change the climate of the school and minimize the custodial impact. Few schools escape having some students who resent the custodial reality; others have many. Even a few can alter the learning dynamic, while larger numbers can destroy it.

Custodial institutions usually have overwhelming numbers of people and limited resources for individualized treatment. To defend themselves, the institutions organize and control life by rigid regulations and routines. Institutions maintain close surveillance at all times to minimize incidents and to insure compliance. Even the physical environment is structured for control, for example, cells or cell blocks (classrooms); isolation (detention rooms). Custodial institutions tend to be tuned to control and assume that everyone in them needs to be controlled. There is little time left for those who have learned to make choices and be responsible for them, or for creating conditions which help all involved to learn to make choices and deal with the consequences—in other words, "learn to be free."

This description does not mean that the Commission perceives *all* American schools as being like prisons. The Commission recognizes as a reality that the profession has to exist in some ways within the context of a custodial institution, even though custodial environments are in and of themselves antithetical to the purposes of education. However, some schools succeed in minimizing their custodial realities, while others show an overpowering concern with law and order and strong elements of custodial behavior. When schools have armed guards in the hallways and require teachers to police study halls and check hall passes, it is not easy to deny the problem. On the other hand, it is satisfying to see the growing number of schools that are persisting in efforts to develop open climates and responsible student behavior, thus minimizing the custodial elements.

It is not easy to be a professional teacher in a strongly custodial environment. *The teaching profession and society will need to make every effort possible to minimize the custodial penchants of schools if we are to realize present commitments to quality education and equal access to educational opportunity.*

MISSION DEFINITION. There is widespread recognition that schools lack adequate definition of their mission and role in society. While many states and school systems do have public statements of goals, they express these in highly general terms and provide little direction for programs or professional behavior. *Communities will have to separate obligations of the school from those of other agencies and institutions. Also, they will have to translate the long-term goals and aspirations into shorter term objectives and reconcile them with existing resources and other inputs.* Such conditions are conducive to the identification of the professional services necessary for attainment of societal goals.

RESOURCES. Though education consumes a substantial share of the nation's resources, it continues to be funded at a level too low for goal attainment. Additionally, existing resources often are not effectively used. The nation neglects teacher preparation and educational innovation at all levels. The American people always have taken a simplistic view of education and of teaching. In earlier periods, the discrepancy between what was expected and what could be achieved was not great. Now, however, expectations grow while conditions become more difficult. Resources are expanded but not enough to make critical differences. Dependence on local funding often means that communities with the greatest needs have the least capacity to meet them.

A low level of resources tends to lock the institution into what it is already doing. Desperately needed are innovations designed to improve efficiency and effectiveness; this will require allocation of funds for development and dissemination.

USE OF TECHNOLOGY. Education involves much communication. Communication in our society enjoys a high level of technological support. Schools, for the most part, have only a meager and primitive technical back-up for their activities. Consequently, the teacher continues in the role of presenter long after this role becomes technologically obsolete. One approach to enlarging the scarce resource of teacher time is use of a multimedia technology. Effective teaching calls for the use of individualized instruction and independent and interdependent student behavior. The use of this approach depends upon making access to learning relatively independent of constant access to the teacher. *Some kind of instructional packaging is needed if this is to occur. Again, technology used wisely and humanely seems the indispensable ally of effective teaching.* Technology is part of the American way of life. A school without it must seem strange to its students. Society owes its schools the resources necessary to enhance education through technology.

MANAGEMENT AND LEADERSHIP. School systems are organized hierarchically much like business and industry. The lay policy board is the school board. The superintendent of schools advises the board and administers policies. Assistant superintendents, principals, teachers, and pupils are successively lower in the hierarchy than superintendents. Central office supervisors and school principals supervise teachers. Accountability flows upward through the hierarchy. Modern organizational theory differentiates between organizations staffed primarily by professionals and those that employ skilled or unskilled labor. The former, referred to as "modern organizations," differ particularly in decision making and in the use of supervision. Professionals possess the technical expertise and are involved in decision making. Administrators preside over the processes, but they do not presume to know enough to make the decisions. Accordingly, there is a strong emphasis on both horizontal and vertical communication processes. For similar reasons, supervision is deemphasized. The source of a professional's authority is expertise. Vertically organized supervision places one professional over another; yet both have the same obligation to be competent, and both draw on the same source for that competence. Peer relationships pervade the modern organization.

It would appear that the organization of schools at present has elements that are antithetical to the development of professional competence. Whether the situation exists because teaching has not become a profession, or whether teaching has been hampered in its professional development by its administration really cannot be answered. However, a different form of organization or a different emphasis in administrative practice will be productive in encouraging professionalization.

USE OF PERSONNEL. Teaching has long been a single-level occupation. Graduating teachers enter a school and take over classes. Forty years later, most of these teachers retire. Little or no role differentiation will have occurred in their lifetimes (though some may be mentors to young teachers or become influential in faculty or school affairs). School systems generally have no means of role specialization, and few invent any.

In the last two decades, some have made strong efforts to break traditional patterns of one-teacher, one-class (or in high school one-teacher, a number of similar classes). While it is true that significant progress has been made in the realm of team teaching, actually a very small proportion of teachers get involved in genuine teaming. The lack of preparation and lack of time for the necessary planning has worked against the plan, as has the lack of differentiation of function and the development of specialization for the function. In other words, teams have been left to develop their own roles and the competencies for them.

Thompson differentiates two kinds of specialization—task specialization and person specialization.[4] Task specialization is equated with craftlike preparation for easily performed and repetitive skills; one worker readily replaces another. Person specialization is more like specialization within a profession; it consists of developing a high level of competence in one or more areas, with the result that the expertise is needed by other professionals. *Teaching should become a person-specialization profession; this will enhance status and enable teachers to become crucial members of teams of specialists. The resulting effect on a professional's self-concept and personal motivation can be expected to be dramatic.*

Brief reference should also be made to other factors of personnel use. There is infrequent use of paraprofessionals and other aides in schools. We expect teachers to do everything, and, unfortunately, even when given alternatives, many teachers still want to.

OTHER CONDITIONS. The school conditions listed and described above should be taken as representative of a broad array, some of greater and some of lesser consequence. They are largely speculative in nature since definitive proof is not available.

Other conditions which might be of equal or greater significance but not singled out for attention here include:

1. The prevalent and still persistent white middle-class orientation of schools.
2. Restrictions on academic freedom to address significant problems and issues as they arise.
3. The tight boundary which separates the school world from the real world.
4. Conditions which constrain the exercise of initiative, individuality, and creativity of teachers.

THE NATURE OF THE PROFESSIONAL TEACHING ACT

Generally, our society perceives teaching as consisting of little more than a lay level of intervention performed in schools by well-meaning, socially safe persons called "schoolteachers." This notion has survived with relatively little change as generations of children have passed through the schools, taking with them—as one of their major and most persistent learnings—this perception of the schoolteacher.

Teachers in Early America

When schools were first established in America, there was no teaching *profession*. History records that teachers—often itinerant—were mostly low-paid males of little education. Many were of dubious worth and character. Citizens, rightly concerned over the welfare of their children, set up "visiting committees" of educated persons to visit the school to see that the teaching was competent and the learning adequate. In the absence of qualified teachers, many marginal persons served.

It was not until the 1830s and '40s that America introduced teacher education from Europe in the form of normal schools. At first, normal school students had less than a high school education; later, high school became a common requirement. Normal schools offered some subject matter and a smattering of pedagogy. Their clientele was mostly female; elementary teaching became predominantly a woman's role. In the late nineteenth century and into the twentieth, normal schools lengthened their periods of preparation to two years. Then, impelled by the growing need for secondary teachers, and by the desire of the society to expand higher education opportunities close to home, they became teachers' colleges and state universities. Teacher education became a significant element in the majority of colleges and universities, both public and private. Unfortunately, however, teaching did not develop a professional preparation program with characteristics similar to other professions.

The public, the teaching profession and the university had not thought of teaching as a professional act demanding knowledge, behaviors, and skills parallel to other developing professions. And state governments, the federal government, and foundations did not give the matter serious attention. Complex forces rooted perhaps in the persistent notions of the early schoolteacher kept the profession of teaching from seriously studying and developing itself. It is true, of course, that teaching is by its nature less precise than other professions; its undergirding disciplines cannot provide the certainties that those of some other professions do. Even here, however, there is much available helpful knowledge that is seriously ignored. Society appears more reluctant to hand over its children to professionals for modification in behavior, thinking, and attitudes than it is to have their teeth preserved and their health maintained by professionals. For whatever reason, a schoolteacher is still a schoolteacher; the concept of a professional educator has yet to emerge.

Development of Other Professions

In America, other professions over the same period of history have made tremendous forward strides from similar beginnings. When "schoolteacher" began, lawyers were those who chose to study law on their own; barbers let blood and used leeches in the treatment of disease; and midwives delivered many of the children who attended the schoolhouses. Markowitz and Rosner provide a few quotations from journals of the late nineteenth century which remind us of our recent past in medicine; the similarity of their tone and critique to teaching is striking.[5]

> [It is] . . . humiliating to make a comparison of the economic and social positions of our leading physicians and surgeons . . . with leading lawyers and other professional men. *Pittsburgh Medical Review* 10 (June 1876): 176.

> The income of many a medical man who has spent years in acquiring a medical education is often less than that of an ordinary mechanic. *Cosmopolitan* 34 (April 1903): 654.

And in his landmark report of 1910, Flexner reported the continuance of these conditions.

> . . . very seldom under existing conditions, does a patient receive the best aid which is possible to give him in the present state of medicine, and that this is due mainly to the fact that a vast army of men is admitted to the practice of medicine who are untrained in sciences fundamental to the profession and quite without sufficient experience with disease.[6]

Progress in medicine came about rapidly only as recently as the early twentieth century, stimulated by the Flexner Report.

More Recent Developments in Teacher Education

The lack of professionalization in teacher education continued with little change through the early years of the twentieth century and into the post-Second World War period. Sputnik (1957) awakened the nation to presumed deficiencies in the schools, and the federal government responded with large-scale efforts to stimulate improved teaching. Because the government assumed that the problem was teachers' subject matter deficiency, it poured resources into curriculum development and academic inservice education, mainly in the sciences and mathematics. Obviously, there was significant upgrading in these subject matter areas, but pedagogy, the professional *act* of teaching, received little attention.

In 1954, the courts began their succession of rulings on rights and education. During the 1960s, the nation's festering social problems erupted into civil rights movements. There was rioting in the streets and parts of cities were burned. Often, schools were targets of violence; sometimes, though, rioters selectively preserved the schools. Possibly, this action symbolized the ambivalent hopes and aspirations people had for schools, and the despair and rage they felt over the schools' inability to teach their children or to provide equal access to educational opportunity. In any case, it was clear that the less privileged groups did *not* perceive their problem to be the upgrading of science and mathematics programs in order to maintain national, scientific, and technological superiority. But schools were so perceived, as were the teachers who served in them.

From that time, the response of the federal government has been to concentrate on alleviating inequities. The government gave serious attention to teacher education for the first time by developing and funding such efforts as Trainers of Teacher Trainers (Triple T), Teacher Corps, The Comprehensive Elementary Teacher Education Models (CETEM) Project, Teacher Centers, the National Institute of Education (NIE), the Education Renewal Project, multicultural education, and bilingual education. Out of these programs and others has come the rapid emergence of the basis for a profession of teaching, with a genuine professional culture.

Models for Teacher Education

As educational historians look back upon the events of the '60s, the federally funded elementary models project (CETEM) could emerge as the most significant single innovative effort. Out of the projects, educators developed 10 models of teacher education. On analysis, the separately developed models were found to have consensus on a number of points:

1. Teaching is a profession; the teacher is a clinician and decision maker.
2. At work, the teacher shares with others the clinical and decision-making tasks; teaching demands team work and collegial relationships.
3. The competencies needed by teachers can be identified, specified as behaviors, and developed through training.
4. Management systems adequate for complex teacher education programs can be developed.
5. Teaching demands a long period of training extending throughout the employment period; effective training programs require collaboration between the several involved parties.
6. Development of the complex competencies of teaching will demand the effective use of both laboratory and field-centered approaches.
7. As an applied scientist, the teacher needs to be well versed in the behavioral sciences which are relevant to the profession.

8. The models—as with all preparation programs—are just early approximations of what is needed.

Out of these models has also come the productive and controversial competency-based teacher education (CBTE) movement, which concentrates on identifying and specifying the knowledges, behaviors, and skills necessary for effective teaching. It is indeed unfortunate that CBTE became engulfed in controversies not of its own making—such as state mandates to use CBTE in all teacher education programs. Professional dialogue on CBTE would have been much more productive in a setting where the issues discussed were educational, rather than political.

Out of the many research and development efforts in teacher education over the last decade have come both a commitment to quality teacher education and an emphasis on new programs and implementation strategies. The use of simulation, protocols, laboratory approaches, and microteaching has added to instructional capabilities on campus. Also, great progress has been made in developing the field-originated part of the program. Teacher Centers have been established to stimulate and coordinate new kinds of collaborative efforts with schools. And teachers in many schools are being prepared to assume "clinical supervision" roles with teacher preparation students. These results have been promising and, in some instances, highly successful. They demonstrate dramatically that the teaching profession can have its professional culture.

The Professional Teaching Act

Learning is a change in the beliefs, values, and behaviors of an individual brought about as a result of experience. Teaching and learning are pervasive; they occur whenever one individual contrives an experience for another in the hope that a desired learning will take place. Professional teachers differ from others who teach in the pedagogical expertise they bring to the task. Ideally, teachers are educated in how to intervene in the experience of others in order to enhance the probability that the desired learnings will occur. It is this expertise in intervention strategies combined with a sophisticated knowledge base that constitute the professional culture of teaching.

Many factors operate simultaneously to determine whether learning will occur. Some of these factors are internal to the individual learner; others are external and subject to control by the teacher. We know much about individuals and how they respond to both internal and external stimuli; social sciences such as psychology (study of the individual), sociology (study of the individual in groups), and anthropology (study of cultures and the behavior of individuals within them) contributed enormously to these understandings. Through the use of these social sciences, through analyzed experience, and through research and experimentation, the teaching profession is increasingly able to predict how individuals will act. These predictions are helpful in making thoughtful decisions on the use of specific teaching strategies.

In common with all professions, teaching is a decision-making and a decision-implementing process. Teachers study each learning case and identify learning needs. Then they consider alternative strategies and decide which ones to use. Implementing the strategy requires highly professional skills; no two learning cases are ever exactly the same. It is because each moment in the teacher's life means complex situations and new decisions that teachers must possess the knowledge, behaviors, attitudes, and skills required of the professional teaching act. A few selected examples of these knowledge bases and skills follow.

SELF-IMAGE OF THE LEARNER. The most important thing that happens to learners is the development of the self-concept or self-image. Out of experience, learners develop perceptions of themselves as able or unable, intelligent or unintelligent, likeable or unlikeable. At any given time, individuals act in ways consistent with the self-image. Some become confident, open to new experiences, and able to cope with problems and challenges. Others, however, experience failures and develop a negative self-concept and low self-esteem. They expect little of themselves and achieve little; learning becomes a continuing problem.

Much development of self-image occurs during the formative early years, before the child comes to school. At this time, children learn about themselves, their pasts, their families, their social class status, and their future possibilities. Adults in the immediate environment strongly influence the developing self-concept by their punitive and judgmental behavior or by being open, supportive, and encouraging. Differences in child-rearing patterns are both idiosyncratic and cultural in origin. Parents, teachers, and others will tend to raise children in the same way as they were raised unless they have an opportunity to learn a different pattern.

Thus, children come to school not only different in ability and capability but different in what their self-image will permit them to do with that ability. It is difficult for the school to change these well-established patterns. Nonetheless, *capable teachers strive continually to improve children's self-images by raising their level of confidence and expectation. The ability to do this well is perhaps the teacher's most important professional attribute.* Professional educators understand the importance of self-image and its relationships to cultural identity;

additionally they cultivate behaviors, attitudes, and skills which stress the positive and enhance the learner's ego. These professional skills do not come naturally; they must be learned.

SELF-IMAGE OF THE TEACHER. Fuller and Bown emphasize the necessity for teachers to be accepting of themselves—to be genuine and sincere persons with a strong professional self-perception. The authors go on to say that "For the child to develop as a person the teacher must be a real person."[7] Cogan, in a perceptive section on the public esteem of teachers and its effect on learning says:

> The esteem in which the general public holds teachers has a profound influence upon what the teachers learn in the course of their professional education, how they teach in school, and especially upon what their students learn.[8]

Cogan does not claim that these are more than questions yet to be answered. There is, however, theoretical and scientific evidence to support his conjecture. In administration there is a principle to the effect that people do not have influence with subordinates unless they are perceived to have status and influence with superiors. The principle would appear to apply to relationships between community and teachers, administrators and teachers, and teachers and students. Esteem from significant others and a strong sense of personal and professional worth on the part of teachers undoubtedly is closely related to teaching competence. It would appear to follow that a first step is to elevate the level of respect and appreciation for the teaching profession in the minds of both teachers themselves and the public.

USE OF GROUPS. Even though all learning is individual and effective teaching is directed toward individuals, the best teaching does not necessarily involve a "Mark Hopkins" on one end of the log and a student on the other. Neither the effective use of resource nor optimal learning achievement is gained by total individual attention. The use of groups for certain purposes can significantly enhance learning. Grouping arrangements can include individuals working alone; two individuals working together as "buddies;" small, ongoing, face-to-face groups working together on a common activity; seminar or laboratory groups; traditional class-size groups; and large group or mass instruction. Teachers need to know and make use of the sociology and psychology of groups, and they also need to be skilled in effective group interventions.

CLASSROOM MANAGEMENT. If teachers are to replace lock-step mass education with individualized and person-relevant learning, skill in classroom management is essential. It is simpler to have children sit while the teacher "teaches" the same assignment from the same workbook to all students who then take the same test. It is far more complicated for a teacher to preside over a number of learners actively involved in a variety of activities, each of which is meaningful for the individual and part of a planned sequence. Teachers need to possess the range of skills needed for both individualized and group instruction.

Skill in the use of classroom groups is an important part of classroom management. Also important is the ability to set objectives, use a variety of materials and media, keep accurate records, and work collaboratively with other professionals and paraprofessionals. The ability to provide structure for a variety of learning activities is one of the teacher's most critical resources, without which independent and interdependent student learning is bound to suffer.

INSTRUCTIONAL STRATEGIES. During the past decade there has been a heightened search for effective instructional strategies. The result has been the appearance of a number of philosophical and conceptual systems, practical approaches, and methods of analysis. Included among these are the following: Flanders Interaction Analysis, discovery learning, affective education, competency-based education, mastery learning, convergent-divergent questioning, individually programmed instruction, positive reinforcement, and open education. Each approach has a high degree of validity; each has proved effective in school settings. Few of these instructional systems, however, have as yet undergone sufficient controlled experimentation or rigorous field study. Dunkin and Biddle, in an exhaustive study of the research on new instructional strategies, found little proof of effectiveness in most of these systems.[9,10] This finding does not mean that all instructional approaches are equally sound or that those tested are unsound. Research on instruction is as problematic as the instruction itself. It does, however, emphasize the need for caution in setting forth solutions to teaching problems.

In spite of the difficulties, teacher educators owe teachers the most professionally defensible knowledge, behaviors, and skills that are available. Within the limits of their resources, teacher educators should:

1. Help teachers to become knowledgeable about available instructional strategies and the evidence of their strengths and weaknesses.
2. Select the instructional knowledge, behaviors, and skills that appear most useful and make them a part of the teacher education curriculum.
3. Prepare all teachers for a lifetime of professional renewal through constant efforts to improve their instructional understandings and effectiveness.
4. Quicken the pace and enlarge the amount of competent research.

THE FUTURE OF THE TEACHING PROFESSION

Whence, where, and whither are questions of critical importance to the teaching profession and to teacher education. The sections above have analyzed teaching in terms of commonly accepted criteria for professions. A wide discrepancy was found between the established older professions—to which status teaching commonly aspires—and the teaching profession as it presently exists in America. A close correspondence was found between the teaching profession and what is described as the semiprofessions.

The tantalizing question then becomes whether teaching as a profession is in an emergent state or whether it is destined for the foreseeable future to remain a semiprofession with all of the limits that pertain thereto. Goode does not equivocate on this issue. He says:

> . . . school-teaching will not achieve professionalism . . . Teachers will doubtless move upward in income relative to other semi-professions . . . all of these [teaching included] will move somewhat towards improving their economic and prestige positions, the journey will not be long and the movement upward not great.[11]

In many ways, the question of status within the hierarchy of professions is false or a nonissue. Status is a consequence of important conditions rather than an important condition in its own right. What the teaching profession needs is a set of conditions which are favorable to the delivery of professional-level educational service to the society and its communities. If these conditions cannot be achieved, then neither can quality educational service. In that case it is society which becomes the loser.

The members of the Commission on Education for the Profession of Teaching do not share the prediction of Goode and Etzioni. We are, however, indebted to these authors for clarifying issues and for illuminating the dimensions of the challenge which professional education faces.

CEPT Position Statement

The Commission shares with the teachers of America the conviction that teaching by its very nature is a profession. That it has not, for very complex reasons, come to maturity as a profession is recognized, even declared. That it can and will self-actualize into a profession which meets all the classical criteria is a matter both of prediction and determination. Indeed, it is the function of this report to stimulate professional and organizational effort in this direction.

The Commission believes that a number of conditions currently are favorable for the profession to make a "quantum leap" forward at this time:

1. The importance of education in society is growing steadily. Increasingly, people recognize learning as "lifelong" and characteristic of our way of life. This development makes it possible to put childhood learning and school learning into a new perspective. Learning is no longer what people "do" to others. Rather, it is a universal process which is necessary, natural, and beautiful; an ongoing happening held in common and shared by child and adult.
2. The knowledge and skills required for teaching are rapidly taking form, and the profession is beginning to take its culture seriously.
3. The organized profession is growing in strength and in the capacity to address the critical questions of the work of teaching, professional quality control, and the broad social issues of education.
4. Teacher education is well through the decade within which it promises to come into its own and into its profession; tremendous progress is being made. Its acceptance within the profession and within the university community appears imminent.
5. Changes in the nature of society and of education within the society have now gone far enough for the public to be able to see that there is need for changes in schools and in the role and function of the teacher. Leadership on the part of the profession could result in early social consensus on the reschooling and professionalization which is needed.
6. There is an emerging capacity for the respective elements within the teaching profession to work together toward common goals.

Concerns Over Professions

Throughout its deliberations, the Commission has been acutely aware of developing societal concerns over the directions that some professions have taken.[12,13] There is substantial evidence that professions have not been as responsive to changing needs as might be expected. They have tended to overspecialize on the one hand and to fail to find means of cutting across specializations on the other. The rigidities of boundaries around existing professions and disciplines have tended to keep collaboration between and among them at a low level. Most serious, perhaps, has been the incapacity to create new professions as conditions change and new needs are generated. In short, professions as institutions have shown the same "steady state" characteristics as have other types of institutions. The consequence is a poorer and poorer fit between what is needed and what is offered.

Despite the problems established professions presently are facing— and adjustment problems are not unique to professions in these times of change and disruption—there can be no acceptable social alternative to professional service and professional organization. To abandon the professions is to deny the quest for improvement in the lot of humanity. For teaching to hold back in its search for quality professional service is to dim the lamps of learning through the land at a time when they hold promise of burning more brightly.

The proper response for teaching is to push forward and, through careful attention to societal need, develop the teaching profession as the model for others in responsiveness and quality service. There is no need to repeat the errors of the other professions. We can indeed, with Robert Frost, take "the road least traveled by" and blaze the trail for others. Education always has been close to the people. It can stay that way and still be served by professionals.

ASSERTIONS

Out of its deliberations the Committee has generated a series of generalizations and positions. These are presented here, in the form of assertions, as summary of what has been presented and preview of what is to follow.

1. Teaching is a profession. In practice it is an applied or clinical science involving services to people; using processes of diagnosis, prescription, and implementation; and characterized by the creative integration of professional knowledge and skill, personal style, and teaching art.

2. Teacher education is the preparation and research arm of the teaching profession.

3. Teacher education is the primary responsibility of (a) the teaching profession and (b) the college or university. Its governance structure should reflect this.

4. In common with other professional programs, the teacher preparation program is most effective when it is located on the campus of a significant college or university. Here it can have the advantage of the scholarly environment which fosters research and creative activities, access to the rich opportunities for liberal learning, teaching specializations in the disciplines, access to the social and behavioral sciences and the humanities which undergird the profession of teaching, the privilege of academic freedom as it pursues its quest for truth and effectiveness, and the rich cultural environment that prevails.

5. Organizationally, the teacher education program operates best when established as a professional school or college on the campus. (When other forms of organization are used, it is treated in the same way as are other professions.)

6. Preparing teachers is a process which transforms educated

persons from lay citizens to professional educators; there is the assumption that the role performance of the teacher will be importantly altered during the preparation process.

7. While recognizing the importance of a liberal education and of specialization in one or more teaching fields, nothing should be permitted to obscure the fact that the difference between an educated person and a professional teacher is pedagogy—the science of teaching.

8. To meet its responsibilities to society, the teaching profession requires a significantly enlarged and expanded initial preparation program as well as much more adequate attention to inservice and continuing education.

9. Teacher educators are an integral part of the teaching profession; as such they should be members of and active participants in the constellation of professional organizations at national, state, and local levels.

10. Teacher education and teacher educators exemplify what they explicate. This implies that the professional college or school can be no less than a model of the best educational practice known to the profession and society—i.e., philosophy, instructional strategies and performance, organization, facilities, equipment and resources, experimentation, and innovation.

11. Professions depend upon the development of a "professional culture" which constitutes the expertise of the professional practitioner.

12. Professional schools of education have as their reason for existence three primary functions:
    a. Adding to the "professional culture" through research and development activities,
    b. Preparing professionals to use the knowledge and skills in the practice of their professions,
    c. Cultivating personal commitments to the social purposes for which education in a democracy exists.

13. Teacher preparation is most effective when it is campus based and field oriented.

14. To be effective, teacher education must be a collaborative effort which involves the university, the organized teaching profession, and the operating schools and school systems, including their communities.

15. As is the case with all professions, the teaching profession has multiple clients. It serves the broader society, the community, and the individual.

a. The profession draws its authority from the broader society which hosts it; its expertise and organization are international and national in scope.
b. Individual teachers have their teaching assignment from a local school or school district which they must satisfy through performance which is at one and the same time professionally defensible and locally effective.
c. The focus of teaching is on the individual who is the ultimate client with a need and right to learn.

16. Because professions both necessarily and desirably have national and international perspectives, because education is a function of the state, and therefore varies in requirements from state to state, and because local schools have needs that derive directly from the nature of the community, there tends to be some discrepancy between the generalized preparation of the teacher and the specific instructional needs of the individual school or school system.

17. It is the responsibility of:
a. The preparation program to prepare teachers with the skills needed to learn to cope with specific community and school situations and needs.
b. The individual teacher, as a professional, to learn what is needed by the community and to adjust performance to community realities.
c. The local education authority to assist the teacher in this accommodation through inservice education, appropriate supervisory assistance, and other means.

18. In its broader sense, teacher education is a lifelong process for the professional teacher. It begins with the experiences students have in schools and in the societies, is professionalized in the preparation program, and continues throughout the professional career.

19. Teachers, as professionals, individually are responsible for keeping up to date and for improving their competence throughout the period of their professional careers.

20. Universities and colleges, professional organizations, and local education authorities share responsibility for facilitating and assisting the teacher with continuing and inservice education.

21. Colleges and universities have primary responsibility for the initial preparation programs of teachers. Employing school systems and other responsible agencies are responsible for inservice education. The individual teacher and professional associations are responsible for continuing professional education. Teacher

education institutions are partners at each stage of the career development process, even though their responsibilities vary.

22. While concentrating its attention on development and preparation, the professional school of education shares responsibility for public enlightenment and for extending assistance into other areas of instructional and educative endeavor.

23. Regardless of the extent to which some aspects of control of education may move toward state or national centralization, the community will continue to have substantial influence on and authority over who teaches in the schools and what their conditions of work will be.

24. All of the direct human service professions hold in common the need for knowledge and skills necessary for people to learn. Because the most significant quality in every helping relationship is a teaching-learning interaction, the profession in general, and teacher education in particular, should recognize this common need and take the initiative in developing collaborative or unified programs across the human service professions to prepare professionals who can function effectively in a variety of human service careers. Only when educators reflect an enlarged view of the settings in which teaching is vital will the profession reach its full maturity.

FOOTNOTES

1. Dan C. Lortie, *Schoolteacher. A Sociological Study* (Chicago: The University of Chicago Press, 1975).
2. Amitai Etzioni, ed., *The Semi-Professions and Their Organization: Teachers, Nurses, Social Workers* (New York: The Free Press, 1969), p. xii.
3. Margaret Mead, "An Anthropologist Looks at the Teacher's Role," *Education* 94, no. 4, pp. 379-82.
4. Victor A. Thompson, *Modern Organization* (New York: Alfred A. Knopf, 1961).
5. G.E. Markowitz and D.K. Rosner, "Doctors in Crisis: A Study of the Use of Medical Education Reform to Establish Professional Elitism in Medicine," *American Quarterly* 25 (March 1973): 83-107.
6. Abraham Flexner, *Medical Education in the United States and Canada* (Boston: D.B. Updike, The Merrymont Press, 1910).
7. F.F. Fuller and O.H. Bown, "Becoming a Teacher," in *Teacher Education. 74th Yearbook of the National Society for the Study of Education*, Kevin Ryan, ed. (Chicago: University of Chicago Press, 1975), pp. 146-72.
8. M.L. Cogan, "Current Issues in the Education of Teachers," in *Teacher Education*, ibid., p. 204.
9. M.J. Dunkin and B.J. Biddle, *The Study of Teaching* (New York: Holt, Rinehart and Winston, 1974).

10. At a conference on research in teaching, held at the Research and Development Center, University of Texas at Austin, November 1975, the research reports were much more optimistic.
11. W.J. Goode, "The Theoretical Limits of Professionalism," in Etzioni, *The Semi-Professions,* p. 281.
12. E.H. Schein, *Professional Education* (New York: McGraw-Hill, 1972).
13. C. Argyris and D.A. Schon, *Theory in Practice* (San Francisco: Jossey-Bass, 1974).

THREE

The Governance of Teacher Education

With the proliferation of organizations that represent the teaching profession and teacher education, there is a tendency to produce babble rather than intelligible sounds.

Everyone stands to gain by the establishment of strong teacher education and a strong profession.

Where education is involved, everyone is involved. There are innumerable agencies, institutions, organizations, and groups which participate directly or indirectly in the governance, support, management, and operation of the formal educational enterprise. The type of changes advocated by this Commission will affect all of these interests. Some will be concerned with the reallocation of power and authority. Some will be interested in the impact of the proposals on the profession, schools, and society. Hopefully, however, all interests will keep in mind the broader interest of society, communities, and citizens. Hopefully, too, there will be continuing commitment to the nation's mission of achieving equal rights for all.

There is in the social sciences a concept called "zero sum." It is a description of a situation where there is assumed to be a fixed amount of some desired commodity or condition. If one of the interested parties gets more of the object, the other will get less. Thus there is an inevitable conflict of interests between the interested parties. The concept of zero sum—so frequently subscribed to unknowingly or knowingly by individuals and groups—often is false. This is particularly true in matters of power and influence. Contesting for right to control often reduces the ability of any to make a difference. The sum of ability to achieve is thus reduced as one cancels out the other.

The Commission holds that the reallocation of authority and responsibility in education recommended in this report is *not* "zero sum." It is exactly the opposite, because thoughtful reallocation will result in the capacity to educate better; thus, we will be increasing, *not* minimizing, our ability to control our social destiny. Because this is what all desire, collaboration toward this end should be the goal of all.

Even as concern for education pervades society, so do organized educational structures appear everywhere. There is a complex legal system extending from the international level to the local community—UNESCO, federal government, state government, intermediate units, local education agencies, and individual schools. Even more complex is the array of academic, professional, service, political, and community organizations which are interested in educational affairs. For practical reasons, this report will concentrate on those organizations which are centrally involved in the educational system: the federal government, private foundations with interest in education, state government, colleges and universities which host teacher education, local education authorities and their communities, and the organized teaching profession.

THE FEDERAL GOVERNMENT

The Founding Fathers rejected the idea of a national system of education. Instead, they left to the states the responsibility for providing educational opportunity for the people. However, under the Constitution's General Welfare Clause, they reserved for the federal government the right to take action in areas where the general welfare of the people and the nation was involved. Also, through the Bill of Rights, they allowed the federal courts to intervene in matters where the rights of individuals were abridged.

The Growth of Federal Participation in Education

Almost 100 years after the founding of the nation (1867), the federal government entered directly into educational affairs, establishing the Department of Education in Washington. This legislation was circumspect concerning state powers, however, since the Department was restricted to collecting and disseminating nationwide data on education. The purpose of the activity was to "aid the people . . . in the establishment and maintenance of efficient school systems, and otherwise promote the cause of education throughout the country."[1]

With the exception of the Smith-Hughes Act and of legislation providing benefits for veterans, participation by the federal government remained largely at the information-gathering and dissemination level until after the Second World War. In 1957, Sputnik created deep concern over the quality of education in the nation's schools, the impact on American leadership in science and technology, and long-term national security. Acting under the broad terms of the Constitution's General Welfare Clause, Congress moved to establish the National Defense Education Act. Also, the National Science

Foundation funded thousands of workshops to upgrade the performance of science and mathematics teachers. In 1965, Congress passed the Elementary and Secondary Education Act, funneling massive amounts of resources into urban school systems. In the late sixties, the government attempted to improve the quality of teacher education and instituted a number of programs through the Education Professions Development Act (EPDA) (1967). By the mid-seventies, however, federal funding for teacher education had significantly declined. Whether this decline was due to deteriorating economic conditions, the alleged surplus of teachers, or to other causes is not clear.

What is clear, however, is that the federal presence in education has been established, presumably permanently. Also, it is well established that the federal courts and the federal government have the power to change education. With the responsibility for delivering education to the citizenry vested in the states, the federal role turns logically toward interventions in pursuit of national goals.

Categorical Aid

In its earlier efforts, the United States Office of Education (USOE) used its resources to give categorical aid. This permitted the "building of lighthouses" to serve as models for others. More recently, Congress has initiated "revenue sharing"—the giving of grants to states to be used, within the intended purposes, as decided by the individual states. It is not for this report to render opinions on general revenue sharing as public policy. It is, however, a matter of serious concern if federal policy causes categorical aid to be diminished. "Lighthouse building" is one of the best ways to promote the public good; sponsorship of efforts to produce new knowledge is another. Resources for these two purposes are not usually provided by the institution or agency responsible for providing or funding educational programs and services. At the level of operational responsibility, resources are usually allocated across the operating units; rarely is there significant attention to research and development since program operations are all-consuming of resources. Without continued federal support, development and research effort will suffer.

The fact that large, bureaucratically organized systems find it difficult to change is well known; less well known is the fact that change in organizations occurs largely through outside stimuli or pressures. Thus, categorical aid can be a most effective external strategy for bringing about change in the public interest and for the public good.

Recommendation

That the federal government, through the use of categorical aid, continue to seek improvements in teacher education, in the teaching profession, and in the public schools.

An Area of Neglect

It is apparent that federal programs in support of the search for better ways to educate teachers and teacher educators have had a significant influence on teacher education practice. New approaches have been developed. Much less successful has been the effort to institutionalize the new programs. The *professional culture* of teacher education has been significantly advanced, but there has been a counterproductive failure to assist teacher education to increase the length of programs so that teachers could learn that culture. This has been the major flaw in the efforts of EPDA and other U.S. Office of Education (USOE) programs. In order to make effective use of the new conceptual insights and instructional techniques, teacher education requires a significantly longer preparation program. With the reduced need for additional teachers, now is the time for the development of programs with longer time spans and different patterns of organization. When USOE established the elementary models project, its declared intention was to fund the testing of those models. It was not able to do so.

Recommendation
That USOE undertake the funding of teacher education models which require preparation time spans more closely approximating the length of training in other professions, in an endeavor to determine the results that optimal models could achieve.

Recommendation
That USOE use its resources to encourage states and institutions to move vigorously in efforts to improve teacher education.

An Area of Troublesome Policy

Whether as a matter of policy or of expediency, federal interventions through grants have tended to minimize the opportunity to really make a difference. Contributions have been less than adequate in amount and for durations which were shorter than required for an effective effort. The structures for lighthouses have been built—perhaps jerrybuilt—but the beacons have not been lighted or kept alight. In consequence, the teacher education landscape is dotted with derelict and crumbling edifices—mute testimony to vacated hopes and frustrated ambitions.

There is at least some reason to speculate that this approach has caused institutions to develop coping behaviors which have frustrated realization of the intent of the programs themselves. The purpose has been the invention and institutionalization of more effective educational systems. Institutions cannot, however, risk their basic stability for transient and ephemeral change thrusts. In the presence of uncertainty, they "hedge their bets" by making the innovative effort simply another project operated on the periphery of institutional purpose and commitment. Regular programs go on as usual. The "soft money" is used to employ temporary faculty who develop and operate the program for its limited duration. Regular faculty are little used; indeed they learn that long-term institutional rewards rarely accrue to project people. The result of this coping behavior is minimal impact; often it is counterproductive.

To make institutional change requires critical mass inputs over a relatively sustained span of time. The development has to be made central to the purposes of the institution. Institutional rewards have to go to those who become involved. The institution has to have reasonable assurance that something better will emerge and survive. Otherwise it cannot risk fundamental change.

The federal programs have not all been of this too-little-for-too-short-a-time nature. The university-based research and development centers and the regional educational laboratories have been notable exceptions; support has continued over some 15 years. Interestingly, it is becoming apparent that these sustained efforts are beginning to yield the kind of research findings which promise to build the professional culture which the teaching profession so badly needs.

A similar approach in other programs undoubtedly would have had similar results. Failure to do so may well have both wasted scarce resources and done as much harm as good.

Recommendation

That federal programs in teacher education should concentrate on critical mass inputs over longer periods of time in order to maximize the probability of success.

Present federal policy is to focus on nationwide problems with concentration on problems of the disadvantaged, according to one federal document.[2] The same paper indicates three types of support: (a) capacity building; (b) supplementary costs; (c) direct support. This Commission holds that educational problems are central to the plight of minorities. Furthermore, the key to the education problem in large part rests with the teaching profession. Until teachers are educated in depth, there is little chance that they will be capable of dealing with the challenges of minority education. The appropriate federal policy in this regard would be capacity-building teacher education programs of the kind suggested in the previous section. To date this has not been seriously tried. (Note again that the elementary models were developed but not tested.)

Research

Critically needed in education is a continuing large-scale effort to add to the knowledge base through fundamental and applied research. Also, the profession needs to develop and disseminate a wide array of workable solutions to persistent educational problems. In the long run, the greatest contribution the federal government can make is through research and development activities. Massive federal resources continue to pour into medicine, engineering, and the sciences. Surely education cannot be perceived as less important.

Recommendation

That the federal government broaden and intensify its research and development efforts in education and in teacher education with the purpose of rapid development of a professional culture for teachers.

Parity

One of the principles developed by USOE for use in the funding of education was that of "parity." The concept originated from the efforts of minority groups to have their interests directly represented in policy making, program determination, and resource allocation. At times, parity has meant *adequately* represented; at other times, it has meant *equally* represented.

Teacher education was one of the early areas where the federal government applied the principle of parity. At first, this included representatives of teacher education, the local education authority, and the community. However, the early policy did *not* recognize the teaching professions. Though the USOE has partially corrected this omission, for the most part teachers and teacher organizations still are not included or adequately represented in the policy-making bodies of institutions, programs, and projects.

Recommendation

That in all federally funded collaborative projects in teacher education, the organized teaching profession be an indispensable partner with the other groups involved.

Education Not the Federal Responsibility Alone

There is a tendency to think almost exclusively of the federal government in connection with funded projects in teacher education and to expect that all areas of need be met. As David Mathews, the newly appointed Secretary of Health, Education, and Welfare, said on the occasion of his swearing-in ceremony:

The hard truth is that we are far from being the sole arbiter of all matters of health, education, and welfare. We are one among many, along with the Congress, the other departments of the executive branch, and a host of state and local agencies that have a responsibility in these matters.[3]

It is for others too to share the burden, the opportunity, the challenge. In the sections to follow attention will be given to some of these other partners in the educational system.

PHILANTHROPIC FOUNDATIONS AND TEACHER EDUCATION

As would be expected, the philanthropic foundations have directed significant attention to the problems of education. Indeed they were active long before the federal government became involved. The foundations also are interested in teacher education even though, as the Ford Foundation has discovered, universities have not been easy to influence.[4] In common with the federal government, foundations have been more interested in innovative action and dissemination than in research; though to a lesser extent, they also have tended to operate in shorter time frames than are needed for meaningful change efforts.

Foundations presently are experiencing hard times. When they recover, they should be urged to give high priority to developing a professional culture for teachers and preparation systems to transmit and sustain the culture. Their efforts will continue to be unsuccessful, however, if they resume the search for quick ways to educate teachers. If they can accept the need for any possibility of a genuine profession of teaching, they could be responsible for achieving it. There is logic to the idea that it is easier to impact education through teacher education research and development than through any other approach.

Recommendation
    That the teaching profession attempt to convince major foundations to concentrate their educational efforts on strengthening teacher education and the teaching profession as the most effective and efficient way to bring about innovation and improvement in schools.

STATE GOVERNMENTS

By the Tenth Amendment of the Constitution, education became the right and responsibility of the states. Acting under this authority, all states have by constitution and/or statute established systems of public education.

Structure for State Governance of Education

Generally, there are lay state boards of education which regulate and set standards for education systems within the provisions established by statutes. Each state has a superintendent or commissioner to administer the educational system under the direction of the state board. Each state also has a department of education composed of professional and support staff, headed by the chief state school officer (superintendent).

Each state, acting at its own discretion, delegates control of education to local communities through the establishment of school districts which are legal and operational arms of the state government. These districts are established, altered, or abolished at the discretion of the legislatures. Their board members are state officials, and their employees are employees of the state. Their properties and funds are owned by the state. Whatever authority they have is delegated by the state. If they wished, states could operate all schools directly from the state capitol.

Both the education of teachers and their licensure are state functions. Normal schools were once state institutions, established and maintained by the state as a part of the public education system. When the function of teacher education was placed within colleges and universities, the state reserved for itself program accreditation and licensure rights—policies which continue the pattern of state influence and control.

Most states have separate boards for the control of higher education. Thus teacher education, unlike either public schools or universities, is usually subject to control from two state agencies. This dual responsibility and control often works to the disadvantage of teacher education.

Teacher Education Program Approval

Each state education department develops, adopts, and promulgates a set of standards which institutions must meet before its teacher education program is approved. This process, which includes private as well as public institutions, is mandatory since only graduates from approved programs can be given teaching certificates. At the time of initial application for approval, and at specified intervals thereafter, there is the familiar sequence of self-study and report, review by a visiting team, and decision by a professional board. Program approval is also the basis of certification.

There is considerable similarity in both program standards and review processes among the states. This is due to the influence of national standards developed by the National Council for Accreditation of Teacher Education (NCATE). Also, the teacher education officers of the state education departments belong to a national organization—the National Association of State Directors of Teacher Education and Certification (NASDTEC)—which works toward common standards and practices.

Though they are capable of insisting on quality in all teacher education programs, state program approval processes often fall short of this in practice. Program approval teams rarely deny approval outright; the few programs which are denied approval soon get reinstated. In the United States, there are between 1,300 and 1,400 institutions with teacher education programs, all of which the states approve. Clark and Marker point out that only about 40 percent of these institutions have been approved by the national accrediting agency, even though "fifty-nine of the sixty largest teacher training institutions in the United States" are NCATE accredited.[5] Many of the small institutions do not seek approval beyond what the state requires; presumably, many would have difficulty meeting the national agency standards while others elect not to.

Though rarely visible, politics is ever present in teacher education, especially at the institutional and state levels. Because teacher education students represent a high proportion of the total enrollment in institutions across the nation, their programs provide strong course registrations for other parts of the institution. Loss of teacher education would be a serious, even mortal blow to many institutions. Because the state right to *disapprove* programs would have serious political repercussions for governmental agencies, they seldom make such decisions. Indeed, they rationalize the lack of rigor on the grounds that the program review process is primarily one of self-study and improvement. Whatever the rationale, many institutions with marginal commitments and/or minimal financial and personnel resources continue to prepare teachers.

Recommendation
That each state insure that only those institutions capable of quality programs in teacher education be permitted to prepare teachers and recommend them for certification.

Certification

All states have regulations which require certification for teaching, and for other educational positions. Eligibility for certification is based upon possession of a bachelor's degree, and completion of specified courses or a program in an approved institution. In some cases, the institution simply certifies that requirements for certification have been met; in others, the state conducts a review of each applicant's transcript. All states have procedures for accepting transfers from other states. Some accept program completion at an NCATE-approved institution in accordance with a reciprocal interstate agreement. Unlike other professions, states have no common external teacher education examination (e.g. the Bar Exam) which the candidate must pass before being licensed.

In times of teacher shortages, state certification agencies commonly have relaxed licensing standards and granted emergency credentials. These practices have permitted school districts to employ persons who have had little or no teacher education while they pursue a part-time program of study. Even though this practice is understandable from the viewpoint of those responsible for staffing schools, its detrimental effect on the professional status of teaching cannot be denied.

Higher Education and Teacher Education

Teacher education has two state masters. State education departments exercise program control over teacher education, while state higher education authorities control the universities and colleges which house teacher education programs. Seldom is there adequate collaboration or even communication between the two agencies. One agency may implement new teacher education regulations and program requirements which have serious budget implications without checking to see that the other agency provides adequate resources. Rarely does the teacher education division of the state agency promote teacher education interests with the higher education agency.

Across the nation, higher education seriously underestimates the needs of teacher education. The financial support level is the lowest provided in higher education. Neither universities nor state education agencies attempt to correct this deficiency.

Recommendation
That state education departments should vigorously represent the needs and interests of university-based teacher education in the state.

Recommendation
In those states where there are separate boards for higher education and the public school education, that there should be a cross-agency group charged with insuring collaborative action in all matters concerning teacher education.

The State and Support for Teacher Education

States are responsible for both teacher education and public schools; as a matter of intelligent self-interest they should insist on a support level for teacher education at least as favorable as that provided for other professions, but this does not happen. Teacher education receives the lowest level of support of all the programs offered in higher education.

. . . though teacher education accounts for about one third of America's college students at any given time, it receives less than nine percent of the support given to higher education. Education departments in humanistic and fieldwork areas receive less per credit hour than conventional departments in other colleges of most institutions. Teacher education in 1972-73 received $1,300 to $1,500 per F.T.E. (full time equivalent) as contrasted with expenditures twice that high and more in other professional areas.[6]

This nation cannot expect to solve its educational problems as long as the states neglect the preparation of teachers. The enormous resources which states invest in public school education can only be less than efficiently used if they do not insure that qualified personnel are available.

Recommendation
That states should give high priority to developing the support levels necessary for quality teacher education in approved institutions.

The State, Teacher Education, and the Teaching Profession

Though the state has a legal responsibility for education and for teacher education, it has the right to make its own determination of how to exercise that responsibility. It can delegate to one or more responsible parties the functions of control of teacher education and teacher certification.

The established professions accept responsibility for governing themselves. This includes preparation, licensure, and surveillance of the ethics and competence of members. Since 1971, the National Education Association (NEA) has been pressing for passage of teacher standards and licensure acts which vest responsibility in state commissions composed predominantly of teachers. At this time, only Oregon and California have moved fully in this direction. Other states are likely to do so soon, while some will prefer variations of the NEA Model Act. It appears that teachers and their associations are ready for substantial steps in this direction.

Recommendation
That all states should develop the means by which the organized teaching profession can be delegated responsibility for establishing professional standards for teacher education, for teacher certification, and for the professional behavior of all education professionals.

COLLEGES AND UNIVERSITIES

Teacher preparation has not always been a function of colleges and universities; only in this century have universities and colleges taken over the responsibility for teacher education. The improvements in teacher education and the teaching profession expected from the new relationship have not occurred, however. Higher education has exploited teacher education for its own interests, while granting it low status, misplacing it organizationally and programmatically, and seriously underfinancing it. Even the vigorous development effort of the last 10 years has not produced much change; teacher education still sits on the academic street corner, tin cup in hand, begging for the capital to market its product.

Higher Education Organization: A Conceptual Model

Universities are institutions established to achieve significant social purposes. The most fundamental of these purposes is the pursuit of *valid knowledge*. All the basic activities of a university are directly concerned with the search for valid knowledge, with its presentation and dissemination, and with its use. It is in protection of this function that academic freedom exists. And it is in the exercise of these responsibilities that professors research, teach, and engage in social criticism.

Valid knowledge cannot readily be described in discrete terms. It is more adequately described as a phenomenon that exists along a continuum that stretches from the search for pure knowledge at one end to uses of that knowledge at the other (Figure 2).

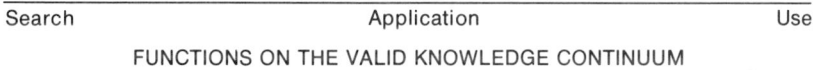

Search	Application	Use

FUNCTIONS ON THE VALID KNOWLEDGE CONTINUUM

FIGURE 2

In terms of people who perform the functions, there will be researchers, developers, and practitioners (Figure 3).

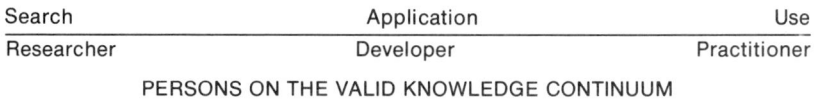

Search	Application	Use
Researcher	Developer	Practitioner

PERSONS ON THE VALID KNOWLEDGE CONTINUUM

FIGURE 3

Scholars in the disciplines perceive themselves as researchers; their interests lie predominantly toward the search end of the continuum. Professional practitioners are primarily concerned with the applied uses of knowledge; hence their interests and activities would fit on the use end of the continuum. Professors in the professional schools on the university campus have a strong interest in developing the valid knowledge base of the profession which they represent; thus their interests will tend to cluster around the middle of the continuum. The hypothesized modality of interests for the three groups can be illustrated by placing curves along the continuum (Figure 4).

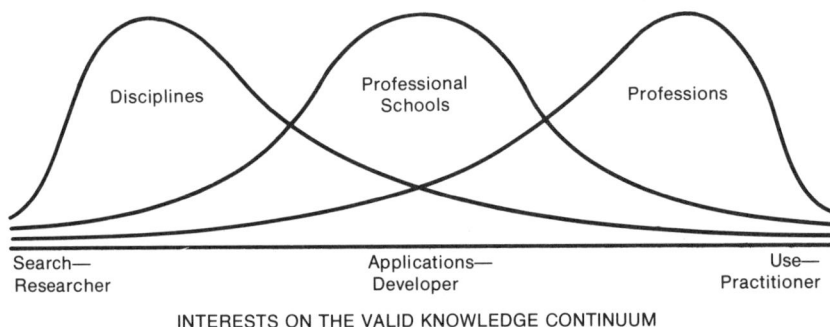

Search—	Applications—	Use—
Researcher	Developer	Practitioner

INTERESTS ON THE VALID KNOWLEDGE CONTINUUM

FIGURE 4

It should be observed that the curves are overlapping and no group is mutually exclusive of the others; any group may be expected to have individuals who regularly or occasionally express their interests at any point along the continuum. Nevertheless, the modal behaviors of the groups could be predicted to fall as conceptualized.

Disciplines and Professional Schools

Universities comprise faculties who represent the disciplines on the one hand, and professional schools on the other. While sharing the basic values of the university, the two groups have different emphases in their academic missions. Each group has a university subculture of its own which is highly functional.

The *disciplines* emphasize pure forms of research, place value on and reward research and related scholarly activities, relate to scholars in the disciplines as their significant referent groups, eschew concern on their part for the practical utility of knowledge, and display the skills and capabilities characteristic of scholars and researchers. The *professional* schools value and undertake research and scholarship, but emphasize the search for socially useful applications of knowledge to professional problems; address the reality represented by the profession by drawing on the contributions of multiple disciplines as well as their own technical culture; place value on and reward those activities which have direct application to the problems of professional practitioners; relate to their own professional faculties and to practitioners as significant referent groups; embrace a concern for the practical utility of knowledge without denying the importance of the

58

knowledge itself; and display the skills and characteristics of professionals who must work with "real world" constituencies.

Most universities will recognize the dual nature of this system, encourage each unit to operate effectively within its own sphere, promote cross-unit activities, and accommodate each in matters of administration and governance. Some institutions may elect to effect a high level of integration among the disciplines and the professional schools. Whatever the approach, it is critical that institutions identify and place each instructional unit in the campus within its appropriate group. For most units this represents no problem. *However, teacher education is a notable exception. It requires the status of a professional school or college but often does not get it. Even when it is named as a professional school, it may not be treated as such. To misplace any unit is to confer role expectations which it cannot meet. Teacher education is not a discipline; it is an endeavor of "studied action."*

Professors of education are professional educators whose graduate programs prepared them for continuing professional service. They expect to be involved in a lifetime of teaching, educational development, and professional service. They do not come to higher education to adopt the lifestyles of academicians in the disciplines. The disciplines exist for a purpose which they serve well—to contribute to the pool of valid knowledge upon which the professions depend. Professions and professional schools exist for a different purpose—to develop and disseminate a professional technical culture suited to the needs of practitioners.

Recommendation

That teacher education be organizationally identified and established within colleges and universities as a professional college or school; it should not be subordinate to or dominated by an academic unit.

Recommendation

That all concerned with the teaching profession vigorously press to improve the status and condition of teacher education on the college and university campus.

Teacher Education in Higher Education

A large majority of colleges and universities have teacher education programs. In larger institutions there usually is a unit called a school or a college of education. Smaller institutions often locate teacher education as a department within a larger academic unit. Some newer institutions are experimenting with other forms of organization which merge professional preparation programs with related academic disciplines. And some institutions are considering a preparation program for human service professionals which would organize groups on the basis of commonality of function.

Teacher education units, no matter how organized, have long been concerned over their status on campus. They have not been able to shed the image of marginal academic respectability which they brought from their normal school past. Neither have they been able to convince the academic community that they have or could have a genuine professional culture which teachers need in the pursuit of their careers. In consequence, teacher education has existed in a "no-man's land" between the disciplines on the one hand and the professional school on the other—on the model presented earlier (Figure 4), in the trough between the respective curves. It has been coveted without being included. And it has suffered the openly expressed disdain of many professors in the disciplines.

The reasons for the continuing low status of teacher education on the campuses are many, complex, and largely speculative. No attempt will be made here to either elaborate or assess them. A list of possible reasons might be useful, however.

1. Failure to overcome the "normal school" image and the hard feelings that were engendered when normal schools were incorporated into or became colleges and universities.
2. An assessment on the part of the academic community that teaching is and will remain a semiprofession and is, therefore, lower on the academic totem pole than the disciplines or the other professional schools. Other marginal units on campus have a similar or more aggravated circumstance.
3. Negative "spin-off" from the ongoing competition for the time of students in teacher education.
4. Difference over whether teaching is an art or a science.
5. Conscious or unconscious realization that to accept teaching as a profession would require teachers in higher education to undergo professional preparation or admit inadequacy as teachers.
6. Failure of teacher education to assert its uniqueness and to develop a distinctive presence on campus.
7. The ongoing closeness of government influence through accreditation and certification which characterizes teacher education and does not characterize other university units.
8. The absence of any outside force which is concerned enough to come to the aid of teacher education politically or institutionally. Most notable is the professional organizations which logically could be expected to do so but do not.

Whatever the reason, the situation can only be assessed as damaging to the teaching profession and in need of urgent attention.

Problems in Self-Determination

Colleges and universities as institutions pride themselves on their decentralized organizational structure and operation. Academic units (colleges and departments) have considerable autonomy, particularly in matters of instruction and scholarly activities. Though there usually is a representative body which reviews programs and courses, there is high expectation that undue interference will be avoided. Unless there are serious questions of quality or propriety, of jurisdictional conflict between units, or of financial or other impact detrimental to some other unit, approval will be granted.

Teacher education, as a college or department, characteristically does not enjoy this privilege of self-determination, however. Part of the situation may be attributed to the status of teacher education on the campus. More arises directly out of a built-in and ever-present conflict of interest between education and other units, notably the arts and sciences colleges and their component disciplines. The conflict of interest is real. Teachers are the only professional students who are required to continue study in the disciplines following completion of the general education requirement. Teaching has its undergirding disciplines as do other professions (psychology, sociology, etc.). In addition, each teacher must prepare in depth in at least one and often two teaching fields. This means that teacher education students are the continuing object of attention of both the disciplines and teacher education. Each group views its contribution to the education of the teacher as critical. Each would enlarge its domain to provide more extensive preparation if it could. This leads to conflict of interest over possession of the student on the one hand and allocation of courses to be taken on the other. Relatively rigid state certification regulations place substantial limitations on the freedom of both parties. After mandated requirements have been met, only a few hours of electives are left over to negotiate.

Teacher education units often complain that they do not have a chance. Faculty from the disciplines comprise a large proportion of the total on campus, at least one half being the usual case. Teacher educators are much fewer in numbers. When votes are called for, education often loses. It is this situation to which Clark and Marker refer when they state that teacher education will never be anything more than an academic major.[7] Who has decided? Certainly not teacher education which has institutional and professional responsibility for the professional component of teacher education. Nor will it be possible to find minutes of meetings to that effect. Instead it is a generalization derived from countless examples in hundreds of institutions over several decades of time. One has to count the times that proposals to enlarge and enhance teacher education have been turned down by academic vote. Impossible to count would be the innumerable times that what was desired, needed, and justifiable was never proposed. It had already been decided.

There appears to be no ready solution to this situation short of expansion of teacher education into longer preparation programs. Even then, however, the conflict could be expected to continue since the appetite of the disciplines would only be whetted.

Universities could resolve the problem internally, but they are unlikely to do so on their own initiative. What remains then is resort to prescriptions from state agencies about requirements for program accreditation and for certification, but even these are subject to influence from the academic community. A third alternative is to shift control of programs to bodies which are professionally oriented and willing to confront for professional gain.

THE LOCAL EDUCATION AUTHORITIES

Though the states have responsibility for education, education in this nation has long been considered a strongly local matter. Early schools were either private or local community efforts, voluntarily established and independently operated. Later the states mandated that local communities provide schools. Still later the state (a) established a state-wide system of local school districts which together included all the state area; (b) made school attendance mandatory; (c) provided partial funding; and (d) began the process of regulating the schools through standards for teacher preparation and curriculum.

Each local school district was placed under a board of school trustees which represented the people. The board was a corporate body; individual trustees had no power except as specifically delegated by the board. It was given the authority to receive the state funds and to raise funds through a tax on property within the district. Unlike municipal bodies, school districts and everything pertaining to them were legally made part of the state education system; whatever they had was not theirs and whatever they did had to be within the specific authority delegated to them by the state or implied therefrom. These conditions continue to the present.

School districts are significant elements in the professional education and growth of teachers. They participate both directly and indirectly. At this time, it would appear that local districts are the most significant single force operating to determine the quality of the profession. Their influence is directed through a number of different activities, of which the following are representative: (a) recruitment, employment, assignment, and reassignment; (b) conditions surrounding the work of the teacher; (c) benefits such as development leave, salaries, and increments; (d) inservice education and related activities; (e) support of the teachers' efforts in lifelong continuing education; (f) personnel policies related to rewards for teachers' self-improvement efforts; and (g) the nature of administrative and supervisory practices.

At present there are wide variations among districts in what they do in teacher development. This is almost certain to attract the attention of the courts as the equality of educational opportunity goal is pursued beyond equalizing the overall resources available. Another situation which can be expected to markedly affect the role of the school district is collective bargaining, which has grown very rapidly and gives indication of including virtually all teachers in the foreseeable future. Each of the items referred to in the paragraph above is subject to negotiation.

Recruitment, Employment, Assignment, and Reassignment of Teachers

As the employers of teachers, school districts constitute the marketplace. The district is always in a position to influence directly the quality of its own program through the choice it makes among available teacher candidates. It can also influence teacher education by making public the competencies and qualities which it values and needs in teachers, and by demanding corresponding inservice and continuing education from the colleges and universities. And, finally, teachers themselves are quick to perceive that rewards come to those who prepare themselves for the specific needs of the district.

Because the teaching profession, the college or university, and the state education agency all control teacher education, programs should not change their philosophies and methodologies only in response to local needs. Teachers entering the profession have a right to a preparation that prepares them for "safe" performance *anywhere,* not just *somewhere.* The teaching profession has the obligation to insure that every teacher has validated, broad-based professional competencies, without which teaching is merely an individually or locally developed craft. This is not to argue that teacher education should be unresponsive to local needs; rather, teacher education should be responsive but only within professional limits. These limits should include electives within the preservice program; graduate offerings related to the local community, but consistent with the continuing education needs of all teachers; and cooperation with districts and schools in inservice work.

Conditions Surrounding the Work of Teachers

Preservice and inservice teachers understand the realities of the workplace. They process formal experiences in teacher education in terms of those realities. For example, prospective teachers will not be interested in individualizing instruction if they believe that in the community where they will teach, individualization is not possible, valued, encouraged, or even permitted. Nor will they plan continuing education or other professional activities after school if they must suffer large classes and heavy burdens every working day. Leadership serves the teaching profession and the schools best when it creates conditions as favorable as possible to success; maintains a climate of commitment, active search, innovation, and openness; and rewards teachers who pursue continually the search for greater effectiveness and proficiency.

Employment Benefits

Local school systems across the nation differ widely in their policies concerning professional renewal benefits for teachers. Some have generous policies; some have none at all. *This Commission believes that one of the most important functions of school district policy is to insure that teachers remain lifelong learners in both their personal and professional lives.*

Teachers often teach in situations which demand broad, educated backgrounds, as well as a need for high professional knowledge and skill. They serve in a world characterized by rapid change and by a continuing knowledge explosion. Also, teachers require a background knowledge of the community they serve. Successful adaptation of professional teaching skills to the local community usually calls for specific job and situation preparation which their previous preparation could not provide.

Unfortunately, teachers are not paid enough to permit them to spend much on personal and professional development. What they need in the way of association memberships, travel to meetings, books, journals, continuing education, formal study and informal activities, self-improvement, and national and international travel simply is not available, particularly for young teachers and heads of households. The employing agency should provide these opportunities on a systematic basis.

Recommendation

That local education authorities view the continuously learning teacher to be as important as the continuously learning child, adult citizen, school board member, or school administrator.

Recommendation

That each school system devote a percentage of its professional salaries budget to providing growth activity opportunities for teachers. As a longer term objective, at least 20 percent should be devoted to this. At least 2½ percent should be available immediately.

This should increase by at least 1 percent per year until 10 percent is reached. The rate beyond this should be based on experience and need.

Recommendation

That the resources for professional development be apportioned in such a way as to have three distinct categories of use: (a) a cumulative account for each individual from which the individual, with approval of plan, may draw; (b) a fund for inservice education upon which the school system and individual schools draw for educational needs specific to the district or school; (c) a fund for continuing education activities upon which teacher associations, the school districts, individual schools, or other groups may draw upon approval by the board of education or the superintendent.

Recommendation

That each school system make a distinction between those activities of professional development that derive from the unique needs of a particular workplace (school; district) and those that are of consequence to a professional regardless of the workplace.

"Inservice" should be used to refer to employment-oriented education. For example, if a school staff decides to use the Individually Guided Education (IGE) program as its approach to individualization of instruction, then the faculty needs to be prepared specifically for this. The school should provide the education at school expense. "Continuing" should refer to activities designed to supplement and extend the preservice education of teachers, and to update them on recent findings and approaches. For example, if teachers feel a need to expand their proficiency in individualization, then they will want to know the latest thinking and practices. Their professional organization might discover the need through its annual needs assessment inventory and declare a high priority. After approval by the policy group and the superintendent, a teaching center might offer a series of workshops.[8] Payment of costs might come from continuing education money from the district funds, payment from the teacher association treasury, and individual contributions (either personal or drawn) from the individual's personal development account in the district.

Recommendation

That the states build into their school finance allocations and apportionment formulas the funds needed for professional development of teachers on ratios similar to those recommended above.

Inservice Education

In the section above, *inservice* was defined as meaning those activities which have as their intended purpose preparation for specific demands which decisions within the system have created. It should be a condition attached to all innovations which are introduced to school systems or schools that adequate specific preparation precede or accompany them. Many innovations are lost for want of this "nail;" much time, energy, money, and potential learning are wasted. Worse, perhaps, is the resulting reluctance on the part of teachers to get professionally "turned on" by suggested innovation for fear it will be "like the last time and the time before that."

Not all inservice derives from innovation, however. There is frequently need to go back and learn to do better what already is being done.

Continuing Education

Continuing education refers to all efforts to expand and update the skills of the individual professional beyond the basic or "safe" level required for entry to the profession. A professional, by definition, is responsible for keeping up to date and competent. This does not mean that the individual does this alone. The employer, out of intelligent self-interest and necessity, contributes directly to continuing education for teachers. Personnel policies of the school district should clearly spell out the expectations and available assistance.

In all professions, organizations offer educational programs for their members by making available studies, books, and journals. Similarly, teacher associations need to expand their activities in this area. Professional schools should continue to contribute to the continuing education options open to professionals by offering graduate and postgraduate work, including credit and noncredit lectures, seminars, and workshops.

There is great need for collaborative action among the several contributors to continuing education. Without such collaboration, overlap and gaps are likely to characterize programs.

Recommendation

That because the "Teacher Center" (by whatever name) appears to represent a great opportunity to facilitate teacher education at all levels and in all respects, it should be the object of serious attention.

Recommendation

That as teacher centers and other such efforts develop, careful attention be given to the allocation of responsibilities to insure the preservation of the integrity of the individual professional and of the profession.

Personnel Policies Related to Rewards

In sound personnel management, rewards accrue for desired outcomes. Learning in schools is the desired process and outcome for both teachers and students. It should be rewarded. It is essential to the learning process in schools that teachers be perceived by children as being avid learners themselves. Otherwise, in their eyes, learning becomes something (like castor oil) that adults impose on children from which they can escape only by becoming chronological adults.

Learning activities should be specified as an objective for each professional in the district. They should receive attention both in the planning for improvement and in the evaluation program.

Administrative and Supervisory Practices

Administration and supervision have long been important elements of the school system. However, there is little evidence that they have made significant contributions to teacher performance or learning outcomes. Much administration and supervision have been "out of sync" with the nature of the school and the professional work force. Potentially, they are critical elements in the education of teachers. In large measure, they determine what teachers will be able to do with the education and experience they already possess. Administrators and supervisors must keep in mind always that schools are *modern* organizations staffed by professionals; learning and teaching are sensitive processes which insensitive relationships often violate; and since learning has personal development both as its process and its intended outcome, emphasis must always be on the formative, helping relationship, rather than on the summative, decision-making side of institutional life.

PROFESSIONAL ORGANIZATIONS

The National Education Association

The National Teacher's Association, established in 1857, was the first national organization of teachers in the United States. Its purpose was "To elevate the character and advance the interests of the profession of teaching and to promote the cause of popular education in the United States." Thirteen years later it merged with other organizations to form the National Education Association (1870). The merger established directions which were to dominate the organized profession for almost 100 years. The new organization included both teachers and administrators, thus establishing the principle that the diverse professional groups involved in education could effectively work together in one organization. Teachers, teacher educators, principals, supervisors, curriculum specialists, superintendents, and higher education personnel came under the NEA aegis. In 1906, an Act of

Congress incorporated the Association under the revised name of National Education Association of the United States.

In the 1960s, however, the situation dramatically changed. Teachers saw themselves as dominated by administrators, professors, and others. Militantly, they began to disassociate those departments which represented professionals other than classroom teachers. These became separate organizations. Individual membership privileges were denied to persons who served on negotiating teams for an employer. It is still too soon to assess the long-term consequences of the splintering of the education professions into separate organizations. In any case, the move probably was inevitable. If the teachers need to use collective bargaining in the desperate search for improved working conditions, it is only natural that they would find administrators in conflict of interest.

The NEA has remained the dominant teachers' organization over its entire history. Its purpose appears in the Preamble to the Constitution of the National Education Association of the United States:

> . . . [the NEA will] serve as the national voice for education, advance the cause of education for all individuals, promote professional excellence among educators, gain recognition of the basic importance of the teacher in the learning process, protect the rights of educators and advance their interests and welfare, secure professional autonomy, unite educators for effective citizenship, promote and protect human and civil rights, and obtain for its members the benefits of an independent, united teaching profession.[9]

Its membership presently includes more than one and a half million teachers—approximately three out of every four public K-12 classroom teachers. There is an effective affiliation with state teachers' organizations, a common dues structure, and a growing ability to act in concert.

Through the early years of its history and into the 1960s, the NEA placed strong emphasis on what Knezevich has called the "professional ethic" and less on the "militant ethic."[10] In recent years its behavior more nearly parallels the development of the American Federation of Teachers (AFT), especially in regard to the new militancy, relationships with administrators' organizations, emphasis on collective negotiations in establishing improved working conditions for teachers, and the decision to be politically active. The AFT had an early advantage over the NEA because although it included administrators in its membership, they were not allowed to hold office. Nor was it associated with AACTE. Also, it had the long experience of the AFL-CIO behind it as an advantage in negotiations expertise. Though the NEA change to militant behavior did follow closely on AFT successes with negotiations and strikes, particularly the 1961 New

York City strike, it should not be assumed that this is a causal relationship since common conditions face both.

While the NEA presently pays much attention to teacher power and to strong efforts to improve working conditions, it appears to give less attention to professional questions including teacher education. In a 10-item list of specific objectives in the most recent NEA bylaws, there is no direct reference to teacher education. The National Commission on Teacher Education and Professional Standards (TEPS)—long outstanding in its professional activities—has been dissolved and incorporated into a new division called Instruction and Professional Development. While it is unwise to infer that the NEA has a diminished interest in professional matters, it has shifted its priorities. In order to survive the challenge from AFT, it has to put its own house in order. Presently, it seeks as much direct power for teachers as possible. One example of its new confrontation strategy was the 1972 withdrawal of the NEA financial contribution to NCATE. This tactic enabled NEA to achieve parity with higher education in matters of teacher education accreditation. Now, teachers participate in all NCATE processes on an equal basis. This episode signals a forward movement in professionalization.

In the NCATE controversy, the NEA lost on the issue of voluntary versus mandatory accreditation; voluntary accreditation continued as the policy. In the meantime, however, the NEA has pressed for implementation of its "1971 Model Teacher Standards and Licensure Act." If this program is successful, the organized teaching profession will be in control of both certification and accreditation in states where it is implemented. And since accreditation of teacher education programs is mandatory in the states, the profession will have achieved control of teacher education. Furthermore, the annual delegate assemblies of the NEA show interest not only in the licensure and accreditation questions, but also in the structure of preparation programs, the establishment of teacher centers, inservice and continuing education for teachers, and practitioner participation in all of these areas. It is evident that NEA is determined to represent the teaching profession, not only in matters of working conditions, but also in the domain of professional performance.

One of the casualties of recent NEA developments has been the lack of involvement of professors of education. It is necessary for those in the preparation arm of the profession to be full-fledged members of the NEA. Professors of education should seek to bridge the gap which exists between them and the NEA.

Recommendation
That professional organizations of teachers recognize the campus-

based teachers in teacher education as fellow professionals and actively seek their inclusion and participation.

The American Federation of Teachers (AFL-CIO)

The AFT originated with the establishment of the Chicago Teachers Federation in 1897, and its affiliation with the Chicago Federation of Labor in 1902. In 1916, the AFL founded and chartered the AFT. Its early growth was slow. A 1956 decision to promote collective bargaining enabled the AFT to rise rapidly in membership during the sixties and seventies. The victory of the AFT over the NEA in the 1961 New York City election and the gains made in New York thereafter were highly visible and probably reduced teachers' anxieties about using labor tactics. By 1975, the "Union" could claim more than 450,000 members.

Though the AFT historically has seemed to be less interested in the professional aspects than in the *working* conditions of teachers, its less visible interest should not be taken lightly. Its publications indicate a breadth of professional interest, a depth in scholarly approaches to problems, and an increasingly important place for teacher education—particularly as it relates to an internship program for beginning teachers.

A United Profession?

The AFT has actively promoted the idea of a unified profession since the early sixties. It continues to seek some kind of merger with the NEA. For a time, the NEA was open to negotiation, but recently, it has rejected further consideration of the matter. The NEA is determined not to be associated with organized labor. In its 1975 Representative Assembly, it reaffirmed its 1974 position which stated that the NEA emphatically did not want affiliation with the AFL-CIO. On the other hand, the AFT believes that only through affiliation with the AFL-CIO can teachers achieve power and influence. Those who predict an eventual merger should not overlook the cogency of the adamant stand the NEA takes against labor affiliation. The NEA has shown much more willingness to learn from the AFT than to identify with it.

Collective Bargaining

The sections above on the two large teacher organizations both indicated emphasis on militancy in behalf of teachers' rights and of favorable working conditions. Collective bargaining, recognized by law, is an important objective of both organizations. Much progress in this direction already has been made. There is a distinct possibility that federal intervention may grant collective bargaining rights to all public employees, including teachers. Higher education faculties also would be covered.

Collective bargaining includes the right to negotiate over working conditions. Responsibilities in connection with teacher education are an important element in teacher working conditions. Experience indicates that teachers in school districts with collective bargaining agreements soon turn their attention to responsibilities with student teachers and other aspects of teacher education. It must be anticipated that negotiated agreements will specify the conditions under which teachers *may* participate.

Included may be:

1. Payment for services.
2. Release time from regular assignment.
3. Right to special preparation for the assignment.
4. Reduced class size.
5. Student teachers and interns only from professionally accredited colleges.
6. Student professional membership.
7. Employment in district of only those students who graduate from professionally accredited institutions.
8. Involvement in the teacher education program.

Though the full implication of collective bargaining as it relates to teacher education cannot presently be foreseen, its significance can be assumed. Much of the freedom colleges and universities have had will disappear. A variety of constraints will be imposed. On the other hand, a new source of power and influence will intervene in the governance and quality control structures of teacher education. Higher standards of preservice preparation can be predicted as can active professional involvement.

Teacher educators have a vital stake in the collective bargaining agreements reached between school districts and the bargaining unit. As a third party, however, they will not have direct access. The only apparent opportunity for participation is collaboration on decisions about demands to be made. This will require initiative on the part of teacher educators.

The American Association of Colleges for Teacher Education

The AACTE is not a genuine professional organization; rather it is a voluntary association of institutions involved in teacher education. At this time, however, it is the major voice of teacher education in the nation. Its approximately 835 institutional memberships—of the 1,380 offering teacher education—include almost all of the large institutions and a variety of smaller ones, both public and private.

More than 85 percent of all teacher education graduates are students of AACTE institutions. The AACTE has no provision for individual memberships. Officially, each institution has from three to seven representatives who receive publications and exercise the institution's voting privileges. Attendance at the Annual Meeting and the privilege of addressing issues is open to all faculty members, whether or not they are appointed representatives.

The forerunner of AACTE was the American Association of Teachers Colleges, founded in 1918. In 1948, through a merger with other groups, AACTE came into existence. From the late '40s through the 1960s, it was a national organization only. Since the early '70s, the Association has been developing state chapters, first at the initiative of interested teacher educators at the state level, and now with official and priority encouragement of the Association.

Over the years, AACTE has been active in promoting teacher education by many means, one of the most significant being accreditation. From 1948 to 1954, AACTE had direct control of accreditation. Then, in 1954, NCATE was established as a joint venture, the major partners being the Association and the NEA. In addition, the Chief State School Officers (CSSO), the National Association of State Directors of Teacher Education and Certification (NASDTEC), and the National School Boards Association (NSBA) were involved. Recent changes have increased the participation of practitioners (NEA) in the NCATE accreditation process. Also, NCATE has been given responsibility for the establishment of standards for teacher education, a function previously performed by AACTE.

The Association maintains an interest in teacher education and keeps a watchful eye on it at the national level. Through publications, commissions, conferences, and the Annual Meeting, it involves teacher educators in numerous ways. It conducts projects with outside funds (e.g., the Educational Resources Information Center (ERIC), competency-based teacher education, multicultural education). From time to time it mounts task forces and study groups to study significant issues. The Board of Directors at the Annual Meeting adopts policy statements and makes recommendations. The AACTE also maintains active liaison with federal agencies and with other associations.

Institutions legitimately involved in teacher education can be members of AACTE by paying the annual fees based on the enrollments and diversity of programs of the individual institutions. There is no requirement that institutions be NCATE accredited although they must be regionally accredited. Consequently, the member institutions include marginally qualified institutions along with the best qualified. This dulls the capacity for taking strong positions on the qualifications necessary to be involved in teacher education, since almost any proposed quality control criteria will offend some institution(s). There have been few ventures calculated to threaten, push, or even strongly stimulate teacher education toward needed improvement. This troubles some who desire stronger stands and more impact in upgrading teacher education and the teaching profession. Nonetheless, organizations comprised of diverse institutions rarely take stands counter to the interests of member institutions. So, in the absence of such a capacity, AACTE emphasizes improvement through leadership, influence, and dissemination.

The danger of AACTE is that other organizations less constrained by a diversity of interests will assume leadership in times of change and stress. This is already happening. Control of teacher education standards has been transferred to NCATE where NEA influence may call for more rigorous evaluation of institutions. The deans of education of state universities, land grant colleges, and large private institutions have organized separately and are active, visible, and influential. (The members of this group also are involved in AACTE.) Some of the state units of AACTE expect stronger positions from the national organization and are actively urging it.

Unless AACTE over the next decade can provide a much stronger impetus to change in teacher education, it will lose out to other groups that have the capacity to do so.

Recommendation

That the AACTE begin to take strong stands on teacher education and other educational issues, even when the stands are contrary to the interests or desires of some member institutions.

Association of Teacher Educators

The Association of Teacher Educators (ATE) includes teacher education personnel in both colleges and universities and other preparation centers. This is an organization devoted to the overall interests of teacher educators. Increasingly, it attempts to involve more field-based teacher educators. Until recently it met conjointly with AACTE; now it holds its annual meeting independently. There are indications that it will seek to be an NCATE partner, and that it intends to be more vigorous in its professional efforts. In the meantime, ATE has not yet caught on as the voice of the individual teacher educator. It deserves backing in its efforts to become so.

Since ATE is financed through individual memberships, it has the potential to become a viable organization for individual teacher educators from the colleges *and* schools. College-based professors of education, adjunct faculty in schools, and cooperating teachers are all in need of this type of organization in order to come together. This link is crucial for the future when one considers the implications of the

teaching center concept, continuing education, and shared governance. Since the goals of AACTE and ATE are similar and since it
makes sense for both AACTE and ATE to provide a mechanism for
institutional and individual membership, a closer working relationship must be established.

Recommendation

That AACTE help to strengthen ATE as an effective organization for individual teacher educators and encourage its return to
close working relations with the Association. A first step to pilot-
test the feasibility of a collaborative relationship would be for
AACTE and ATE to locate their offices together.

TOWARD A COLLABORATIVE EFFORT IN GOVERNANCE

Governance Mechanisms

*In accordance with the principles of professionalization, the profession
should make every effort to decrease the extent of state dominance, and
increase college and professional control of teacher education.* To be effective in increasing professional control, the university and the teaching profession must establish governance mechanisms on such issues
as accreditation and licensure systems. Another approach should be
to set up joint committees to make policy decisions about teacher
education and to insure effective implementation. To be sure, governance of important aspects of the teacher education program is the
legitimate prerogative of the entire teaching profession, but the university also has concerns and responsibilities.

Collaborative Mechanisms

The principle of accountability requires taking other interests and
needs into account. Schools, teacher education, and professional organizations become parity partners because each needs the other in
the use of schools for field experiences, and in setting up continuing
and inservice teacher education programs. This collaborative arrangement can be formalized through an organizational structure called a
teacher center. There are six partners who collaborate in the operation
of a teacher center: (a) teacher education, (b) the schools, (c) teacher
organizations, (d) the university, (e) the school board and the community, and (f) the state or intermediate state agencies.

Teacher centers are governance mechanisms; they are not places. (See
figure 5.) However, governance groups can establish places where
teacher education occurs. In such physical centers, an array of preservice, inservice, and continuing education can take place as each

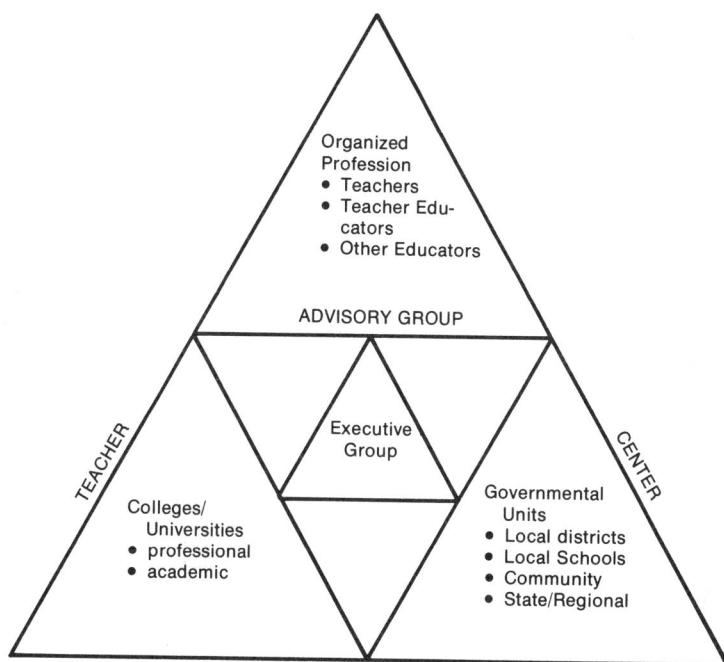

FIGURE 5
A MODEL FOR TEACHER CENTER GOVERNANCE

of the major partners assumes responsibilities that fall within its jurisdiction (See Appendix A.).

Who Speaks for the Teaching Profession?

With the proliferation of organizations that represent the teaching
profession and teacher education, there is a tendency to produce
babble rather than intelligible sounds. Vested interest conflict between competing groups often adds to the confusion. Some governance procedures, especially negotiations procedures, clearly call for
prime spokespersons. Other procedures require no such unity. In the
absence of agreement on who is to represent the profession, a composite group should be formed from those groups having legitimate
interests. Teacher centers already demonstrate that the big issues of
jurisdiction do not have to be present in normal day-to-day operations. The real world of parents, children, and schools cannot stand
by forever awaiting resolution of whether we are to be a "union" or
"profession," administrator or teacher, teacher educator, or school-
based profession.

This chapter began with references to "zero sum." It can well end
with the same. Everything is to be gained by deciding on basic principles and by collaborating to get them implemented. Everyone stands

to gain by the establishment of strong teacher education and a strong profession.

Sobering Up

Questions of governance are heady wines. In their presence one tends to be persuaded and thereby conclude that others are also convinced.

Clark and Marker are not alone in their pessimism over the ability of the profession to do what clearly needs to be done. They say:

> . . . we are pessimistic about the likelihood of positive changes which will be affected in the field over the next decade. (p. 73)

> In this framework of organized irresponsibility there is not only an endless opportunity to avoid accountability, but a rational posture which is available to each partner in the enterprise to justify the avoidance. (pp. 75-76)

> Those who would reform teacher education by exhorting these partners to join together in a cooperative relationship do not recognize that "even paranoiacs have enemies." (p. 80)[11]

Corwin, in the same publication, is cautiously more optimistic.[12]

The members of this Commission recognize the forces which stand in the way of change. We are, however, convinced that the time is right for an all-out effort. What is needed is a catalytic element capable of starting the release of the tremendous energies necessary for action. No less miraculous things have been thought possible before.

Recommendation

That responsibility for teacher education in the states be delegated to the teaching profession and to the colleges and universities, with the state providing only the needed support services.

Recommendation

That governance mechanisms for teacher education in the form of teacher centers be established for teacher education institutions or contiguous groups of institutions and funded through the regular support formula or budget.

FOOTNOTES

1. Roald F. Campbell, *R & D Funding Policies of the National Institute of Education* (Washington, D.C.: National Institute of Education, 1975), p. 109. See also papers presented at a November 1975 conference on research in teaching held at the R & D Center, The University of Texas at Austin, to be published as a theme section in the Spring 1976 *Journal of Teacher Education.*
2. Office of Management and Budget (OMB) working document headed "The Fiscal Year 1977-1981 Forward Plan," mimeographed, 1975.

3. "Mathews Reflects on Roles of HEW at Swearing-in," *Higher Education and National Affairs*, August 15, 1975, p. 1.
4. *A Foundation Goes to School* (New York: The Ford Foundation, 1972), p. 52.
5. D.L. Clark and G. Marker, "The Institutionalization of Teacher Education," in *Teacher Education. 74th Yearbook of the National Society for the Study of Education*, Kevin Ryan, ed. (Chicago: University of Chicago Press, 1975), pp. 53-86.
6. "Teacher Education in America," draft copy of a report of the Study Commission on Undergraduate Education and the Education of Teachers (Lincoln, Nebr.: University of Nebraska Press, 1975), Chapter V, p. 7.
7. Clark and Marker, "Institutionalization," p. 76.
8. G.W. Denemark and J. Yff, eds., *Obligation for Reform: The Final Report of the Higher Education Task Force on Improvement and Reform in American Education* (Washington, D.C.: American Association of Colleges for Teacher Education, 1974).
9. *NEA Governance Instruments 1975-76* (Washington, D.C.: National Education Association, 1975), p. 4.
10. L.A. Netzer, et al., *Education, Administration, and Change* (New York: Harper & Row, 1970), p. 63.
11. Clark and Marker, "Institutionalization," pp. 73, 75-76, 80.
12. R.G. Corwin, "The New Teaching Profession," in *Teacher Education*, K. Ryan, ed., pp. 230-64.

FOUR

Designing the Career-Long Preparation of Teachers

Professors of education
should exemplify what they explicate.

The design of teacher education should include
a continuous interlocking relationship
between practice and theory.

The profession should rid itself of institutions
unable to provide adequate life space to prepare teachers.

Fundamental to the design of any educational program is an understanding of its goals and objectives. Planners of preparation programs must comprehend professional roles if learning experiences are to be consistent with role requirements. Role requirements are always more easily understood when institutions are stable and when there is consensus regarding social values and expectations. Usually, the professions themselves largely determine the role definitions, and condition the views held by others. However, the task of designing a teacher education curriculum is complicated by divergent views both from within and outside the profession.

DIFFERING PERCEPTIONS OF TEACHING AS CHALLENGE TO THE TEACHER EDUCATOR

Views regarding teaching and the status of teachers vary considerably. Lortie suggests that

> Teaching seems to have more than its share of status anomalies. It is honored and disdained, praised as "dedicated service" and lampooned as "easy work." It is permeated with the rhetoric of professionalism, yet features incomes below those earned by workers with considerably less education . . . Teaching from its inception in America has occupied a special but shadowed social standing . . . real regard shown for those who taught has never matched professed regard.[1]

Many lay citizens view education as important but do not attach comparable status to the role of the teacher. Speculating on the effects of low public teacher esteem, Cogan suggests two "self-fulfilling prophecies." First, teachers will internalize a low opinion of their work; and, second, students who share the negative views of teachers expressed by their parents will learn less effectively than if their education had been conducted in an atmosphere of high esteem for teachers and schools. Also, indifferent and negative public attitudes toward teachers make the following very difficult: recruiting strong candidates for teacher education, maintaining a high level of motivation, and securing adequate resources to support quality preparation programs.[2]

Another difficulty is the many preconceptions of the teacher's role held by the student. College students have had at least 12 years of schooling in which to shape their views of schools and teachers. And during that time they have developed many limited or unfavorable views of teachers and teaching. Thus, the task of the teacher educator becomes very complex because it entails not only teaching a technical range of knowledge, behavior, and skills, but also altering earlier negative perceptions. To fail is to perpetuate images of teachers grossly incompatible with the professional demands teachers face.

Past experience represents such an overwhelming influence on teacher candidates that they are likely to think about teaching exclusively as a formal classroom activity and remain unaware of such broader professional responsibilities as curriculum development, community relations, and program evaluation. Unfortunately, prospective teachers' preconceptions about schools and teaching are often accurate. Their inaccuracy is not with classroom realities, but with the ideals professionals set for themselves.

The professional socialization of teachers differs significantly from other professions. The long period of association with schools and teachers prior to professional status provides students with a high level of *informal* socialization. In contrast, medicine entails only infrequent and limited contacts with physicians before professional studies begin. The *formal* professional socialization of the physician, however, is much more extensive than that of the teacher and makes greater use of the undergirding disciplines in preprofessional curricula.

Hostility or indifference toward teacher education from faculty members in other academic units further complicates the task of a college of education. Some professors are so hostile in their attitudes toward teacher education that students are negative about their professional studies even before starting them. Some faculty openly advise their ablest students that they would be "wasting" their talents by preparing for teaching. When such attitudes prevail, they often result in inadequate resource allocation to teacher preparation. Although the financial survival of many small colleges and of some departments in large universities is dependent upon their enrollments in teacher education, institutional budgets seldom reflect this. Priorities for staff and facilities point elsewhere, lending credence to Stone's observation that teacher education is a "stepchild," largely unwanted by the colleges.[3]

Most unfortunate is the tendency of the teaching profession to accept low public and academic assessments of its worth. Too many teachers view themselves merely as clerks and technicians, rather than professionals charged with one of the most complex and demanding responsibilities imaginable. Low public esteem for teaching, limited perceptions of the teacher held by teacher candidates, frequent indifference or disdain for teaching in higher education, and acceptance by the teaching profession of itself as a craft present a challenging and troublesome context in which to design quality teacher preparation.

Absence of a Professional Culture

Observers often view the act of teaching as requiring only common sense and familiarity with subject matter. They perceive teaching to be innately artistic and thus incapable of reproduction through any systematic preparation program. Unfortunately, the teaching profession has rarely challenged these views of teaching. Through most of its history, teaching has been dependent upon personal insights, without the underpinnings of empirical study of systematic theory. In 1975 we reached the end of an era. Society now demands a new breed of teacher—a well prepared, highly motivated professional capable of understanding a broad range of learning problems and of designing and implementing curricular and instructional strategies to solve them.

A PROFESSIONAL VIEW OF TEACHING

The professional view of teaching emphasizes its demanding complexities. These complexities require rigorous preservice preparation to be the foundation for career-long professional development. Teachers need to be well educated in liberal or general studies, since *all* school teachers are teachers of general education. They must also be well versed in the disciplines connected to their teaching fields and their learning implications for students. Teachers also require intensive preparation in the conceptual frameworks within which teachers can develop diagnostic and planning skills. A broad repertoire of teaching behaviors and skills must be another major focus of teacher education, incorporating both theoretical and experiential components.

To assist beginning teachers to understand the relevance of generic skills and theoretical components to specific community and school needs, preservice preparation programs should provide elective options for every student, enabling study in depth of at least one local, regional, or national subculture. Such study should be linked to a broad framework of sensitization to cultural differences and their implications for teaching and learning. All of these program components are essential to the preparation of a teacher. Each contributes to the shared, systematic, and scientific knowledge base for pedagogical decisions— the hallmark of professional teaching behavior. Without such a base, teachers remain forever captives of limited personal experience, whether their teachers' or their own.

Importance of a "Safe" Level of Beginning Teacher Skills

The concept of safety to the client is important to every profession, including teaching. Obviously, the profession cannot realistically expect a mature level of professional performance from beginning teachers. However, the profession must establish consensus on the professional culture required to *begin* the practice of teaching, and the means to assure career-long professional development.

Safety to the client does not always imply a comfortable relationship. At times, a professional will have to confront, challenge, and even upset clients. It does mean that whatever is done with clients is based on the professional's sound knowledge of theory and skill in practice. Neither does the concept of safety imply satisfaction with minimum levels of teaching performance. Rather, because it expects more of its teachers, the profession must accept nothing less than a safe level of initial competence from its beginners. Scheffler points out, ". . . the standard we use to specify a skill or competence in a given context need not eliminate *further* distinctions of relative proficiency or independent references to mastery or to greatness . . . . Knowing how to do something is one thing, knowing how to do it well is . . . another, and doing it brilliantly is still a third . . ."[4]

Recommendation
That every beginning teacher be able to perform the essentials of teaching at a safe level.

MAJOR COMPONENTS IN THE EDUCATION OF TEACHERS

General or Liberal Studies

Students preparing to teach enter the university, like all other students, through a program of general or liberal studies. But liberal education is of special significance to teachers, for it should meet their professional as well as personal needs. As teachers of general education, they will use subject matter to clarify modes and areas of choice for students who will soon be citizens, parents, and adult consumers. Liberal education for teachers should not be different from the liberal education of other students unless the differences represent extended opportunities for prospective teachers to explore the interrelationships of knowledge and their implications for teaching and learning. Unfortunately, liberal studies sometimes fail to help students experience decision making and choice, the creation of personal meaning, and the use of evidence and logic. Too often general studies are narrow, sketchy introductions to disconnected subjects with an overemphasis on nomenclature and classification systems. Separation of information from real-world problems and issues still characterizes too much of general education today.

The importance of general education for teachers is to help them become learned persons. Because they are responsible for the intellectual development of children, teachers themselves must be interested in ideas and capable of understanding them in broad conceptual contexts. Teachers must understand the nature and interrelationships of knowledge.

Recommendation

That all prospective teachers participate in an experience focusing on the nature and implications of knowledge, in conjunction with general education studies. Taught by an interdisciplinary team, students will consider alternative ways of knowing, unique structures of knowledge in the different fields, linkages among concepts in the various disciplines, and the implications of these ideas for teaching at elementary and secondary levels. The instructional team should include at least one member from professional education along with appropriate representation from other behavioral and social sciences.

Preeducation in the Undergirding Disciplines

Teacher education has been slow to move in the direction of preprofessional studies paralleling curricula in medicine and law. Yet the complex nature of teaching requires an adequate theoretical base rooted in the several disciplines from which it draws, e.g., psychology, sociology, anthropology, and philosophy.

When disciplines "undergird," they do two things: they *strengthen* the conceptual and valuational grounds for professional practice, and they *support* development of a level of personal understanding and involvement that distinguishes the professional from a technician. The demands upon professional courses for both foundational and applied knowledge are so great that they can neither function without the contextual knowledge of the undergirding disciplines nor assume responsibility for providing it in the professional sequence.

Recommendation
That all teacher education programs include a preeducation component designed to provide necessary contextual knowledge from the undergirding disciplines.

Limitations of the Undergirding Disciplines as Traditionally Taught

As conventionally taught, the disciplines are vulnerable to four types of criticism. First, the disciplines are too often taught as separate and rigorous bodies of knowledge, each with its own self-sealed boundaries, established research standards, and exclusionary initiation rites. Instead of emphasizing the concepts, facts, values, and procedures which might overlap with other disciplines, the disciplinarian is likely to call attention to the highly idiosyncratic type of inquiry which exists within each specialized discipline. It is not unusual to hear students in professional programs claim that experimental psychology or sociology or economics appears to have little in common with each other. Indeed, few students are capable of identifying the cross-cutting conceptual and methodological principles which unify the separate subject matters. Actually, few faculty members are capable of such a unifying task. In a society where educators must continually marshal data, principles, and procedures from all the knowledge areas to help people with a variety of problems, educators can no longer tolerate the isolation of one body of knowledge from another.

Second, the criticism of the undergirding disciplines usually made by disgruntled students is that these studies are too theoretical and divorced from the real world of professional practice. Argyris and Schon hold that political scientists or philosophers, to mention two examples, are too preoccupied with weaving elaborate "espoused theories"—those conceptual rationales people usually give when asked to explain their actions but bear little correspondence to their "theories in use." "Theories in use" include the operational assumptions we make about the everyday world which eventuate in the ways we actually deal with people and things.[5] It is rare that people ever examine closely their "theories in use."

Thus, while students may hold an espoused theory about the innate goodness of all people, some actually assume that young people are untrustworthy and treat them accordingly. This disjuncture between elegant "espoused theories" and "theories in use" has heightened in recent years because many academic disciplinarians have either stubbornly refused—or been unable—to translate their espoused theories into tangible professional practice. This is an era of accountability,

83

a time when educators are struggling to find the best "fit" between what they assume about people and their institutions and how they act on those assumptions. Faculty members must help professionals merge theory and practice more creatively, consistently, and congruently than has been the case.

The charge of discrepancy between espoused theories and theories in use points to a void between what educators profess to know and believe and what they actually do. In the years ahead, educators will be required to search for ways to reconcile contradictions between personal ideals and public actualities. Thus far, the disciplines have been of little help in the reconciliation of these contradictions.

Third in criticisms of the disciplines is that they tend to stress disproportionately the intellectual acquisition of subject matter to the exclusion of their personal meaning (emotional, intuitive, normative) for the professional practitioner. Very few of the disciplines have been helpful in demonstrating how the educator's private beliefs and values (about self, others, what constitutes effective teaching and learning, helping, and why people behave the ways they do) emerge from, and are clarified by, the subject matter under study. Subjects like history and physics, to mention but two, have traditionally been taught as inert and specialized bodies of facts, totally purified of any "unscholarly contaminants," i.e., personal implications for students. What effective educators will require in the years ahead, however, are strong justificatory beliefs about their professional activities. But first, teacher educators must help their students to discover the personal meaning of ideas and subject matter, encouraging them to translate these personal insights into significant public actions. Disciplinarians will have to spend much more time helping students to engage in "personal belief and value clarification," and exploring the best ways to construct the guiding ideals which can assist them in successfully coping with the enervating, day-to-day ordeals typical of so much professional work.

Fourth, where the disciplines have been most vulnerable to criticism, especially from educators, has been in their austere concern with value neutrality and objectivity at the expense of any kind of explicit commitment to social ideals. Starr has remarked that the social sciences have rendered themselves almost impotent; they steadfastly refuse to speak of social purposes, ultimate values, morality, or the meaning of human existence. Instead, they are preoccupied with technical issues; refining ever more precisely their methods, vocabulary, concepts, style, and strategies of presentation.[6] What educators will need in the years ahead are not narrow, pragmatic reasons for being professionals. Recent research confirms that a high percentage of new teachers are looking toward their training to expand their social awareness and foster a profound sense of purpose. This research also shows that preprofessional students resist efforts—however well-meaning—to convert them into functional technicians only.[7]

Teacher Preparation in Academic Specialization

Another important component of teacher preparation is study in the academic specialization areas. Programs preparing secondary teachers, and an increasing number preparing elementary teachers, require candidates to do substantial work in subject areas. This is usually done in courses *outside* the college of education. Students with academic and professional objectives generally enroll in the same classes together, although the sequence of courses appropriate for a teaching major is often different from regular academic majors. Representatives of the academic and teacher education faculties frequently agree on the distinctions between the sequence for the teaching versus the nonteaching majors, although in small institutions such distinctions may disappear because of limited offerings.

Many of the criticisms of the undergirding disciplines are relevant to preparation in the academic specialty fields. Academic faculty sometimes assume that when secondary education majors learn the research procedure, logic, and content of an academic specialty, their ability to think analytically, act wisely, and excite others about the value of the discipline will follow. Some faculty also assume that knowledge of a subject matter is sufficient preparation for the teaching of it. Courses designed primarily to meet the needs of majors who intend to continue on into advanced graduate study in that field often neglect the concerns of other students with different professional objectives. As a consequence, generations of new teachers have gone forth perpetuating concepts of subject matter and of teaching that are abstract and ill-suited to the learner.

The preparation of teachers, like that of nurses, social workers, doctors, and counselors, requires a mastery of subject matter which is human-service *functional*. Not only do teachers need to know the technical language and the concepts of their disciplines; they require an "in breadth" understanding of how a subject matter can be useful to students in discovering personal levels of meaning, and how students can translate this meaning into humane daily action. However, functionality of subject matter does not imply different subject matters for different student populations. As Smith, Cohen, and Pearl observe:

> No matter what his social environment, an individual must learn—and go on learning, at least minimally—how to get along in a technological, urbanized society, a society that requires scientific knowledge, social and political understanding, and a variety of skills and social techniques.[8]

85

Of critical importance to the subject matter preparation of teachers is attention to the broad principles and generalizations of a subject, rather than concentration on a maze of specific topics.

Recommendation
That principles be the "constants" of academic study. Facts should be the variables, organized around the broader principles.

If such teaching is necessary in public schools, instructors must exemplify it in the universities. No longer can college professors be content to teach only the "data" of their disciplines. They must show students the *illuminative* properties of the disciplines. Professors can no longer grudgingly carry out teaching assignments as the price they pay for research opportunities, or reluctantly work with teacher education students whom they view as "anti-intellectual."

A Conceptual Framework for Planning the Professional Components of Teacher Education

The following illustration (Figure 6) lists seven categories of objec-

OBJECTIVE ↓ MODE →	CLASSROOM	LEARNING	RESOURCES	CENTER	LABORATORY	FIELD	MODEL	MENTOR
KNOWLEDGE								
ATTITUDES—VALUES								
BEHAVIORS—SKILLS								
INDUCTION TO PROFESSION								
PERSONALIZATION								
PROFESSIONAL LITERACY								
CONTINUING DEVELOPMENT								

FIGURE 6
FRAMEWORK FOR DESIGNING CAREER-LONG
PROFESSIONAL PREPARATION OF TEACHERS

tives for the education of teachers, and six categories within which instructional modes may be grouped to meet those objectives. A brief discussion of these objectives and instructional modes follows. Any one instructional mode, or a combination, may contribute to each of the professional objectives. While the model is meant primarily to reflect preservice preparation, it is also relevant to the continuing professional development of the teacher. Each of the professional components—foundations of education, teaching behaviors and skills (both generic and specialized), elective subcultural study, and field application—can be considered in light of the objectives and instructional modes.

The Foundations of Education: A Professional Component

The central weakness of foundational studies has been the tendency of many foundations professors to look at their fields as if they are full-blown disciplines, each with its own highly specialized conceptual framework, investigative procedures, and research methodologies. Philosophy of education or history of education courses are sometimes taught as if they were separate, disconnected disciplines designed to provide students with depth of understanding in a single field, or to train students to think about education in a narrow, "discipline-specific" way. Thus, most students fail to see the interplay between the study of education as a discipline and the practice of education as a profession. Some foundations professors refuse to become involved with value prescriptions, field experiences, or the problems of practitioners—which they perceive as residing *outside* the analytic or descriptive functions of the discipline.

The "discipline" approach is a retreat from what should be the basic purpose of all foundational studies in education: to provide interdisciplinary and conceptual illumination of the issues, problems, and procedures confronting contemporary educators everywhere so that more professional and humane public action might ensue. Thus, students must explore the hidden value dimensions of education practices and policies. Also, students must develop a well-formulated belief system to serve as a principle of selection for instructional materials, teaching procedures, and curricular content. The student must develop a sense of social purpose—an activistic concern for the sociopolitical *ends* of the educational experience which invest professional decisions and procedures with ultimate meaning and conviction.

Foundational studies must be *interrelated.* The more specialized and isolated each of the academic disciplines becomes, the more necessary it will be for foundations faculties to reintegrate the subject matters for sound educational judgment and action. Educators face a welter

87

of problems and issues too complicated to be solved within the framework of a single discipline. To solve educational problems requires broad intelligence, contextual knowledge, and integrative vision.

Recommendation
That a series of changes be made in the formats, conceptual frameworks, and delivery modes of the undergirding disciplines, whether taught in the preeducation component or in professional foundations courses. To support and strengthen teachers, the undergirding disciplines must become interdisciplinary; unifying in concept and practice; less obscure and more human service functional; problem-based, featuring "theory in practice" modes of inquiry; original and bold in developing explanatory hypotheses; personal and clarifying in terms of beliefs and values; socially activistic and mission centered; and experimental in teaching procedures and delivery modes.

Importance of a Professional Knowledge Base

Fundamental pedagogical knowledge is of central importance in the preparation of professional teachers. *The Commission asserts that effective teachers gain understanding and control of classroom events mainly through theoretical and empirical knowledge.* In turn, they gain an appreciation of important concepts as they see them work in school situations. A frequent criticism of teacher preparation programs is that they are too theoretical. The Commission holds, to the contrary, that they may not be *sufficiently* theoretical. What is necessary is the continuous interplay of theory and practice.

Teachers are more likely to understand and appreciate concepts only if they are linked with the study of actual behavioral situations. *The Commission proposes not that all teachers be researchers but that professional programs develop the teacher's capacity to understand and consult appropriate research before making instructional decisions.*

Developing a Repertoire of Teaching Behaviors and Skills

A professional teacher is one who possesses a broad repertoire of classroom behaviors and skills, grounded in professional and academic knowledge. Educators must also develop skills in the performance of teaching through practice in a controlled training environment.

The demanding task confronting beginning teachers requires a reasonable level of proficiency in the behaviors of teaching. Beginning teachers with a safe level of instructional competence are likely to maintain self-confidence through the trying experiences of their first year. Without generic teaching behaviors and skills, new teachers are likely to become discouraged and either leave teaching or settle upon narrow techniques simply to "survive" in the classroom. *The Commission believes that without the development of effective performance skills, teachers will remain preoccupied with survival matters rather than broader educational concerns.*

A number of instructional skills are generic. Others are a function of specific subject matter or particular learner needs. Many formulations of generic teaching are available to the curriculum planner in teacher education. Smith, Cohen, and Pearl identify as minimum skills the ability to perform stimulant operations (question, structure, probe); manipulate the different kinds of knowledge; perform reinforcement operations; negotiate interpersonal relations; diagnose student needs and learning difficulties; communicate and empathize with students, parents, and others; perform in, and with, small and large groups; utilize technological equipment; evaluate student achievement; and judge appropriateness of instructional materials.[9]

Generic teaching skills developed at the University of Houston include 33 competencies listed under 11 broad categories (See Appendix B.). Burdin describes the wide range of roles played by teachers as follows:

> They know how to conduct needs assessments. They know the objectives of democracy and its strategies. They know about present and future. They know how to utilize effectively people, time, space, equipment, and materials for instructional purposes. They know how to assess teaching and learning. They lead, and they follow. They function in places called schools; they function equally well as educators in other settings. They can design learning activities with rather high probabilities for attaining publicly announced learning objectives. They are competent. They are accountable.[10]

The Importance of Teacher Values and Attitudes

Not only must preparation programs develop teaching skills and a knowledge of theoretical and empirical concepts, but they must foster humanistic educational values and attitudes. Indeed, the central task of teacher education is to provide teachers with a philosophy of education that will help them to think seriously and continuously about the purposes and consequences of what they do. This entails being aware of the value system of a particular educational environment, as well as the effects of a personal value system on a school environment.

The distinction between "espoused theories" and "theories in use" implies the use of values clarification for prospective teachers. It is unwise to promulgate impressive value statements for students to endorse or to suggest that values are personal matters outside the scope of professional preparation. Neither is it enough to study the classical philosophical schools. Instead, prospective teachers need to induce operational values from real school situations, and to test the consequences of assumed values. Cogan realizes the importance of operational values for teachers and the difficulty in fostering those values in the training program. He believes:

> If we are to seek teachers who in class will be creative, democratic, integrative, learner-centered and the like, then . . . it will probably be more economical to select by whatever methods are available those candidates for teaching who manifestly or latently exhibit the qualities we seek.[11]

While the Commission accepts Cogan's endorsement of values in the selection process for teacher education, it recognizes the difficulty of obtaining reliable evidence on values and the danger of simply reproducing the value patterns of those engaged in the selection.

Personalization in Teacher Education

Teachers are different from one another. The establishment of generic skills essential to the professional repertoire of every teacher does not deny the individuality of teachers. Teacher educators have long since abandoned the notion that teachers should be interchangeable parts in a production line. Instead, teachers must develop their own styles, techniques, and materials consistent with their personalities, experiences, and abilities. Teachers need much latitude in the instructional modes and materials they employ.

Recommendation

That all prospective teachers make use of their own interests, talents, and styles in developing beginning teaching behaviors and skills.

Induction into the Profession

Socialization into the profession happens when teacher candidates experience actual teaching responsibilities, and when they associate daily with professionals. Teacher education must provide socialization opportunities for students in professional ethics and values, legal obligations of schools and teachers, certification requirements and procedures, relationships between supervisory personnel and teachers, the history and role of professional organizations in teaching, and continuing professional development opportunities associated with conferences, publications, and other activities. Professors who see themselves and are viewed by the profession as members of the teaching profession can enhance greatly the process of induction.

Professional Literacy

Professional literacy familiarizes teachers with current educational issues and professional concerns. Effective teachers interpret the schools to the citizenry, and serve as analysts of community interests to the schools. Financing public education, citizen participation in educational policy decisions, school board-professional association views on negotiations, and educational trends in other nations are examples of topics which contribute to the professional literacy of teachers and enable them to participate more intelligently in public discussion on these issues.

Recommendation

That teacher education programs provide opportunities for teachers and teacher candidates to become knowledgeable about important educational and sociopolitical issues, and capable of interacting effectively with concerned citizens in the consideration and resolution of such issues.

Establishing Habits of Inquiry and Continuing Learning

When teachers develop inquiring minds and commitment to continuing learning, they are able to contribute to the profession throughout their lives. Most teacher educators talk about the need for teachers to be experimental and exploratory in their work. However, most preparation programs are prescriptive and didactic in form. Thus, we must develop at least a beginning competence in research and inquiry skills among prospective teachers.

Recommendation

That teacher candidates study alongside faculty who have mastered research and scholarship skills, and who can encourage prospective teachers to develop their own inquiry and research skills.

INSTRUCTIONAL MODES IN TEACHER EDUCATION

Teacher Educators as Models of Effective Teaching Behavior

The teaching in a college of education should be a model for the kind of practice expected in the schools. *Professors of education should exemplify what they explicate.* This means that college instructors must incorporate the same principles of instruction in their own teaching that they wish to engender in their students. If teachers are to become competent professionals, they must be prepared by competent teacher educators. Course outlines, learning modules, lectures, demonstrations, evaluation practices, and student advising should all exemplify principles of effective teaching.

Teacher Educators as Mentors

Interviews with teachers and other professionals often disclose a strong influence in their development by one of their own teachers. Teachers are more likely to identify a *person* than a course or program as a key influence in a career decision or personal development. Though such persons may have been called "advisors," they actually functioned in a role far more significant than simply program planning. The mentor-student relationship is a collegial one, exemplifying an acceptance and friendship well beyond the usual narrow academic consultation. The mentor is a model, not simply of a variety of teaching modes, but of the humane professional. Arrowsmith argues the case eloquently:

> Charisma in a teacher is not a mystery or nimbus of personality, but radiant exemplification to which the student contributes a corresponding radiant hunger for becoming . . . . Such embodiment may be personal, rational, and contemplative, or activist and public. What matters is the integration of significant life and knowledge, of compassionate study and informed conduct. The teacher in this sense goes where the action is, where his example is most needed.[12]

Recommendation
That teacher education transform the present status of mentoring as a largely unplanned and uncontrolled dimension of teacher education to a deliberate effort to enhance and strengthen such relationships through faculty recruitment, development, rewards.

The Classroom Mode

The Commission believes that both personnel and program factors are essential to effective teacher education. The college classroom provides the teacher education counterpart to the public school environment where the beginning teacher will work. And, just as elementary and secondary teachers can make classrooms exciting environments for learning, so too should college instructors make their college classrooms rich and varied settings for the study of teaching.

The Learning Resource Center and Laboratory

The regular classroom must be enriched by close ties to a learning resource center (LRC) and to both campus- and field-based laboratory experiences. The LRC can provide a rich range of resources such as books, films, tapes, records, protocol materials, data banks, computer-

92

assisted instruction, educational games, curriculum guides, and instructional materials. The LRC also supports individual study, so critical to the development of independent thinking and learning associated with every teacher professional.

The teacher education classroom should be a laboratory for the study and development of teaching knowledge and skills. This laboratory should be expanded to include instructional procedures such as microteaching, simulation, modeling, and demonstration. These procedures help students to confront a controlled reality by concentrating on particular teaching-learning behaviors until they attain adequate levels of skill and confidence. When students do encounter the complexity of a regular classroom, they will have experienced a planned series of teaching acts in a minimally threatening environment, with immediate feedback and experienced supervision.

Recommendation

That because teacher education is best when it is campus based and field oriented, there be an expansion of efforts to develop protocol and training materials that record real situations and illustrate ways of responding to them consistent with appropriate conceptual frameworks.

The dichotomy that "know-what" learnings should be campus based, while "know-how" learnings should be field based, is a false one. Effective teacher education incorporates both field and campus experiences in applied and foundational learning. The potential is great for protocol materials and microteaching procedures to bring reality to the campus environment in a context which allows for deliberate analysis, deletion of redundancies and irrelevancies, related situations drawn from different locations and time periods, and closer linkages between theory and practice.

A Continuum of Field Experiences to Link Professional Knowledge and Skills

Recent literature on teacher education suggests that the university cannot train teachers and therefore should give up its claim to offering technical education in education areas and assign it to schools, industry, and community agencies.[13] *This Commission unequivocally rejects such views, believing instead that the place to initiate basic and enduring reform in professional preparation is at the university, not away from it.*[14] But the issue is not either/or. Schools and colleges must collaborate if teacher education is to be effective. There is no magic in field experiences. Professional training is not significant simply because it is "out there." It is valuable only if it has been carefully planned, interpreted, and linked with appropriate conceptual frameworks. *The Commission believes that the design of teacher education should include a continuous interlocking relationship between practice and theory.* Involvement with teaching should begin as soon as students enter a teacher preparation program. Useful direct experience, with simultaneous study of useful knowledge, divided into achievable goals for beginners and gradually increasing the difficulty of the role, is the ideal form of preparation. Students should have many choices, at whatever age they choose, to engage in the real affairs of schools and communities.[15]

Improved Supervision of Field Experiences

The complexity of the field experience demands effective direction and supervision. Existing practices are mostly ineffective and require radical change. Student schedules often compel assignment to schools immediately adjacent to the campus. Overcrowding at these schools results in assignment of aides and student teachers to personnel inadequately prepared for such key responsibilities. Another difficulty is the considerable time which college supervisors spend in travel to and from the schools where their students teach. Thus, they have relatively little time to spend in actual observation and consultation with the student and cooperating teacher. Changes in the roles played by college and school personnel seem inevitable.

Recommendation

That the establishment of some teacher education centers be located away from the campus, employing well-prepared, professional supervisors who retain continuing teaching responsibilities with a local school system and serve as adjunct or part-time members of one or more college faculties.

Some present university supervisors could assume full-time responsibility for the field centers, while others could concentrate on in-service training activities with classroom teachers.

Differentiated Responsibilities in the Classroom

In addition to the *professional* responsibilities of the teacher, there are also important teacher functions which are technical, clerical, and custodial. These functions may influence significantly the learning environment of the classroom. They require, therefore, that professional teachers have final responsibility for such functions, whether carried out by teachers or by support staff. Many technical functions associated with teaching, such as reproduction of materials, organizing field trips, and evaluating homework assignments, may not demand a high level of professional skill, but the failure to conduct them professionally can impede learning. *The Commission reaffirms* not only the importance of professional functions being carried out by highly qualified teachers, but also the importance of classroom maintenance functions being under the supervision of a qualified professional. The Commission encourages continued development of differentiated staffing arrangements which allocate some of these duties to aides and paraprofessionals in order that teacher professionals may devote their energies to the diagnostic, prescriptive, and evaluative dimensions of the teaching process.

The Need for Special Emphasis on Children with Learning Disabilities

Society has only begun to realize its obligations to children with learning disabilities. In most states, the educational needs of a majority of children with learning disabilities remain unmet. Schools need large numbers of teachers who have the preparation to engage in diagnostic and remedial procedures with all of their pupils, and the time to do so. The current emphasis upon "mainstreaming" of childen with a variety of learning disabilities places an increased obligation on all teachers to develop basic understandings and skills to promote learning among a broad range of children. Such teaching requires time as well as training. Staffing arrangements must permit teachers to use their higher order skills to meet the needs of these children.

STUDY OF A SIGNIFICANT SUBCULTURE

The teaching profession has multiple clients, including the broader society, the community, and the individual. Because the profession is national and international in its perspectives and obligations, it is concerned with the generalized preparation of teachers. In contrast, school systems are rooted in particular communities, and seek teachers to meet their specific instructional needs. The result is sometimes a discrepancy between the preparation of the teacher and the instructional needs of a school or school system. Some of this discrepancy is inevitable, even desirable, in that every teacher needs an appropriate mix of generic and particular professional learnings. A preservice teacher preparation program that provides no opportunities for its students to practice in, and adjust their performance to, community realities is unlikely to have many of its graduates survive the first year of teaching. However, a preparation program geared entirely to the particular needs of a single school or school system will produce narrowly provincial teachers who are technicians, not professionals. The professional teacher must be capable of functioning effectively in a particular school and community environment, and also capable of functioning effectively if the character of that environment changes, or the teacher is employed elsewhere.

Limitations of Community- or Ethnic-Specific Teacher Education

Some people advocate community-specific and ethnic-specific teacher education in order to satisfy the needs of segments of our population neglected by many current teaching practices. They recommend that education programs for teachers be community based and community controlled with the following characteristics: (a) teachers-to-be, at the time of recruitment, should select one or more culture-specific areas to master; (b) teacher education programs should be authorized only after a particular community has defined a program—the need for it, its content, and the terms on which it will be acceptable; (c) the role in teacher education for institutions of higher education should be region specific, and their mission should be to work with local education agencies to develop programs for satisfying educational needs articulated by their various communities; and (d) training programs should use anthropological models that view a specific community or region without ethnocentric bias or, more positively, with the eye of the citizen who has the interest of the area and its children at heart.

While the educational problems this approach seeks to remedy are serious ones, and the objectives commendable, the consequences of a narrowing of teacher competencies could be disastrous. This viewpoint is reminiscent of the early growth of public education in America, and is not a satisfactory solution to the education problems of a large, pluralistic, urban society. A community-specific or ethnic-specific approach to teacher education is inherently dangerous because polarization and animosity are already rampant among ethnic groups and social classes. Such an emphasis reinforces differences and perpetuates the biases of individual communities and ethnic groups, intensifying rather than reducing the strife within American society. If our society is to survive, the nation's major institutions must deliberately seek the enlargement of shared values among broader circles of our citizens. Teacher educators must build into preparation programs the idea that both core values and individual freedom should be preserved within a matrix of cultural pluralism.

Many schools have failed adequately to meet the needs and expectations of our diversified society. Many schools have failed to prepare the children of white middle-class suburbia, and the Black or Chicano child of the ghetto, to function effectively in a highly technological, multicultural, and ever-changing society. Teacher education programs often neglected or totally ignored the concepts of community and ethnicity until the civil rights movement of the sixties. Then, educators used *community* as a code word for "inner-city" and "ghetto," and *ethnic* for "Black" or some other minority group. If community or ethnic concerns were dealt with at all over the last decade, it was usually within such a limited context. Large numbers of teacher training programs included components that attempted to give preteachers the "inside story" on a specific community or culture group situation— usually urban, Black, poor, and more recently, the Native American. These efforts have been less than adequate.

Teacher education programs must deal with the concepts of community and ethnicity concretely and comprehensively, if we are to have skilled professional educators who are sensitive to the pluralistic nature of society. The proponents of community-controlled, community-based teacher education programs, and those with an exclusive focus on particular ethnic minority studies, suffer from the same short-sightedness. Both make theoretical and operational assumptions based on limited and narrow definitions of *community* and *ethnic*.

We believe that teacher educators must define community and ethnicity in the broadest sense, including all segments of society and the infinite number of variations within each. And because all of us live in a multicultural society, developers of teacher preparation programs must help students devise and test strategies to cope with the real-world demands arising from a broad range of community and ethnic concerns.

The Commission agrees with proponents of community-based, community-controlled teacher education who hold that communities must be involved in the policy planning process for education—from goal setting to evaluating outcomes.

Recommendation
That all parties devise mechanisms where communities, local education agencies, and institutions of higher education work together to reconcile their varying perceptions of what education should be. Responsible, open collaboration among all constituencies must occur in order to build responsive, pluralistic programs.

Recommendation
That teacher education programs provide students with conceptual structures concerning teaching and learning which cut across ethnic and community boundaries. Also, that all teacher education students study and experience in some depth at least one of the local, regional, or national subcultures.

Methodology relevant to specific ethnic-community issues must become as important a part of the curriculum as the acquisition of other teaching competencies. Students must have a basic understanding of America's historic, sociological, and economic developments which have created today's pluralistic society. Students must become sensitive to cultural differences among children, and to the obligation of the school to make the most of such differences rather than viewing

97

them as undesirable discrepancies from a monolithic cultural norm. Also, preparation programs should deal concretely with a comprehensive problem-solving *process* for resolving community-ethnic specific issues. *The Commission emphasizes, however, that while communities are unique in many ways, they also share many commonalities. And, some educational processes remain constant across all communities and ethnic groups.* The Commission shares Holbrook's view:

> The prisoners of Attica, in calling out "We are men," appealed to *humanitas* [the universal], not to their ethnicity. Our laws presuppose *humanitas* for their ultimate ethical justification, even if they fail to embody it totally. Even when we decry the universality of *humanitas* in the name of ethnic concreteness, we assume that those who disagree with us can understand what we are saying. Thereby we refute at one level what we assert at another level. Without the universality of *humanitas* we could not disagree, not even about ethnicity.[16]

THE IMPORTANCE OF ADEQUATE "LIFE SPACE"

Teacher education suffers from serious inadequacies in the "life space" available to carry out the demanding task of preparing professional teachers. In time, facilities, personnel, instructional and research materials—even in access to quality instruction in other academic units—teacher education programs require greater resources than presently allocated. It is important to understand the limitations on curricula imposed by the cramped, seriously inadequate life space which teacher education programs presently occupy. *The magnitude, intensity, and direction of the efforts needed to prepare a teacher reach far beyond present resources.* Teachers in training need:

1. A sequence of study in the disciplines which undergird teaching.
2. An in-depth examination of a significant subculture within a context of broad cultural awareness.
3. More effective integration and expansion of theory and practice.
4. Field experiences which illuminate educational theory and course work and extend practice.

The life space demands imposed by these needs necessitate a careful analysis of the different populations served by colleges of education. Every institution must examine its objectives in light of the cost of necessary resources. Teacher education programs which lack sufficient resources and, thus, compromise quality standards must either secure the resources or be abandoned (See Appendix C.).

Many colleges of education attempt to provide instructional service in several, or all, of the following categories:

1. Preparation programs for elementary and secondary teachers leading to initial certification in those fields.
2. Preparation of educational specialists in a variety of fields (e.g., counseling, administration, research, and college teaching).
3. Continuing professional development for teachers.
4. Inservice needs identified by area school systems.
5. Preparation of paraprofessional school personnel.
6. Programs for personnel employed by, or interested in working in, nonschool agencies having educational functions (e.g., museums, educational television, churches, community recreation groups, and industry).
7. The study of educational processes and institutions as a part of general education (the motivation of an increasing number of parents and other citizens).

Future educational developments will continue, even intensify, these service demands. However, if institutions lack the appropriate resources to offer good programs, there will be a deterioration of quality standards in all. Also, if colleges of education conserve instructional resources by enrolling students with widely differing objectives in the same course, then subject matter will become irrelevant. For example, mixing junior college faculty who desire instructional improvement with students seeking certification-type professional courses can only result in a compromise that reduces usefulness for all professionals.

Most colleges of education, committed to quality standards but confronted with limited resources, will place their highest priorities on programs leading to teaching certification and to the preparation of related school specialists. However, significant changes in supply and demand will cause a reordering of priorities in many institutions.

Recommendation

That every college of education identify its objectives, determine the resources necessary to achieve those objectives at a quality level consistent with the demands of our profession, and then establish realistic priorities for the size and diversity of programs those resources can support.

Recommendation

That teacher preparation for initial service be conducted in a five-year sequence, combining both bachelor's and master's degrees.

This plan will provide the "life space" urgently needed for adequate preparation in general education, academic specialization, preprofessional social and behavioral sciences, educational foundations, subculture study, and an appropriate blend of campus and field experiences emphasizing effective instructional strategies. *The Commission is not recommending simply an expansion of existing liberal arts and professional components into an additional year of study. Instead, it is urging a bold new commitment of time, energy, and resources for an entirely original structure to prepare teachers.*

The Internship

One of the critical problems of teacher education is the absence of opportunity to exercise professional responsibilities under direct and continuous supervision during an internship. Other professions find a planned internship essential. The demanding nature of teaching suggests a similar need.

At least the first year of teaching should be in an internship role. Beginning teachers should be given responsibility comparable to experienced teachers but under the direction of supervisors who are available for assistance as needed. Assigning interns to schools in small groups (at pay levels somewhat below those for regular teachers) and providing a specially prepared experienced teacher as intern supervisor is a relatively inexpensive but effective approach which has already been tested in a number of locations. Teacher education assistance from the university should be continued through the internship period, both through supervisory collaboration and through more structured continuing education experiences. Continuing certification should be withheld until after successful completion of the internship experience.

Recommendation
That the internship in teacher education be defined as a minimum of one year of supervised employment and that it be made an integral part of all teacher preparation programs.

Needed: Continuity of Preservice, Inservice, and Continuing Education—The Critical Nature of the Early Years of Teaching

The early years of teaching are crucial to the professional development of teachers. The support they receive from other professionals can influence greatly the attitudes, effectiveness, and subsequent professional growth of the new teacher. Teachers who are trying new things need many opportunities to talk about their work with each other. New teachers' willingness to use a range of approaches to teaching will level off or stop if they are left alone to face classroom problems. Often, the need to survive becomes the major force for continuing to use whatever seems to have worked—without further exploration of instructional alternatives or reflection on the long-range consequences of teaching behavior.

The new teacher's need for professional support requires that the university (which provided preservice preparation), professional organizations, and employing school system all provide help. The university and professional organizations can help in assisting teachers to reconceptualize their roles during times of great change. The employing school system can help by supporting teacher centers which draw on the expertise of a variety of professionals in order to develop and refine teaching skills. While there is broad agreement that schools need to be more effective than they have been and that teachers must initiate change, it is unlikely that a new teacher, acting alone, can be an agent of reform.

Taking strong issue with some in teacher education who gear their programs to an idealized view of schools and of teaching, Smith and Orlosky argue that "it is mischievous, deliberately, to maladapt a teacher to the school for those who are so maladapted cannot survive in it, let alone reform it."[17] However, the problem requires a balanced approach since intimate contact with school reality, without benefit of the perspective of new values and theories, will foster a teacher's adjustment to what *is* rather than stimulating visions of what *could be*. *New teachers must come to teaching both with a capacity to survive and a willingness to work toward building professional relationships that will support reform.*

Teacher Preparation for Institution Building

The knowledge and skills important for effective teaching include an understanding of the school as a social institution, and the teacher as an institution builder. Colleagues, administrators, parents, and students all exert a powerful press upon the new teacher. Preparation programs must help beginning teachers to understand these environments and provide the continuing education to aid teachers to become skillful in receiving and giving colleague support.

Colleges of education should extend their formal contact with beginning teachers through their initial year of teaching. This plan could reduce the "culture shock" of the new teacher, blur the artificial distinctions between preservice and continuing education, and provide for collaboration between school and college personnel. Presently, many new teachers function in a professional desert, abandoned by the institutions where they received their preservice education, and neglected by overburdened school supervisory personnel. By sharing university resources with school systems, and allocating additional resources to this critically important area, teacher education could touch the professional lives of teachers when they are most responsive to new learning.

Professional Learning in the Immediate Teaching Environment of the Beginning Teacher

In addition to a mastery of generic teaching skills, new teachers will need to become familiar with the policies and practices unique to their school systems. Methods of record keeping, the system's reading program, the scope and sequence of the total curriculum, provisions for handling various learning disabilities, and supervisory roles and procedures are some examples of a school system's practices. School systems should assume responsibility for instruction in these practices through teacher centers, workshops, and extended conferences. These learnings build upon the general learnings of the university-based program and provide the necessary familiarity with a particular school's procedures. They also ease adjustment to a new setting, raise the level of confidence of new teachers, and increase the likelihood that new teachers will try a broader range of instructional techniques.

The Differing Emphases of Preservice Education, Inservice Education, and Continuing Professional Development: A Summary

Preservice education should emphasize the generic knowledge, behaviors, and skills that enable beginning teachers to function at a safe level in a wide variety of settings. Preservice education should be a direction setter for beginning teaching and for further professional growth. It should stir interests, stimulate inquiry, and initiate commitment.

Inservice education should meet the needs of the school system. While the continuing education needs of individual faculty members may not be at odds with the training needs of a school system, nevertheless, needs of the system should be paramount. School systems should undertake periodic reviews to determine staff training needs. The emphasis on school system needs as the locus for inservice education is a considerable departure from the common pattern of accepting any college credit without regard to its relevance. *The Commission is not proposing that colleges and universities be uninvolved in inservice teacher education.*

Recommendation

That school systems become the chief locus for inservice education in order to keep this phase of staff development maximally responsive to school and community needs. Area colleges should expect to participate regularly in the planning and to contribute resources when they are relevant and available. The primary role of the college of education, however, should be to prepare public school personnel competent to carry out assessments and research basic to such programming.

Continuing Professional Development

Continuing professional development reaches beyond the support of beginning teacher efforts to apply teaching knowledge and skills to particular school and community situations. It reaches beyond the meeting of specific school system needs through inservice education. Its function is the development of professional teacher-scholars, capable of high levels of diagnosis and prescription; coordinating the instructional efforts of other professional and paraprofessional associates; and exercising leadership in school, community, and the profession. Continuing professional development aims at proficiency, at mastery, even at brilliance in the performance of instructional responsibilities.

While the chief responsibility for continuing professional development must rest with the individual teacher and the organized profession, the major vehicle for carrying out professional development objectives still doubtless remains the graduate programs of the colleges and universities, enriched by the collaboration of school systems. Professional organizations can contribute to the substantive experiences as well as to the design of professional development standards through publications, conferences, and other educational activities.

This phase of professional growth should integrate the educational experiences of the teacher-scholar with those of other specialists pursuing advanced degrees at the university. At this stage, the programs of teacher-scholars can be differentiated to support the development of specialized knowledge and skills important to the balance of a school instructional staff. *The Commission believes that programs in continuing professional development should lead to advanced degrees or certificates having professional designations paralleling those employed in other professions such as medicine and law.* The teacher-scholar degree candidate should be required to demonstrate mastery of the knowledge contributing to effective diagnosis of teaching and learning problems as well as mastery of the skills associated with application of such knowledge in a manner whch fosters learning.

EXPANDING THE APPLICATION OF PROFESSIONAL EDUCATION BEYOND THE SCHOOL

Other community agencies are involved in educational programs requiring well-trained teachers. Society is finally starting to recognize the needs of students who, for a variety of reasons, benefit from educational programs outside the regular offerings of schools and colleges. Teachers who work with these students need many of the traditional understandings and skills required of educators; these teachers must apply these skills in different environments and with a variety of learners.

Ylvisaker identified a number of recent developments suggesting new directions for colleges of education.[18] These included:

1. Educational entitlement providing every adult American with an annual allocation available for a broad range of educational activities. (A bill in the New York legislature proposes $100 per individual annually for all persons over 26 years of age.)
2. An early, family-centered education.
3. Educational use of the mass media.
4. Integration of work and learning.
5. Consumer education and the growing emphasis upon self-education.
6. Training and retraining professional, paraprofessional, and governing personnel.
7. A broadened definition of "educators" to include school board members, trustees, judges and their clerks, legislators and their staffs, and others playing significant roles in the learning process.

Clearly, these developments necessitate a new kind of teacher—a "human service educator"—a highly diversified professional who, because of appropriate pedagogical knowledge, values, and skills, will be able to help others realize their best human, professional, and societal potentials. Today, human and social needs are expanding, there is the prospect of real structural change in the institutions that serve people, and resources are declining. Under these circumstances, the public is calling increasingly on educators to undertake a greater variety of professional tasks with learners of every age and type, in settings as diverse as nursing homes, storefront social action agencies, social welfare offices, and factories.[19]

Rapidly expanding human service areas require a broad range of professional knowledge and skills. There is growing evidence to suggest that a number of generic competencies are relevant to all the human service professions. Cole and Lacefield, in a study of skill domains for the helping professions, found that certain skills beneficial to teaching were also important to other professional fields. A sampling of students, faculty, and practicing professionals in counseling, social work, home economics, allied health, and dentistry evaluated those skills relevant to effective professional practice (See Appendix D.). Cole and Lacefield found that:

> generally, the professional-technical skills and the interpersonal regard skills were seen as being most professionally relevant by all disciplines . . . . Value clarification was consistently perceived as

less relevant than other skill domains . . . The social-behavioral science groups tend to perceive value clarification as more professionally relevant than the medical science groups.[20]

Recommendation

That colleges of education seek resources to expand their program formats and philosophies to include the preparation of other human service professionals in addition to teachers, administrators, and counselors for public school settings. Also, colleges of education must develop new collaborative relationships with other professions in order to foster new attitudes and skills and reduce the parochialization of excessive specialization.

THE EDUCATION OF TEACHER EDUCATORS

The education of teacher educators is largely ignored in the professional literature. *The Commission holds that the education of teacher educators should emerge principally from the needs of the personnel they prepare.* Teaching is a complex activity with ambitious objectives and demanding skills. Teacher education must be accepted both as pre-service preparation and a professionalizing process which continues through the career of the teacher. Teachers must be capable of diagnosing learning problems, developing curricular materials, experimenting with instructional procedures appropriate to the needs of a wide range of individuals, and evaluating the outcomes of these activities.

The complexities and responsibilities of the teacher's role are obvious. Yet, an analysis of the graduate preparation of most teacher educators discloses that few have participated in programs specifically designed to meet these complexities and demands. In their own training, most teacher educators specialize in a single graduate department with little understanding of the interrelationship of the separate specialty areas.

Recommendation

That in addition to in-depth study in a single area, teacher educators study each specialization in an in-breadth context. Teacher educators must become more knowledgeable about, and sensitive to, the relationship of their own specialty to all other specialty areas in professional preparation. This can be accomplished by a broad foundational experience in pedagogy and the supporting disciplines, designed to provide teacher educators with an awareness of the contributions of their own area of specialization to the broad context of teacher preparation. Without such a background, teacher educators will leave to each student the impossible task of integrating the miscellany of learnings into a coherent whole.

The Liaison Role of the Teacher Educator

Teacher educators must become familiar with the world of the teacher and the variety of functions a teacher discharges in the school and community. Teacher educators must also function effectively in the world of higher education. They must be capable of applying the knowledge and research in higher education to the problems of schools and teachers. Teacher educators must relate to both school professionals and to university academicians and be able to cope with the ambiguities and strains this dichotomous relationship generates. Exclusive affiliation with one group would obviously reduce such tensions. Unfortunately, it would also deprive the teacher educator of the chance to meld theoretical and applied knowledge and to serve as a liaison agent in the necessary collaboration between schools and higher education.

Major Components of Professional Knowledge

Many authors who describe the components of professional knowledge agree that it should have the following minimum dimensions: an underlying conceptual and/or scientific base; an applied, problem-testing and problem-solving component; and a technical culture which includes performance skills and professional attitudes. Dunkin and Biddle synthesize these components of knowledge into a useful model for research on teaching, and for designing appropriate knowledge for the education of teacher educators.[21] According to their model, all classroom teaching can be broken down to four major variables. *Presage variables* include all teacher characteristics which affect the teaching-learning process (personal, professional, technical training). *Context variables* include those environmental characteristics to which teachers must adjust, and about which teacher educators can do little. *Process variables* include the actual procedures of classroom teaching. And *product variables* include the outcomes of teaching resulting in behavioral and attitudinal change. The model is especially helpful because it suggests the kinds of knowledge all teachers must possess. Presage knowledge necessitates general sociological, psychological, and anthropological understanding. Context knowledge requires the same understandings applied to a specific environment—the classroom-school-community complex. Process knowledge requires a technical understanding of learning theory, behavior change, and teaching methodology. And product knowledge calls for evaluation and prescription skills.

In many respects, a college of education *is* a school and subject to the same variables as those which affect the teaching-learning process in elementary and secondary schools. The parallels suggest that teacher educators will benefit from the study of teaching in their own classes as well as in the classrooms of the schools they serve.

A Broad View of the Education Process

Another task of teacher educators is to associate with the general public and to understand the educational processes which go on *outside* the schools. In one sense, *schooling* is concerned with specific learning tasks in a formal setting. *Education* is broader, involving learning those tasks which relate to the total living experience. Most learning, in this sense, takes place *outside* formal frameworks, vis-à-vis the family, church, press, theatre, television, and peers. Thus, the competent teacher educator must develop professional skills in relating to, and influencing, all citizens concerning these broader teaching-learning processes.

The Teacher Educator as Exemplar of Effective Teaching

Teacher educators should practice what they preach—exemplify what they explicate—if they are to be effective in working with prospective and experienced teachers. Teacher educators who exhort their students to individualize instruction, cultivate a taste for research and scholarship, and develop team-teaching skills—while employing none of these approaches themselves—are unlikely ever to persuade students to adopt new teaching styles or new ways of thinking about education.

Teacher educators must apply to themselves all that they advocate in the preparation of elementary and secondary school teachers. One way to develop teacher educators who are exemplars of effective teaching is to impose rigorous selection standards in the faculty recruitment process, by requiring evidence of highly successful teaching experience. Another way is to provide supervised college teaching internships with peers, and with one or a group of experienced faculty members. Graduate teaching assistantships will be helpful only if they are properly designed and coordinated. Without orientation, joint planning, continuing supervision and regular feedback, graduate assistantships usually represent cheap instruction for the college, and trial and error learning for the graduate assistant. Finally, teaching must take place in a team setting. The complexity of teacher education makes the stereotype of the autonomous teacher working alone with a standard size class of students totally anachronistic.

Linking Research and Teaching

Teacher educators must be actively involved in research and

scholarship which is thorough and pertinent to teaching and learning. Teacher educators must be more than consumers of other people's educational research; they must be productive researchers themselves.

The Commission urges all teachers to be students of educational processes—productive scholars who research the teaching-learning experience— as well as preparers of personnel. If teacher educators are only trainers, then teacher education is likely to become mere verbal exhortation and mechanical routine. If the objective of education is to produce citizens capable of independent thinking and inquiry, then teachers and teacher educators must themselves be independent thinkers.

Commitment to the Professional Preparation of Teachers

Data from the Study Commission on Undergraduate Education and the Education of Teachers reveal that there is low commitment to teacher preparation by faculty members in many teacher education institutions. Many believe that their priorities should be to train graduate students, provide a broad liberal education, and do research.[22] There is nothing wrong with those teacher educators who perceive liberal education to be of major importance to teachers. Rather, the trouble lies with those teacher educators who assume full responsibility for liberal education themselves, and, as a result, are unable to devote their full energies and resources to the compelling work of professional education.

Dangers of the Self-fulfilling Prophecy

Unfortunately, the low self-esteem of teacher educators for their own work is an outgrowth of the inferior status which American higher education has long assigned to the preparation of teachers. Some teacher educators who question the importance of their own field begin to seek ways to achieve conventional academic stature. Also, some students who prepare for teaching in what they perceive as an "inferior" academic environment show little regard for the importance of their training. The pervasive low self-esteem of teacher educators and their students results in a self-fulfilling prophecy: the assignment of inferior status to professional education. *Teacher educators must break this cycle of low esteem and low performance. The profession must attract teacher educators who will exemplify the ideals they profess and commit themselves enthusiastically to the work they do.*

Cultural Pluralism and Advocacy of Human Rights

Teacher educators must maintain a profound commitment to human rights, particularly the rights of children. Unfortunately, teacher educators have not always been conscious exemplars of human rights. Few actively advocate the rights of minority groups or promote cultural pluralism. Today, leaders ask the education profession to develop in students those attitudes and beliefs which support cultural pluralism as a positive social force. Thus, the education of teacher educators must be substantive enough to develop a respect for the culture, lifestyles, and contributions of nonmainstream cultures. Teacher educators also need a commitment to universal human values in order to promote harmonious coexistence.

The profession must reaffirm its commitment to multicultural education and cultural pluralism. We could find no better statement to guide the future than *No One Model American*, developed by the AACTE Commission on Multicultural Education and adopted by the Board of Directors of AACTE in November 1972. The statement begins by saying:

> Multicultural education is education which values cultural pluralism. Multicultural education rejects the view that schools should seek to melt away cultural differences or the view that schools should merely tolerate cultural pluralism. Instead, multicultural education affirms that schools should be oriented toward the cultural enrichment of all children and youth through programs rooted to the preservation and extension of cultural alternatives. Multicultural education recognizes cultural diversity as a fact of life in American society, and it affirms that this cultural diversity is a valuable resource that should be preserved and extended. It affirms that major education institutions should strive to preserve and enhance cultural pluralism. [23]

Colleges of education have a special obligation to set an example for other colleges by aggressively seeking and hiring faculty from minority groups and providing educational access to students from minority groups. A multiracial, multicultural faculty and student body is essential if multicultural education is to become a reality rather than just a concept.

The Commission believes that teacher educators, as advocates, must respond with a sense of urgency to move the concepts in No One Model American *from thought to action in all aspects of professional preparation and the organizations that represent the teaching profession.*

Women's Rights Movement and the Profession

Women in the teaching profession have felt the consequences of prejudice and discrimination in the larger society. While women have not been systematically excluded from the teaching profession historically, they have been relegated to subordinate positions in education at all levels. Few women have achieved formal positions of leadership in public schools, postsecondary institutions, or professional organizations. Where women have achieved positions of influence in education, they tend to occupy professional roles which are less prestigious and lower paying than positions held by their male counterparts.[24]

The profession must go on record as being unalterably opposed to any ideology, hidden or declared, which forces women to suppress their capabilities. *Contrary to some views, the Commission believes that a preponderance of women is not a liability to becoming a profession, especially when viewed in the context of the present women's rights movement. The success of this movement in the decade ahead will be one of the major factors in determining whether or not teaching achieves the status of a profession.* In linking its ultimate fate with the rise of the women's movement, the teaching profession will assure its own constant renewal. In the years ahead, both women and men must be called upon equally to contribute the knowledge and skills necessary for the continuing revitalization of the profession. Teacher educators must exemplify what they explicate in human rights as well as in teaching strategies, both on the campus and in schools and communities.

Informed Perspective on Schools

Rapid changes in schools, changing patterns of behavior of the young, the growing influence of the community on schools—these and related trends mandate that teacher educators need a thorough and current knowledge of schools. Unfortunately, college responsibilities permit teacher educators to pay little attention to actual school settings. Regular exchange of school-based and college-based personnel can enrich both learning environments and results in continuing professional development opportunities for both groups. Also, regular adjunct faculty appointments for qualified school personnel (who have their work load adjusted for teacher education) can insure an updating of knowledge about the schools. Reimbursement for these assignments can take the form of college-based personnel doing actual public school teaching, materials development, curriculum consultation, and other service tasks.

The Need for Continuing Education

All teacher educators, like their public school counterparts, need lifelong professional development. This necessitates such "renewal" experiences as sabbatical leaves, teacher exchanges with public school personnel, and research involvement. *The Commission endorses the need for the continuing education of teacher educators if faculty are to be skilled in relating both to colleagues in the academic disciplines and to public*

110

school educators, talented in applying concepts from the disciplines to the resolution of school problems, capable of blending teaching and research interests so that one illuminates the other, and skilled in a broad range of instructional procedures to demonstrate exemplary teaching.

FOOTNOTES

1. D.C. Lortie, *Schoolteacher. A Sociological Study* (Chicago: The University of Chicago Press, 1975), p. 10.
2. M.L. Cogan, "Current Issues in the Education of Teachers," *Teacher Education: 74th Yearbook of the National Society for the Study of Education,* Kevin Ryan, ed. (Chicago: University of Chicago Press, 1975), pp. 204-9.
3. J.C. Stone, *Breakthrough in Teacher Education* (San Francisco: Jossey-Bass, 1968).
4. I. Scheffler, *Conditions of Knowledge: An Introduction to Epistemology and Education* (Chicago: Scott Foresman, 1965), pp. 95-96.
5. C. Argyris and D.A. Schon, *Theory in Practice: Increasing Professional Effectiveness* (San Francisco: Jossey-Bass, 1974), pp. 3-19.
6. P. Starr, "The Edge of Social Science," *Harvard Educational Review* 4, no. 4 (November 1974): 383-415.
7. P.A. Olson, ed., "Analysis of Carnegie Commission Survey Data Completed," *Study Commission Newsletter* (Lincoln: University of Nebraska, January 1975).
8. B.O. Smith, S.B. Cohen, and A. Pearl, *Teachers for the Real World* (Washington, D.C.: American Association of Colleges for Teacher Education, 1969), p. 111.
9. Ibid., p. 71.
10. J. Burdin, "The Changing World and Its Implications for Teacher Education," *Teacher Education: 74th Yearbook of the National Society for the Study of Education,* Kevin Ryan, ed. (Chicago: University of Chicago Press, 1975), pp. 295-304.
11. Cogan, "Current Issues," p. 227.
12. W. Arrowsmith, "The Future of Teaching," *The Liberal Arts and Teacher Education: A Confrontation,* D.N. Bigelow, ed. (Lincoln, Nebr.: University of Nebraska Press, 1971), pp. 40-42.
13. J. Bowman, et al., eds., *The University Can't Train Teachers.* USOE Superintendents and Principals Subcommittee of the Study Commission on Undergraduate Education and the Education of Teachers (Lincoln: Nebraska Curriculum Development Center, University of Nebraska, 1972).
14. R.J. Nash, and E.R. Ducharme, "The University Can Prepare Teachers —An Unfashionable View," *The Educational Forum,* November 1974, pp. 108-9.
15. D.C. Corrigan, *Some Value Premises to Consider in Developing Performance-Based Strategies for Maximizing the Humane in Education* (Prepared for the AACTE Leadership Training Institute on Performance-Based Teacher Education, Boston, Mass., December 12, 1974), p. 6.

16. C.A. Holbrook, "The Erosion of Humanitas," *World View*, July 1974, p. 37.
17. B.O. Smith and D.C. Orlosky, *Socialization and Schooling* (Bloomington, Ind.: Phi Delta Kappa, 1957), p. 157.
18. P.N. Ylvisaker, Memorandum to Members of ACESEULGC Legislative Liaison and Planning Committee (Harvard University Graduate School of Education, June 9, 1975).
19. R.J. Nash and E.R. Ducharme, "A Futures Perspective on Preparing Educators for the Human Service Society," unpublished manuscript (Burlington: University of Vermont, Spring 1975); also R.J. Nash "Humanistic Teacher Education: A Future Look," *AACTE Bulletin* 28 (August 1975): 3.
20. H.P. Cole and W.E. Lacefield, "Skill Domains for the Helping Professions," unpublished manuscript (Lexington, Ky.: College of Education, 1975).
21. N.J. Dunkin and B.J. Biddle, *The Study of Teaching* (New York: Holt, Rinehart and Winston, 1974), pp. 38-52.
22. Paul A. Olson, ed., *Study Commission Newsletter*, January 1975.
23. AACTE Commission on Multicultural Education, "No One Model American," *Journal of Teacher Education* 24, no. 4 (Winter 1973): 264-65.
24. "The Molding of the Nonsexist Teacher" (Theme), *Journal of Teacher Education* 26, no. 4 (Winter 1975).

FIVE

Quality Control

*The profession must become more consumer oriented
and less practitioner protective.*

*During the last quarter of the twentieth century,
the range of educational settings,
needs, and personnel will expand.*

*Accreditation should be mandatory
for all institutions preparing teachers.*

INDIVIDUAL/PROFESSIONAL

Teaching will not become an established profession until it develops creditable quality control policies and procedures. Each of the dimensions of the "quality control" question must be examined, including recruitment, selection and "entry to profession" criteria, individual certification, supply and demand, institutional/programmatic accreditation, and resources for adequate life space to prepare professionals. These factors are discussed in this chapter.

RECRUITMENT

"Quality control," in its customary business and industrial uses, implies that those seeking to impose such measures actually have control of the process. When teacher educators speak about quality control, they speak from the vantage point of "controlling" no more than 25 percent of student preparation. No profession leaves so much of its training to others. A profession that controls so little of its preparation seriously compromises quality control. Furthermore, it is difficult to develop a sense of pride in a profession with only the junior and senior years available for training. A profession so vague in defining its role and function and so impotent in its control of training will continue to face recruitment problems.

Colleges of education have rarely applied strict criteria for entry to teacher education or the profession. Recruitment has historically

113

been a quantitative issue, rarely a qualitative one. With the exception of the last five years and the depression period, the nation has had a *shortage* of teachers. Unfortunately, periods of surplus produced no clear criteria for selection. Thus, the situation continued where admission processes were perfunctory, at best, compared to the established professions.

Recruitment based on any criteria other than variable levels of standardized test scores and high school ranking has been the exception. Generally, the profession has employed permissive recruiting practices. While it is true that, in the past, many teachers underwent four-year preparation programs called teacher education, it is also true that many teachers made late-career decisions and were as welcome as those who declared early. There is a lack of clear evidence, however, that early or late declarations are critical elements in making better practitioners. This absence of evidence concerning recruitment makes it difficult to validate teaching as a profession. It is further complicated by ease of entry, a point which Rivlin recognized a number of years ago: "Why should any superior student aspire to a position anyone can achieve?"[1]

Recruitment and selection have *not* been major concerns of the teaching profession. Even though Master of Arts in Teaching programs in the fifties and sixties had elaborate recruitment mechanisms, they were slanted almost exclusively toward academic and cognitive matters. The profession rarely considers such attributes as social concern, experience with youth, commitment to learning, self-image, and community interests, even though it holds these qualities in high value. There is little evidence to support whatever vague selection processes the profession has used. Even the recent decline in teaching positions has not provoked a profession-wide discussion regarding the qualities candidates need in this constricted market.

The profession must find and support more effective guides for recruitment and selection. Current trends toward lifelong learning, recognition of the varieties of ways that people learn, value of human relationships, and respect for person suggest the kinds of teachers society needs. The profession needs new methods for finding these qualities in prospective candidates. Scholastic Aptitude Test scores, rank in class, and grade-point averages are necessary but not sufficient criteria for quality selection of candidates. Evidence of voluntary social efforts, avocations that relate to effective human relationships, experiences that indicate growing self-concept, sense of responsibility for others, and tolerance for uncertainty and ambiguities are equally important criteria.

Recruitment, Diversity, and Selection Criteria

Recruitment for teacher education must reach a widely differentiated population base. America is still a pluralistic society, and its schools must reflect this diversity. "Affirmative action" policies speak to this issue, but the declining job market could make it easy for institutions to consider only those applicants who fit the traditional criteria. This is not likely to produce the range of people desired. Thus, the profession must develop new selection criteria. *The Commission cautions against the danger of a tightened job market being the rationale for which diversity is denied. The profession must be conscious of the need to insure diversity as well as the need to influence directly the quality of personnel.*

Teacher education also has the responsibility of justifying each student's admission by verifying each student's ability to succeed in the teaching profession. The simple act of choosing to become a teacher does not confer the automatic right to become a teacher. Candidates must demonstrate, at a number of specific points prior to actual professional entry, that they possess the necessary skills, knowledge, and values for successful professional practice.

Indiana State University has developed a process for admitting and retaining candidates. Although there is no intrinsic magic in any flow chart, ISU's chart specifies particular points along the professional continuum where informed judgments should occur. Unfortunately, the history of teacher education is replete with failures because teacher educators have not intervened effectively with candidates of little promise. However, the advantage of the ISU flow chart is that now teacher educators can develop informed, professional judgments about students at all stages of the training experiences (See Appendix E.).

Recommendation

That the profession develop workable ways of insuring that only the ablest teach. The advantage of procedures for admission and selective retention employed by institutions like Indiana State University is that, for the first time, candidates can be helped to determine whether they possess the necessary professional commitments, characteristics, and skills.

CERTIFICATION

One of the great issues of the 1980s will be professional certification. What follows are some key assertions concerning the issue of certification:

1. *Certification is not a lifelong license. Permanent certification is an anachronism.* Because every professional must develop continual renewal through a program of lifelong learning, it is incongruous for a profession to certify people for life. No one design for periodic recertifications will be sufficient for all states and institutions. What is important, however, is that the profession of teaching commit itself to the concept of continual recertification by using

as many means as possible to insure that educators remain up-to-date, effective practitioners.

2. *The granting of certification should be a shared, professional process.* Certification is not the sole responsibility of state departments, professional teacher groups, higher education institutions, or local communities. It is the responsibility of all these groups, a relationship that requires collaboration, feedback, and mutual assistance.

3. *The state must be the source for formal certification; the profession must develop, recommend, and monitor a professional educator's continuing education.* This process will exemplify the collaborative process because it combines a legally recognized source and a professional group to insure the lifelong learning of the educator.

4. *Certification implies a "safety-to-the-client" concern.* Much certification procedure and rationale speak to what *candidates* have learned and what *candidates* have experienced. Certification must emphasize the advantages and benefits for potential *clients*. *The profession must become more consumer oriented and less practitioner protective.*

In the *Griggs v. Duke Power Company* decision,[2] the Supreme Court held that it was discriminatory to use unvalidated tests and educational requirements in selection of employees, and that employers must demonstrate a valid relationship between such requirements and performance on the job. If the concepts inherent in this court case, and other court cases of a similar nature, are transferred to the field of education, the teaching profession will be required to validate the process of certification of individuals through performance criteria. Teacher education will have to show that there is a direct relationship between program objectives and successful performance of the teaching act. Furthermore, such legal decisions will have far-reaching implications for admission to college, matriculation into a professional sequence, and criteria for program completion, as well as certification.

SUPPLY AND DEMAND

The issue of teacher surplus and shortage is often oversimplified. For many years, the United States had a severe teacher shortage. The number of people minimally qualified to teach was fewer than the number of available positions. Unfortunately, much discussion today tends to create a misunderstanding of the meaning of such key terms as "shortage," "surplus," and "supply and demand." The national data have built-in limitations. Colleges report the number of individuals who are graduated, and local education agencies report the number of positions available. Thus, the public learns about the shortages or oversupply of staff and classroom teachers in certain subject fields. But what the public does *not* learn about is the severe "shortage" of highly qualified, exemplary education personnel which still persists. School systems continue to point out that while applicants meet the minimum certification requirements of the state, they still do not meet their own local standards, standards which are becoming higher and more demanding. The positions may be filled, but not always by people with the professional expertise or qualifications that school systems need.

Teacher-Learner Needs

The question of *need* further complicates the matter. While schools appear to be devoting more of their resources to planning, few school systems actually make continuing, systematic, and comprehensive assessments of needs. Needs assessment remains relatively unsophisticated, and so, consequently, does the public's understanding of the true "surplus" or "shortage" of teachers. The reports of local education agencies on teacher "surplus" are merely indications that budgeted positions have been filled. These reports may not reflect the *true* needs of students and communities. In truth, the gap is widening between what their needs are and what communities are willing to support financially.

When viewed in relationship to the educational needs of today's children and youth, it is difficult to accept the current talk about a teacher surplus. For example, about half of the communities in the United States are without kindergartens. Preschool education is nonexistent in most parts of the country, even though research shows that the first five years of life largely determine the characteristics of the young adult. Large numbers of physically and mentally handicapped children are being neglected. Almost half of the adult population 25 years old and over is functionally illiterate. The high schools have less than one counselor for 500 students. And there are hundreds of overcrowded classrooms, resulting in shallow teacher-pupil relationships and widespread student anonymity. Furthermore, the National Center for Careers in Education indicates that 31 of 50 states report a shortage of special education workers; 21 states indicate deficiencies in industrial arts and vocational-technical fields; and almost all states indicate shortages of teachers in environmental education, cultural studies, bilingual education, and adult education. Moreover, practically all minority schools indicate a shortage of minority culture teachers.[3]

Finally, Graybeal notes that if the nation were providing the necessary resources for society's needs, then, in 1974, there was a need for 799,250 qualified teachers; 332,750 teachers were available, and only 154,450 were hired. What has resulted are significant nationwide gaps in educational services that make the issue of educational equality

117

specious. Many communities still lack kindergartens, special education services, adult learning centers, and a host of other legitimate educational needs (See Appendix F.).

A Futures Perspective on Teacher Surplus

When viewed from the aforementioned conditions, current statements about the teacher surplus are faulty because they totally misunderstand what society needs in the present and what it will need in the future. Future social needs will necessitate the emergence of a variety of new careers hitherto not even imagined by planners for education.

If schools are to become personalized learning centers, they will require a variety of personnel with diverse talents. Teaching teams will include specially trained professionals who will work not only with children and youth but with other teachers. For example, the teacher will be less of a content specialist and more of a specialist in the nature of learning and the use of learning resources. Teaching staffs will include research associates, learning diagnosticians, visual literacy specialists, computer-assisted instructional specialists, systems analysis and evaluation experts, specialists in simulation and gaming techniques, information systems and data base designers, and community education teachers.

In the world of the future, teachers and other education personnel will perform a broad range of human services originating from community-school centers—they will be street workers; they will teach in settings which include both children and parents; they will collaborate with social service personnel in corrections, mental health, and rehabilitation agencies; they will be part of a professional team whose goal is to create healthy human communities. It is indisputable that during the last quarter of the twentieth century, the range of educational settings, needs, and personnel will expand. American society is undergoing radical change toward becoming a human service society. This development has serious implications for all of teacher education, requiring that the profession alter significantly.[4]

The challenge for teacher education will be to develop training programs to meet the unique professional and nonprofessional needs of these diverse groups. *In the future, colleges of education will have to develop at least four types of programs:*
1. Programs which will continue to prepare those who seek certification as public school teachers, administrators, and counselors. This group undoubtedly will constitute the largest percentage of the student population.
2. Programs which will serve those who choose to study education as a liberal discipline, rather than as vocational training. The em-

118

phasis will be on the examination of education as a subject matter field, derived from the social sciences, arts, and humanities.

3. Programs which will serve teachers—broadly conceived—in a variety of work settings *outside* orthodox public school classrooms; this will include such "educators" as early childhood specialists, industrial trainers, human service professionals, union organizers, and even parents.

4. Programs which will be directed toward teachers in formal educational settings other than conventional elementary and secondary schools. This will include teachers in preschools, alternative public and private schools, and in such postsecondary institutions as universities and community colleges.

The prospect for a broader training constituency actually faces teacher educators with an increasing consumer demand for an expanded professional training—this in spite of all the hysteria about a teacher surplus. In reality, the supply and demand issue confronts the profession with both paradox and promise.

The number of institutions preparing teachers and the number of students majoring in education are decreasing at a rapid rate. Clark indicates that the number of institutions with teacher preparation programs dropped from 1,441 to 1,380 during the past year.[5] Recent enrollment data show that in universities, education majors dropped from 37.5 percent in 1968 to 24 percent in 1974. Projections showed a drop to lower than 20 percent in 1976.[6] It is not necessary that 1,380 institutions of higher education prepare teachers because it is unlikely that all of these institutions can provide the necessary resources to train professionals. If the institutions which cannot provide the "life space" and professional commitments to make teacher education a top priority are withdrawing from teacher education, then that is good. However, it would be disastrous if institutions which have the greatest potential for providing the necessary resources and commitments would withdraw their commitment to teacher education. This would leave the preparation of education personnel to those institutions least capable of responding to the challenge.

It is uncertain whether institutions are withdrawing or continuing in teacher education for economic or professional reasons. *The profession must make sure that the institutions that can provide quality professional teacher education remain committed to that mission.* The worst thing that could happen is that many people with creative social and intellectual characteristics who wish to contribute their talents to a life of human service will be denied entry to the teaching profession.

Recommendation

That the profession go far beyond thoughts of institutional and personal survival and seriously consider the following assertions concerning the reform of the profession:

1. It is time to develop humane, rigorous criteria for entrance into the profession.
2. There will be a continuing need for highly prepared, multiskilled, strong, flexible teachers.
3. The profession should continue to voice the view that schools are presently understaffed to meet current needs of the society, and that the "oversupply" of teachers is as much a result of society's irresponsibility toward social issues as it is a result of lower enrollment in public education.
4. To remain vital, the profession of teaching needs the presence of new, committed people.
5. There are emerging roles in society that will require the presence of highly trained personnel to work in human services. Teacher education candidates, with their commitment toward people and services, are ideal for these roles. Such an accommodation will require imaginative, professional leadership.
6. The pluralistic nature of our society requires the continuing infusion into teaching of people with a wide variety of ethnic backgrounds.
7. The continued withdrawal of institutions, public and private, from teacher preparation will place increased burdens for quality on the remaining institutions.

INSTITUTIONAL/PROGRAMMATIC QUALITY CONTROL

Existing alternatives concerning institutional and programmatic quality control of teacher preparation include initial chartering by state agencies; accreditation of institution and program by voluntary, nongovernmental agencies; accreditation by the state department of education; federal eligibility reviews to establish lists of institutions meeting federal standards for funding; certification of teacher education graduates through the approved program approach; and internal institutional reviews carried out periodically under college and university regulations, or initiated by the institution's administration or academic council.

While the state chartering of institutions varies in rigor from state to state, generally this process has been of little consequence in the control of institutional quality. Cardozo points out the contrast between the laxity associated with the chartering of educational institutions, and the vigorous regulations involved in initiating a transportation system. He observes that:

> If you want to operate a bus system in a city, a railroad across state lines, or an international airline, you can find elaborate prescriptions in governmental statutes and regulations describing what you have to do before you can start and how you must operate when you

get going. If you want to start a college or university, however, you may find a few regulations concerning the organizational structure the community requires of you; but you will not find statutes or regulations telling you what standards you must follow in providing education leading to a degree. This is because government has left the adoption of those standards and the evaluation of performance to the educational community itself.[7]

The profusion of "diploma mills" in a number of states dramatizes the ineffectiveness of the state chartering system in insuring quality. This ineffectiveness represents a deliberate social policy, since one of the basic traditions of this nation has been freeing higher education from political interference. And, because of this political noninterference tradition, nongovernmental agencies assume accreditation responsibilities.

Although each alternative for quality control of teacher preparation has potential, specialized program accreditation and certification through the approved program approach have had the most impact on institutions and programs. What follows is an examination of these two procedures.

SPECIALIZED PROGRAM ACCREDITATION

Current *national* accreditation of teacher education through the National Council for Accreditation of Teacher Education (NCATE) accepts, as a given, regional accreditation of a total institution. This policy keeps NCATE from becoming involved with total institutional evaluation, in additional to specialized program accreditation. Since preprofessional students take so many courses outside the professional school, NCATE has to rely upon the merits of general institutional accreditation procedures or else develop an expanded accreditation process. NCATE costs already represent a significant financial drain upon institutional resources. Several land-grant universities recently reported institutional costs in excess of $100,000 for the teacher education accreditation process. When multiplied by the number of different professional schools and specialized fields subject to accreditation, the expense to a university can be enormous.

Alternatives to Rising NCATE Costs

A few alternatives are possible. One alternative concentrates on the effective performance of the products of such programs, with correspondingly less emphasis upon admission procedures or program content. Another develops a data collection system relevant to institutional management decisions, as well as to accreditation review. Presently, institutions are developing data bases to help them manage their limited facilities, personnel, and monies more efficiently. They are also attempting to document the cost effectiveness of programs. All of these pressures necessitate the formulation of a comprehensive data system.

Unfortunately, in spite of these alternatives, NCATE continues to demand data in a format and time cycle unsuitable for institutional decision making. *What is needed is consolidation of management data needs with accreditation review needs, in order to eliminate needless duplications, reduce costs, and provide a current data base for accreditation reviews.* The 10-year cycle of NCATE reviews is inconsistent with the changes in many programs of teacher preparation. Yet, shortening the cycle with existing procedures and costs is impractical. Management and accreditation data bases must be shared and kept current if unreasonably large NCATE teams are to be reduced in size. Accreditation must emphasize a sharing of the experience and professional judgment of a small group of professionals from other institutions, instead of bogging down a huge group in data collection and verification. As education becomes more innovative and multifaceted, accreditation will become even more difficult.

Purposes of Accreditation

The fundamental purpose of accreditation is to insure adequate and safe minimum standards. Such standards provide assurance to prospective students and employers. A second objective for accreditation is institutional self-improvement. The emphasis on safe minimum standards raises the issue of the *voluntary status* of teacher education accreditation. One of the unique characteristics of the quality control process in American higher education has been its reliance upon voluntary, nongovernmental accreditation procedures. However, in other professions the impact of accreditation has been so marked that what is theoretically a voluntary process has become in fact compulsory. In teacher education, with nearly 1,400 colleges and universities engaged in preparing teachers, only about 40 percent have submitted programs to NCATE for review.

Undoubtedly, some of the variation between the accreditation of teacher education programs and other professional fields can be attributed to state departments of education accrediting programs within a particular state. Another factor in the low ratio of nationally accredited programs in teacher education is the tendency to accept institution-wide accreditation as sufficient quality control for teacher preparation programs. However, if accreditation is to insure essential minimum standards and safe performance levels, what assurance does a system of voluntary accreditation provide when only two-fifths of the training institutions participate? *The Commission believes that the*

*best alternative to present, inadequate quality control measures is not ex-
pansion of either federal or state government involvement but rather increased support and involvement of the organized teaching profession,
including teacher educators, in the accreditation process. However, such
expanded responsibility must be accompanied by closer, more effective collaboration with colleges of education.*

Accreditation and Other Problems

Because teacher education covers such a range of disciplines, subject fields, and related specialties, it is difficult to identify the appropriate professional bodies to serve on the governing and policy boards
of accrediting agencies. There is a tendency for fragmentation to occur
as representatives establish different standards for each subfield. The
result is a general weakening of the whole accreditation process. The
Joint Committee on Accrediting, a forerunner of the National Commission on Accrediting, listed the following as the major problems of
accreditation: too many agencies, much duplication, costly evaluation, overemphasis on quantitative and superficial standards, domination by outside groups, and procedures which tend to destroy institutional rights and freedoms.

Proffitt has argued that accreditation should be primarily concerned
with the public interest.[8] Historically, accreditation has been inwardly
slanted to satisfy the needs of educators and institutions. A profession's total control over entry into that profession and the delivery of
service has always been a source of tension with the public. In the
future, both the public *and* the profession must determine entrance
criteria and service delivery standards. Shared responsibility will
guarantee that the profession is concerned with the public welfare and
not preoccupied exclusively with self-protection and self-enhance-
ment. The future will see increasing interaction between the public
and the professions. The public will oversee the professions through
representation on the govering councils of professional associations,
accrediting bodies, and licensing boards. Even the profession of teaching will be ventilated by the regular input of public interest.

*The Commission makes the following assertions concerning program ac-
creditation:*

1. *Accreditation should remain nongovernmental in nature.*
2. *"The profession" needs to be redefined to include college-based teacher
   educators as legitimate members and appropriate representatives.*
3. *The expanding responsibility of accrediting agencies to the public requires public representation on the governing councils of professional
   associations and accreditation agencies.*
4. *Accreditation procedures should provide full disclosure to the public.*
5. *Accreditation processes must be specific, detailed, and current to insure*

quality, but not so complex that they will drain off resources from the preparation programs.

6. *Accreditation processes must become less campus oriented, and less fragmented by traditional degree distinctions.*
7. *Accreditation processes must place major emphasis upon the products of training programs.*

Recommendation
That once the aforementioned conditions are met, accreditation be mandatory for all institutions preparing teachers.

THE APPROVED PROGRAM APPROACH TO CERTIFICATION

Another quality control mechanism is the certification process. The certification of teacher education graduates is usually an institutional programmatic matter because of the use of program approval procedures. Program approval starts with the development of broad curricular guidelines by a state department of education; institutions then submit their programs for review to the state department of education. When certification approval is given, then the institution certifies that its graduates have completed a program and are qualified for a teaching license.

Legal Challenges

A recent report points out the legal vulnerability of the program approval approach: ". . . one can only question what a dean or a chairman of education may be certifying or what he may believe he is certifying when he signs the statement or a state application for certification. . ."[9] Current legal challenges of institutional requirements require that teacher educators must specify more clearly the professional competencies which the programs claim to develop. Litigation is being brought against those agencies which refuse to grant certificates to individuals on the grounds that they have not completed a required sequence of preparatory courses. These refusals are merely arbitrary unless certification authorities can document the beneficial outcomes of such requirements in improving teaching skills.

Prework Certification

Certification recommendations are often necessary prior to a record of a candidate's successful teaching sequence. Thus, it is important for the profession to develop a multistaged certification plan so that institutions can recommend initial certification vis-à-vis a candidate's potential to *begin* the practice of teaching. Provision should be made

124

for subsequent continuing certification, at least one year later, depending on a positive evaluation of a teacher's capacity to perform in a full-time teaching assignment. Multiple-stage certification focuses certification recommendations on relevant data, rather than on unwarranted extrapolations from campus performance to field practice.

Student teaching may provide a clear indication that a teacher candidate is suited to one type of student or one kind of community setting. However, the actual certificate granted seldom delineates a candidate's specific competencies.

Recommendation

That programs identify the special skills of the candidate, as well as the professional potentials still undeveloped, and make this information available to prospective employers as relevant employment data.

Two provisos must be added to the above. Colleges of education, as their resources permit, should continue to provide educational experiences for persons who may not desire or qualify for a school assignment. Certification programs, although a principal focus of colleges of education, need not remain their only function when the need for personnel with the knowledge and skills of professional education expands dramatically in industry, communications, and in other human service agencies. Also, much teacher education presently does not fit the competency mode. In such instances, programs should exemplify all the more clearly the instructional values, attitudes, and behaviors they seek to develop in students. Attempts to mandate competency-based programs through state-wide certification regulations are likely to deter rather than enhance institutional efforts to clarify and improve the outcomes of their programs.

A Multilevel Approach to Teacher Certification

The complex and changing nature of the teacher's task and the required continuing professional development make necessary a multilevel approach to teacher certification. Such an approach in turn demands mechanisms for expanded collaboration among representatives of preparing institutions, the organized profession, state education agencies, and employing school systems.

Recommendation

That a three-level plan for teacher certification be established which provides initial certification for the beginning teacher; continuing certification for the teacher whose experience, professionally evaluated, documents effective performance; and professional certification representing high levels of proficiency in the diagnostic, analytic, and leadership skills associated with a teacher-scholar.

Primary responsibility for initial certification should reside in the colleges and universities, with significant assistance from field-based personnel. The second level of certification, designed to prove that a teacher is a competent practicing professional, should rest heavily upon field evaluations of the candidate by professional colleagues from the school system and the organized profession. The third level should document a candidate's capacity to coordinate the teaching and learning efforts of others, and to adapt instruction and curricula to the needs of students from different backgrounds. For this stage, the university and the organized teaching profession should play major roles, supported by cooperating school systems. Each level will continue to relate to a state education agency, but with full recognition that major responsibilities be assumed by professionals in organizations, school systems, and colleges and universities.

The three-level plan entails a profession-wide commitment to the concept of generic abilities shared by all teachers, and necessary at prescribed safe levels for beginning teachers. It requires evaluation of teachers' capacities to apply the generic competencies to particular situations and contexts. And it expects that career teachers will engage in continuing professional development and document an advanced level of diagnostic, prescriptive, and instructional leadership skills.

While the approved program approach to teacher certification has proved more satisfactory than the transcript analysis approach, recent challenges are likely to push teacher education programs to state objectives more clearly, and to document the relevance of specific experiences to these objectives. Certifying agencies, while stopping short of mandated competency-based certification programs, are likely to demand that all preparation programs be clearer about evaluating their graduates in terms of stated program objectives.

Institutional Initiative in Quality Control

Another quality control alternative involves periodic, internal institutional reviews, often initiated by the institution's administrative or academic council. These periodic evaluations of college programs frequently involve university colleagues, representatives of other institutions with similar objectives and responsibilities, students, and clients who use the programs' services. While the format for such reviews is often flexible, they commonly address the extent to which program efforts are consistent with a unit's established objectives. As institutions extend their involvement in inservice and continuing education, and as they utilize off-campus centers for teacher education, internal institutional reviews will have to allow for greater practitioner participation. This involvement will have to come at the point when a program's objectives are being established, as well as in subsequent implementation and evaluation stages.

Internal review is a commendable process because it encourages self-improvement. However, when it is added to regional, national, professional, and state accreditation reviews, it represents a serious drain upon the resources of an academic unit. Institutions will have to establish common data bases and conceptual frameworks for assessing program efforts. These will permit considerable economies of time and energy; they will also prove more useful than the cyclical reviews usually undertaken by accreditation agencies.

RESOURCES

While the ultimate test of high quality programs is the effectiveness of the program's product, the importance and complexity of the training task demands a level of resource allocation and an institutional commitment far beyond what has typified many programs in the past. No longer can the profession condone continuation of training programs where the principal motivation is economic necessity. The price of inadequate training efforts is too high. Some institutions capable of providing quality preparation in the liberal arts, but unable to offer adequate professional programs, will seek collaborative relationships with other institutions where resources are available. These collaborative relationships could insure a high level of quality in professional preparation. The profession must encourage more rapprochements of this type, if quality control in teacher education is to improve.

The resources question is complicated by current methods of funding teacher education by state agencies. State education departments control certification and new program approval; however, state funds appropriated by legislatures in many instances are not allocated to universities or colleges on a line item or program budget basis. Certainly, there are wide discrepancies between what state agencies expect from teacher education and the way individual universities allocate resources. There are demands for programs by the state but little follow-through on providing sufficient funds for development and maintenance of these programs by higher education institutions.

One reason teacher education does not get its fair share of state allocations on the college or university campus is because there is a strong tendency for teacher education to be under the control and domination of the academic disciplines, which have little understanding of, or sympathy for, professional teacher education. Under their value system, pedagogy is not a high priority; hence, teacher education receives a disproportionately lower share of the financial resources. This situation exists whether teacher education is organized as a professional school or as a department of the arts and sciences unit. Rarely is teacher education financially healthy under such conditions. Like Cinderella, teacher education sits in the ashes receiving the leftovers.

Costs

Teacher education receives the lowest support per credit hour of instruction of any professional education program funded in universities. Olsen documents this in the Report of the Study Commission on Undergraduate Education and the Education of Teachers (Appendix C), after examining the Carnegie Commission Study and the National Center for Higher Education Management profiles. This comparison of full education programs for teachers and programs for students in other professional programs shows that the cost per full-time equivalent (FTE) in education programs is lower than that in other professional sequences. Furthermore, more than 60 percent of teachers-in-preparation attend institutions of low quality, according to he Gourman ratings and college ratio ratings; and even in Carnegie-rated high quality institutions, support for teacher education is less than for other programs (See Appendix C.).

A glaring example of the lack of equity in funding professional schools can be seen in a recent study by the University of Vermont of the costs of medical education, which determined how much it should charge per student for residents of other New England states which send their students to the University of Vermont under a reciprocal agreement. The study set the cost of medical education at $10,500 per student per year and rising at about 6 percent annually. National medical education cost figures gleaned from other medical schools were used to determine this figure. The *Report of the Commission on the Financing of Medical Education* (1973) notes that the annual cost of educating a medical student ranges from $16,000 to $26,000.[10] These figures include the cost of research and hospital clinical experiences, as well as the cost of operating a medical school. The cost of pure instruction is lower, according to the Vermont study; however, it is generally assumed that a minimal amount of research and clinical experience is required for a medical student.

Of the approximately 2,400 four-year higher education institutions in the United States, 1,380 now prepare teachers. The very number of institutions aggravates the problem, for it dilutes the impact of these already scarce resources among many institutions only minimally committed to preparing teachers. Even a cursory review of institutions reveals that many have not provided the resources or demonstrated the commitment necessary to prepare teachers adequately. *In the next five years, the profession must develop life space criteria necessary for an institution to be an active participant in teacher education and work to elimi-*

nate those institutions unable or unwilling to provide the necessary resources to prepare professionals.

Special Considerations in Funding Teacher Education

The complex, demanding nature of teaching requires a preparation process that is expensive to administer. Colleges of education offer most of their instruction at upper-division and graduate levels, but funding procedures often fail to take into account the significance of that difference from other colleges, which offer much work at the lower-division levels, sometimes taught by graduate assistants. Classroom and laboratory space is allocated as if education courses were parallel to social science courses, which have little need for specialized space or equipment. Teacher education programs have unique requirements generated by microteaching, demonstrations, simulation, instructional materials production, and team teaching.

The success of the preparation process depends upon the involvement of school-based teachers who provide supervision of teacher education students. Yet many institutions provide only token or no remuneration for this vital service and are without funds to maintain an effective educational program for supervisors of student teachers and interns. Elementary and secondary school teachers are generally expected to carry out such supervisory duties in *addition* to their regular classroom assignments, rather than having time released and paid for by the college or university, which often sees the field experience as the capstone of professional preparation.

Sometimes university administrators view operating costs of teacher preparation programs as unduly high, failing to appreciate fully the complexity of designing and implementing a sequentially designed program of field experience which moves from observation through tutorial and assistant roles to full-time teaching responsibilities. Generally, teacher educators are unable to state clearly either the real costs of the field experience component of teacher education or the relevance of the varied planned experiences to the major components of the preparation curriculum. This situation must be rectified if the field dimension of teacher education is to receive adequate funding.

The growing demands of school systems and teacher organizations for off-campus courses, workshops, consultation, and other support from professional education faculty pose an even more serious problem for funding of colleges of education in the future. The expanding demand occurs at a time when the financial resources available to higher education have leveled off. While undergraduate enrollments in teacher education have dropped at many colleges and universities, graduate, off-campus, and noncredit continuing education enroll-

129

ments in many cases have more than matched the numbers lost and are generally more expensive to staff.

Most education faculty spend a larger proportion of their work load engaged in service to field constituents than is true of university personnel in other colleges, with the exception of colleges of agriculture which usually have an extension service budget to provide resources and faculty load time for such programs. In colleges of education, such service is largely provided to public institutions. It is frequently offered without charge, making every expansion of field service an increased demand upon already limited resources. Even in such mundane matters as secretarial and telephone service and in-state travel, the obligation to retain a close collaborative relationship with school systems and professional organizations generates a need for greater budget support.

Leadership and service to schools is essential if colleges of education are to fulfill their responsibilities as the preparation and development arm of the profession. The total university should realize that it has a stake in the fulfillment of this mission since schools are its feeder system. Further, direct links must be established with teachers, counselors, and administrators if the university is to maintain a positive image with the schools.

Lack of Data

A recent review of surveys of higher education and teacher education disclosed a lack of comparative data (with the exception of the Olson materials reported above and in Appendix C) on what it costs to prepare a teacher. Particularly lacking is the necessary cost data on field experience.

In the context of increasing competition for resources in higher education, it is essential that teacher educators develop an adequate data base for program and budgetary planning. The unique needs of professional programs in teacher preparation require comparisons among such programs in institutions with similar responsibilities and aspirations.

Recommendation

That all teacher education institutions support and provide information to the AACTE (MINFO) system designed to establish a data base for teacher education.

The information in the system will be only as good as the member institutions provide.

Rationale for New Resources

This report calls for major revisions in teacher education, starting

130

with initial professional preparation and extending through the life-time career of teachers. New resources, as well as a reallocation of existing resources, will be necessary to move these ideas from thought to action.

Inputs into the education process have their greatest economy and impact when introduced at the source, which is teacher education. Without adequate inservice and preservice preparation, none of the reforms described in this report will take place. Teachers, like other professionals, need the opportunity to learn new knowledge, skills, and attitudes before they can change their behavior.

Recommendation

That funding be made available to state institutions through revised formulas based on program budgets at least equal to budgets provided other professional programs (e.g., medicine and law). Furthermore, states should move swiftly to provide adequately for the continuing education of teachers. All participating parties must be appropriately involved, i.e., teachers; the organized teaching profession; teacher preparation units; and various governmental units at state, intermediate, and local levels.

Funding should be provided for the operation of Teacher Centers and for the preparation of teachers who collaborate with the college or university in the teacher education program. Teacher Centers should be operated from special federal grants or from an improved state formula. The training of cooperating teachers should be similarly financed. It is important that colleges of education, which have as their first priority teacher education, be the recipients of funds for such research and preparation programs.

States and the federal government, in accordance with their responsibilities for education, should provide their share of the resources needed for the ongoing conduct of preparation, research, development, innovation, and dissemination. Simultaneously, the federal government and appropriate state agencies must not cut present appropriations for teacher education. In fact, appropriations must be expanded to make possible the "life space" systems envisaged in this report, and to provide for the continuing education needs of the more than 2 million teachers in schools and the thousands of others who are "educators" in other community agencies. In a society whose most constant characteristic is changing human needs, teachers more than any other professional group must have the opportunity to stay up to date.

FOOTNOTES

1. H.N. Rivlin, "If I Had My Way," in *The Education of Teachers*, Official Report of the Kansas Conference, University of Kansas, Lawrence, June

23-26, 1959 (Washington, D.C.: National Education Association, 1959), pp. 110-15.

2. Griggs v. Duke Power Company 401 U.S. 424 (1971), as discussed in *Study Commission Newsletter*, Study Commission on Undergraduate Education and the Education of Teachers (Lincoln: University of Nebraska Press, May 1974), p. 5.

3. D.C. Corrigan, "Do We Have a Teacher Surplus?" *Journal of Teacher Education* 25, no. 3 (Fall 1974): 196-8.

4. E.R. Ducharme and R.J. Nash, "Humanizing Teacher Education for the Last Quarter of the Twentieth Century," *Journal of Teacher Education* 26, no. 3 (Fall 1975): 222-8.

5. D. Clark and E.G. Guba, "A National Study of the Role of Schools, Colleges and Departments of Education in Knowledge Production and Utilization," Ongoing study, Indiana University, 1975.

6. Frank Skinner, et al., "Census Survey Shows Education Major Drop," *Higher Education and National Affairs* 23, no. 13 (March 29, 1974): 4.

7. M.H. Cardozo, "Recent Developments in Legal Aspects of Accreditation," *Journal of the American Medical Association* 213, no. 4 (July 27, 1970).

8. J.R. Proffitt, "Professions and the Public: A Crossroads of Interest," *American Journal of Medical Technology* 37, no. 1 (January 1971): 3.

9. Study Commission on Undergraduate Education and the Education of Teachers, Paul Olson, ed. Draft copy of final report, "Teacher Education in America" (Lincoln: University of Nebraska, 1975), pp. 19-20.

10. "Report of the Commission on the Financing of Medical Education," Program/Cost Study of the Dean's Office (College of Medicine, University of Vermont, 1973).

Reflections

Because every helping relationship requires
generalizable skills and understandings
in a variety of teaching and learning systems,
then every human service professional
must first and foremost be an effective educator.
The most significant interaction in
every human service activity
is a teaching-learning component.

Professionalism

The Commission recognizes that there are multiple problems implicit in a too-easy acceptance of *professionalism* as a guiding ideal. At its worst, professionalism connotes exclusion, self-protectiveness, excessive specialization, self-aggrandizement, formalism, authoritarianism, hierarchy, and mystification. Obviously, this is *not* the professionalism the Commission urges for educators. At its best, professionalism combines a high quality of basic knowledge, informed practice, and social commitment with a profound, individual dedication to helping people enrich their lives in their own best ways.

The Commission's hope is that educators will continue to enlarge the meaning of professionalism so that it becomes more democratic, client-nurturing, and political than that which presently characterizes the established professions. In this regard, educators will have to consider the possibilities for enhancing professionalism inherent in cultural pluralism and multicultural education, the women's movement, the rise of teacher militancy, and the expansion of consumer consciousness. Educators must realize that professionalism is still an evolving ideal— neither owned nor fully defined by the established professions. Ultimately, professionalism's worth as an ideal depends on how well educators can encourage self-determination on the part of all learners and social groups.

Teacher Self-governance

The Commission predicts that the more professionalized teachers become, the more they will seek a broad range of autonomy for them-

133

selves vis-à-vis representative governance groups. In the future, if teacher organizations are to advance a professionalism which is democratic, theory based, self-governing, client centered, and political, then some caveats are in order. The teaching profession must be wary of linking itself to organizations which are excessively bureaucratic, where leadership is solidly entrenched. Also, the profession must be cautious about forming liaisons with organizations which skirt controversy by assuming neutral stances on social issues, which tend to footdrag on programs which promote cultural pluralism and the rights of minorities, and which preoccupy themselves more with narrow self-interests than with strong client advocacy. In the future, educators will have to think of collective bargaining as something more than simply a process to provide increased material benefits. Educators will have to use collective bargaining as a mechanism for bringing about organizational reform—as a way to challenge and change school systems when they are racist, sexist, and child-destructive, or when they arbitrarily abridge the academic freedom of teachers. *The Commission believes that teacher self-governance will move closer to becoming a reality only when the public is convinced that an increase in teacher rights will be accompanied by greater teacher responsiveness to the needs of the clients which the profession is dedicated to serve.*

The Professional Culture

The Commission has placed a great emphasis on the existence of a professional culture which embodies sophisticated and generalizable technical procedures and conceptual frameworks. We are dismayed that many teachers still possess a quasi-professional repertoire which is crude and obsolete—largely a collection of folklore. We insist that a professional culture for educators is developing rapidly. Especially during the last decade there has been a proliferation of worthwhile teaching models, learning paradigms, planning systems, and evaluation processes. *We also realize that this developing professional culture is still in its early stage.* Thus, we urge the teaching profession *not* to underestimate the enormous task ahead of constructing valid, generalizable teaching and learning principles. *The entire profession, with the leadership of the college preparation arm, must continually engage in further study of what constitutes "safe" and sound teaching and learning.*

Competency-Based/Humanistic Training

The Commission is aware of the apparent dichotomy which exists between its technical emphasis on competency-based teacher education (CBTE) and its philosophic commitment to humanism. Actually, the dichotomy is a false one. CBTE is a technical means meant to

134

achieve a major end—the development of highly knowledgeable, socially committed, multiskilled, and humanistic professionals. And because a profession's means and ends are always inseparable, competency-based training processes must themselves exemplify the best qualities and practices of the humanistic professionals they mean to produce. Too much of the recent CBTE debate within the profession has been political and semantic. Vested interest groups have wasted inordinate amounts of time quibbling over fine semantic distinctions, and constructing endless prescriptive checklists of teaching behaviors. *It is time to refocus the CBTE dialogue on the inseparability of means and ends in the preparation of education professionals.* Competency-based training processes will be truly humanistic only when professionals emerge who possess a healthy self-image, a flexible repertoire of technical skills, a defensible and wide-ranging knowledge base, a bold social commitment, and a genuine concern for helping people. If this does not happen, then the profession must reconsider the validity of CBTE procedures. It is in the spirit of the mutuality of means and ends that the Commission speaks of humanistic CBTE in the preparation of education professionals.

Inservice and Continuing Education

The Commission emphasizes the central role that the college preparation arm must take in the continuing education of its professionals. Historically, the university has educated teachers-in-service by offering a series of recertification programs, institutes, and traditional courses. Recent events, however, suggest that continuing education must become more creative and flexible than these traditional forms. Increasing teacher militancy concerning the right to define their own professional needs and offer their own reeducative programs has given rise to the Teacher Center. While possessing great potential as a continuing education mechanism, the Teacher Center is meant primarily to be an inservice device (neither exclusively geographical nor fixed in function) designed to deliver college and community resources, get professionals together, and form a network of available educational services. *Colleges of education must not surrender their continuing responsibility to develop and disseminate the professional culture through every mechanism possible, including the Teacher Center.* Neither the public schools nor the colleges can live in splendid isolation. Preservice, inservice, and continuing education are interrelated components of *one* professional delivery system and require the active involvement of the teaching profession *and* the preparation arm.

Technological and Social Changes

Although the Commission is conscious of the need to understand and utilize sweeping technological and social changes, we do not advocate that the profession blindly conform to these changes. Some changes are themselves so questionable that educators must challenge them vigorously. An education calculated solely to adjust learners to "changing technological realities," or to the demands of the job market can only eventuate in further anomie, dehumanization, and an absence of purpose and zest in contemporary living. During the last quarter of the twentieth century, teacher educators will have to be wary of placing technological needs over human needs. When appropriate, human service education must stress personal resistance as well as social adaptation, self-determination, and fulfillment, as well as career survival skills. In the future, professionals will have to be as mindful of their clients' personal, social, and political development as they are of the intellectual and occupational. *Education for people's sake does not serve predefined technological ends.* Rather, it provides individuals and social groups with the principles and skills necessary for achieving their own greatest self-realization. Finally, an education geared exclusively to technological changes risks distracting teachers from the resolution of our most pressing personal and social problems—the function which education (our most human experience) must ultimately serve.

Human Service Education

Throughout this report, the Commission has advocated an approach to teacher education which is human-service functional. Recently, many social analysts have predicted the emergence of a client-centered human service society with a concomitant greater role for human service professionals and consumption of their services. One major ramification of this prediction is that a new kind of professional will have to be prepared to be highly experimental in helping approaches, diverse in skills and understandings, politically adroit in dealing with agencies and bureaucracies, collaborative in planning with clients, liberated from intractible role definitions, and affective in working with people. *This Commission believes that because every helping relationship requires generalizable skills and understandings in a variety of teaching and learning systems, then every human service professional must first and foremost be an effective educator. The most significant interaction in every human service activity is a teaching-learning component.* Consequently, in the years ahead, colleges of education will have to become more concerned with the ways all human service professionals are prepared, and with the ways their services are conceptualized and delivered to the public.

136

The next step for colleges of education is to reorganize their curricula and develop delivery systems which will produce a new kind of teacher—a "human service educator." A human service educator is an effective teacher—at times a counselor, a human rights activist, a political ombudsman, a stimulator of human potential, and a group organizer. Whether through subject matter, human relations skills, or specific technology, a human service educator is able to help people discover more effective and satisfying means to improve themselves and their social institutions. In the sense that human service educators are helping people to learn a variety of skills, understandings, and values, then every human service educator is a teacher.

The ultimate objective of a revised teacher preparation system is to produce fully qualified professional educators who can move easily and horizontally within many human service careers—from classrooms, to counseling sites, to storefront social action agencies, to senior citizens homes. Needless to say, the current oversupply of teachers could be alleviated if educators were to diversify and begin to expand their developing human service opportunities. Thus, the central question for colleges of education is not "How can we continue to survive?" but "How can we help all professionals who work with people in any helping capacity to become more effective teachers?" *The Commission reasserts its conviction that only when educators reflect an enlarged view of the settings in which teaching is a vital function will the profession of teaching reach its full maturity.*

CHALLENGE

The Commission on Education for the Profession of Teaching believes that the American people face a crucial choice concerning their schools. Either they reaffirm their faith in education through increased financial and psychological support, or they will experience the end of public education.

In order to earn this support, the profession of education must radically improve its beliefs and practices. For complex reasons, the professional culture (the technical procedures and conceptual base) has continued to retain large elements of conventional wisdom and craft practices. The failure of the teaching profession to advance beyond this stage is a major cause in the inability of the schools to meet the educational challenges of modern times. Teachers have not been prepared to deal effectively with the bewildering anomalies of American life. The schools themselves have not been designed to overcome these problems.

Throughout this report, the Commission has held that contemporary educators must demonstrate a high degree of professional skill and understanding. Unfortunately, preservice, inservice, and continuing education have been slow to enhance the overall quality of present professional performance. Today, little about the profession— its philosophy, organization, curricular procedures, governance, and management systems—comes even close to addressing contemporary realities. What the profession needs is a totally new set of concepts regarding the nature of the emerging human service society, its educational demands, the kinds of delivery systems necessary to provide public access to continuing educational opportunity, and the types of professional personnel and training required to reform public education in America. What passed as adequate teacher education in simple times simply does not suffice in the more complex society. If our country's educational system is to thrive—even survive—it must have a preparation and research arm that is striving to create the future, not just accept it.

It is the proper function of professional service organizations to examine themselves and the society they inhabit in order to reform the beliefs and practices of each. When service institutions have genuine doubts about their roles or serious misgivings about the directions their society is taking, it is the responsibility of the organization to propose sincere alternatives. It is in this spirit that the Commission has reexamined the question of educational adequacy for the last quarter of the twentieth century. It is also in this spirit that the Commission has explored the issue of the professional preparation of teachers. The Commission has proceeded with this task with the genuine hope that the profession will be able to reeducate itself.

In this year of 1976, the teaching profession faces unprecedented challenges. Whether the issue is seen as survival, continuance of what we have, or moving forward to a new professionalism, the need is the same. Tremendous dedication and effort are necessary. This report calls upon the teaching profession in general, and teacher education in particular, to put forth that effort. We close this report with a folk saying which the Commission found on the wall of a small Vermont coffee shop one morning. It expresses eloquently the task which faces professional educators in the years ahead:

"Everything cometh to he who waiteth, so long as he who waiteth worketh like hell while he waiteth."

> What the profession needs
> is a totally new set of concepts
> regarding the nature of the emerging human service
> society, its educational demands,
> the kinds of delivery systems necessary to provide
> public access to continuing educational opportunity,
> and the types of professional personnel and training
> required to reform public education in America.

138

BIBLIOGRAPHY

*Bookshelf for Teacher Educators on the Profession of Teaching

Allen, W.C., Cady, L.V., and Drummond, W.H. "Performance Criteria for Education Personnel Development: A State Approach to Standards." *Journal of Teacher Education* 20, no. 2 (Summer 1969): 133-135.

American Association of Colleges for Teacher Education. *Professional Teacher Education.* Washington, D.C.: American Association of Colleges for Teacher Education, 1968.

American Association of Colleges for Teacher Education. *Recommended Standards for Teacher Education.* Washington, D.C.: American Association of Colleges for Teacher Education, 1969.

*American Association of Colleges for Teacher Education. *Time for Decision in Teacher Education.* AACTE Yearbook 1973. Washington, D.C.: American Association of Colleges for Teacher Education, 1973.

American Association of Colleges for Teacher Education Commission on Multicultural Education. James Kelly, Chairman. "No One Model American." *Journal of Teacher Education* 24, no. 4 (Winter 1973): 264-5.

American Bar Association Special Committee on Evaluation of Disciplinary Enforcement. *Problems and Recommendations in Disciplinary Enforcement.* January 1970.

American College Testing Program. "Trends in Choosing Majors." *Activity* 13, no. 1 (January 1975).

American Federation of Teachers. *Commission on Educational Reconstruction.* Glencoe, Ill.: Free Press, 1955.

American Philosophical Society Library. *Medicine and Society, Contemporary Medical Problems in Historical Perspective.* Philadelphia: American Philosophical Society Library, 1971.

American Philosophical Society Library. *Medicine and Society, 1972, Four Symposia in Current Problems.* Philadelphia: American Philosophical Society Library, 1973.

Andrews, T.E. "New Directions in Certification." Paper submitted to Improving State Leadership in Education Office, Denver, Colo., September 1970.

Andrews, T.E. *New Directions in Certification. Improving State Leadership.* Olympia, Wash.: Washington State Board of Education, 1970 (ERIC Document No. ED 043 796).

Annual Progress Report on Teacher Education. Billingham, Wash.: Western Washington State College, September 1970.

Antell, W. and Lynch, P., eds. *Indian Educational Leadership: A Conference Report.* Oct. 2-5, 1973. Las Cruces, N.M.: New Mexico State University ERIC Clearinghouse on Rural Education and Small Schools, 1975 (ERIC Document No. ED 104 588).

---

*Titles with asterisks are titles recommended to teacher educators and librarians for their basic bookshelf on the profession of teaching.

*Argyris, C. and Schon, D.A. *Theory in Practice: Increasing Professional Effectiveness.* San Francisco: Jossey-Bass, 1974.

Arnstein, G.E. "Bad Apples in Academe." *American Education* 10 (August-September 1974): 10-14.

Arnstein, G.E. "Ph.D. Anyone?" *American Education* 10 (July 1974): 6-11.

*Arrowsmith, W. "The Future of Teaching." In D. Bigelow, ed. *The Liberal Arts and Teacher Education: A Confrontation.* Lincoln: University of Nebraska Press, 1971.

Ashby-Davis, C., et al. *Participatory Governance and the Education Profession: Three Module Clusters.* Prepared by Fordham University in cooperation with the National Education Association, New York, 1975.

Atkins, J.M. and Raths, J.D. *Changing Patterns of Teacher Education in the United States.* Report prepared for Directorate for Scientific Affairs. Organization for Economic Cooperation and Development, University of Illinois, February 1974.

Axelrod, J. *The University Teacher as Artist.* San Francisco: Jossey-Bass, 1973.

Bagley, A. *The Professor of Education: An Assessment of Conditions.* Minneapolis: Society of Professors of Education, 1975.

Banks, J.A. "Teaching for Ethnic Literacy: A Comparative Approach." *Social Education* 37, no. 8 (December 1973): 738-50.

Barber, B. "The Sociology of Professions." *The Professions in America.* Boston: Houghton Mifflin, 1965.

Bhaerman, R.D. *Which Way for Teacher Certification?* QUEST Paper Series, #2. Washington, D.C.: American Federation of Teachers, 1969.

*Bowman, J., et al., eds. *The University Can't Train Teachers.* Lincoln: Nebraska Curriculum Development Center, June 1972.

Braun, R.J. *Teachers and Power; The Story of AFT.* New York: Simon and Schuster, 1972.

Brook, R.H. *Quality of Care Assessment: A Comparison of Five Methods of Peer Review.* Washington, D.C.: U.S. Government Printing Office, 1973.

Broudy, H.S. "Teaching—Craft or Profession?" *The Educational Forum* 20, no. 2 (January 1956): 175-84.

Brown, L.A. and Fair, J.R. "Architecture for Non-Architects." *Journal of Architectural Education* 37, no. 1, pp. 21-33.

Bulger, R.J. *Hippocrates Revisited. A Search for Meaning.* New York: Medcom Press, 1973.

Burdin, J. "The Changing World and Its Implications for Teacher Education." In K. Ryan, ed., *Teacher Education: 74th Yearbook of the National Society for the Study of Education.* Chicago: University of Chicago Press, 1975, pp. 295-304.

Burdin, J. and Lanzillotti, K., eds. *A Reader's Guide to the Comprehensive Models for Preparing Elementary Teachers.* Washington, D.C.: American Association of Colleges for Teacher Education and ERIC Clearinghouse on Teacher Education, 1969.

Bureau of Labor Statistics Report, *The Houston Post,* September 1, 1975.

Burnett, C.W., ed. *Legal Problems in Higher Education.* Lexington, Ky.: Bureau of School Service, March 1974.

Burrow, J.G. *AMA: Voice of American Medicine.* Baltimore, Md.: Johns Hopkins Press, 1963.

Cahn, L. and Hayden, J. "Educator and Occupational Therapist." *American Journal of Occupational Therapy* 26 (July-August 1972): 249-51.

*Campbell, J.K. "Up from Pedagogy." *Intellect,* July-August 1975, p. 42.

The Carnegie Commission on Higher Education. *The Campus and the City: Maximizing Assets and Reducing Liabilities.* New York: McGraw-Hill, 1972.

The Carnegie Commission on Higher Education. *Governance of Higher Education: Six Priority Problems.* New York: McGraw-Hill, 1973.

The Carnegie Commission on Higher Education. *Higher Education and the Nation's Health Policies for Medical and Dental Education.* New York: McGraw-Hill, 1970.

The Carnegie Commission on Higher Education. *The Purposes and the Performance of Higher Education in the United States: Approaching the Year 2000.* New York: McGraw-Hill, 1973.

The Carnegie Commission on Higher Education. *Sponsored Research of the Carnegie Commission on Higher Education.* New York: McGraw-Hill, 1973.

*The Carnegie Commission on Higher Education. *Toward a Learning Society: Alternative Channels to Life, Work, and Service.* New York: McGraw-Hill, 1973.

Case and Company Management Consultants. *Methods of Compensation for Architectural Services.* Washington, D.C.: American Institute of Architects, June 1969.

Case, C.W., and Olson, P.A., eds. *The Future: Create or Inherit.* Study Commission on Undergraduate Teacher Education and the Education of Teachers. Lincoln: University of Nebraska Press, 1974.

Cassidy, H.G. *The Sciences and the Arts.* New York: Harper and Brothers, 1962.

Chacko, G.K. *Alternative Approaches to National Delivery of Health Care.* Philadelphia: Operations Research Society of America, Health Applications Section, 1972.

Chambers, P. "Role Conflict as Functional: A Re-appraisal of the Tutor's Role in Teacher Training." *Education for Teaching* 88 (Summer 1972): 41-47.

Clark, D.L. "A Conceptual Basis for Collaboration." In ATE Bulletin #4, *Emerging Concepts for Collaboration. Selected papers.* Washington, D.C.: Association of Teacher Educators, 1975.

Clark, D. and Guba E. "A National Study of the Role of Schools, Colleges and Departments of Education in Knowledge Production and Utilization." An ongoing study funded by the National Institute of Education. Bloomington: Indiana University.

Ciampa, B.J. "Academic Pecking Order: An Examination of a Myth." *California Journal of Education Research* 25 (January 1974): 32-36.

Cogan, M.L. "Current Issues in the Education of Teachers." In K. Ryan, ed. *Teacher Education: 74th Yearbook of the National Society for the Study of Education.* Chicago: University of Chicago Press, 1975.

Coggeshall, L.T. *Planning for Medical Progress Through Education.* Evanston, Ill. (now Washington, D.C.): Association of American Medical Colleges, 1965.

Cole, H.P. *Process Education.* Englewood Cliffs, N.J.: Educational Technology Publications, 1972.

Cole, H.P. and Lacefield, W.E. "Skill Domains for the Helping Professions." Lexington, Ky.: College of Education, 1975. Unpublished manuscript.

Coleman, J.S., chairman. Report of the Panel on Youth of the President's Science Advisory Committee. *Youth: Transition to Adulthood.* Chicago: University of Chicago Press, 1974.

*Combs, A.W., et al. *The Professional Education of Teachers.* Revised ed. Boston: Allyn & Bacon, 1974.

Combs, A.W., et al. *Helping Relationships*. Boston: Allyn & Bacon, 1971.

Conrad, D., Nash, R., and Shiman, D. "Foundations of Education—the Restoration of Vision to Teacher Preparation." *Educational Theory* 23 (Winter 1973): 42-55.

Constance, J.D. *How to Become a Professional Engineer*. New York: McGraw-Hill, 1958.

Continuing Education Guidelines for State Nurses' Associations. New York: American Nurses Association, 1974.

Conway, J.A., Jennings, R.E., and Milstein, M.M. *Understanding Communities*. Englewood Cliffs, N.J.: Prentice-Hall, 1974.

Cooke, W.R. *Mercer County Teacher Education Center*. Princeton, W. Va.: Mercer County Schools, 1971 (ERIC Document No. ED 046-868).

Corrigan, D.C. "Do We Have a Teacher Surplus?" *Journal of Teacher Education* 25, no. 3 (Fall 1974): 196-98.

Corrigan, D.C. "The Future: Implications for the Preparation of Education Personnel." *Journal of Teacher Education* 25, no. 2 (Summer 1974): 100-107.

Corrigan, D.C. "Humanizing Education—Goals and Processes." Address presented to the annual meeting of the Association of Teacher Educators, Chicago, February 21, 1974.

Corrigan, D.C. "Some Value Premises to Consider in Developing Performance-based Strategies for Maximizing the Humane in Education." Prepared for the American Association of Colleges for Teacher Education Leadership Training Institute on PBTE, Boston, December 12, 1975.

Countryman, V. and Finnan T. *The Lawyer in Modern Society*. Boston: Little, Brown, 1966.

Counts, G.S. *The American Road to Culture*. New York: John Day, 1930.

Cox, A. "Lawyer's Profession." *New York Southern Bar Journal* 46 (October 1974): 415-20.

Cox, P.W.L. and Mercer, B.E. *Education in Democracy: The Social Foundations of Education*. New York: McGraw-Hill, 1961.

Cruickshank, D.R., ed. "The Education of Teacher Educators." *Theory Into Practice*, December 1974, p. 13.

Davies, D. *Citizen Participation in Education: Annotated Bibliography*. New Haven, Conn.: Institute for Responsive Education, 1974.

Dean, A.V. "The Board Acts on the Role of Women in Architecture." *AIA Journal*, March 1975, pp. 33-34.

Decker, B. and Bonner, P. *PSRO, Organization for Regional Peer Review*. Cambridge, Mass.: Ballinger Publishing Co., 1973.

Denemark, G.W. "Improving Teacher Education: Some Directions." *Peabody Journal of Education* 49 (October 1971): 4-11.

Denemark, G.W. "A Proposed Common Professional Core for the Preparation of Teachers." In W.E. Drake, G.W. Denemark, and H.J. Hermanowicz, eds., *Professional Courses for Teacher Certification*. Cedar Falls, Iowa: State College of Iowa, 1967, p. 22.

Denemark, G.W. "Teacher Education: Repair, Reform, or Revolution?" *Educational Leadership* 27 (March 1970): 539-43.

Denemark, G.W. and Espinoza, A. "Educating Teacher Educators." *Theory Into Practice* 13, no. 3 (June 1974): 187-97.

*Denemark, G.W., and Yff, J., eds. *Obligation for Reform: The Final Report of the Higher Education Task Force on Improvement and Reform in American Education.* Washington, D.C.: American Association of Colleges for Teacher Education, 1974.

Derbyshire, R.C. *Medical Licensure and Discipline in the U.S.* Baltimore: Johns Hopkins Press, 1969.

Dickey, F.G. "Recognizing and Monitoring Professional and Specialized Accrediting Association." Paper presented at Northwest Association of Secondary and Higher Schools Annual Meeting, Portland, Ore., December 2-5, 1973.

Dickey, F.G. "The Social Value of Professional Accreditation." *Journal of the American Medical Association* 312 (July 1970): 592.

Dorros, S. *Teaching as a Profession.* Columbus, Ohio: C. Merrill, 1968.

Drake, D. "Culture and Education: Mexican American and Anglo American." *Elementary School Journal* 74 (November 1973): 97-105.

Dreeben, R. *The Failure of Teaching: Schools and the Work of Teachers.* Glenview, Ill.: Scott, Foresman, 1970.

Ducharme, E.R. and Nash, R.J. "Humanizing Teacher Education for the Last Quarter of the Twentieth Century." *Journal of Teacher Education* 26, no. 3 (Fall 1975): 222-28.

Dummont, M.P. "The Changing Face of Professionalism." *Social Policy* 1, no. 1 (May-June 1970): 26-31.

*Dunkin, M.J. and Biddle, B.J. *The Study of Teaching.* New York: Holt, Rinehart and Winston, 1974.

Elvin, H.L. "Colleges of Education: Their Achievements and Prospects." In F.L. Hilliard, ed., *Teaching the Teachers: Trends in Teacher Education.* London: George Allen and Unwin, Ltd., 1971, p. 34.

Etzioni, A. "Schools as 'Guidable' Systems." In V. Haubrich, ed., *Freedom, Bureaucracy and Schooling.* Washington, D.C.: Association for Supervision and Curriculum Development, 1971, p. 42.

*Etzioni, A., ed. *The Semi-Professions and Their Organization: Teachers, Nurses, Social Workers.* New York: The Free Press, 1969.

Flexner, A. "Is Social Work a Profession?" Paper presented at the Forty-Second Annual Meeting of Charities and Corrections, Baltimore, Maryland, May 1915.

*Flexner, A. *Medical Education in the United States and Canada.* Boston: D.B. Updike, The Merrymont Press, 1910.

Foshay, A.W., ed. *The Professional as Educator.* New York: Teachers College Press, 1970.

*Freeman, L. "Some Legal Developments and Their Possible Impact on the Future of Education." Paper of the Study Commission on Undergraduate Education and Education of Teachers, Lincoln, Nebr., February 10, 1974.

Freeman, L. "Training Document on Legal Issues: Part I." Paper of the Study Commission on Undergraduate Education and the Education of Teachers, Lincoln, Nebr., June 1973.

Freidson, E. *Profession of Medicine, A Study of the Sociology of Applied Knowledge.* New York: Dodd, Mead, 1973.

Frinks, M.L. "Planning and Effecting Improvements in the Preparation and Certification of Educators: Emerging State Relations and Procedures." Paper submitted to Improving State Leadership in Education, Denver, Colo., July 1971.

Gajewsky, S. *Accreditation: Review of the Literature and Selected Annotated Bibliography.* Montreal, Quebec: McGill University, 1973 (ERIC Document No. ED 093 054).

Garner, M.A. "Power and Ideological Conformity: A Case Study." *Journal of Sociology* 79 (September 1973): 343-63.

Gartner, A. and Riessman, F. *The Service Society and the Consumer Vanguard.* New York: Harper & Row, 1974.

Geiger, J.J. "Educational Implication of Changing Methods of Health Care Revision." *American Journal of Diseases of Children* 127 (April 1974): 554-58.

Gibson, R.D. "Legal Education: Past and Future." *Manitoba Law Journal* 6 (1974): 21-38.

Glante, L., et al. "Medical Practice, Medical Education and the Law." *Journal of Medical Education* 49 (September 1974): 810-901.

Goode, W.J. "The Theoretical Limits of Professionalization." In A. Etzioni, ed., *The Semi-Professions and Their Organization: Teachers, Nurses, Social Workers.* New York: The Free Press, 1969, pp. 266-313.

Goodlad, J.I. "Knowledge, Pre-collegiate Education and the Preparation of Teachers: Perspectives on the National Scene." In W.A. Jenkins, ed., *The Nature of Knowledge: Implications for the Education of Teachers.* Milwaukee: School of Education, University of Wisconsin-Milwaukee, 1962, p. 88.

Goodman, R., ed. *Professional Standards Review Organizations.* Los Angeles: University of California at Los Angeles, 1975.

Gousha, R.P. "Teacher Education and Organizational Behavior." Address presented to Indiana University Conference on Teacher Education, November 1974.

Graham, R. and Royer, J., eds. *A Handbook for Change: Recommendations of the Joint Commission on Medical Education.* Philadelphia: Wm. F. Fell, 1973.

Greenbaum, W. "America in Search of a New Ideal: An Essay on the Rise of Pluralism." *Harvard Educational Review* 44 (August 1974): 411-40.

Haberman, M. "Educating the Teachers." In V. Haubrich, ed., *Freedom, Bureaucracy and Schooling.* Washington, D.C.: Association for Supervision and Curriculum Development, 1971, p. 285.

Haberman, M. "Extention of Equity in the Governance of Teacher Education." Milwaukee: School of Education, University of Wisconsin, 1973 (ERIC Document No. ED 079 271).

*Haberman, M. *Guidelines for the Selection of Students into Programs of Teacher Education.* Research Bulletin 11. Washington, D.C.: Association of Teacher Educators and ERIC Clearinghouse on Teacher Education, 1972.

*Haberman, M. and Stinnett, T.M. *Teacher Education and the New Profession of Teaching.* Berkeley, Calif.: McCutchan Publishing Corporation, 1974.

Hansen, H.R. *Medical Licensure and Consumer Protection.* Washington, D.C.: Group Health Foundation, 1962.

Hansen, J.H., ed. *Governance by Consortium.* Syracuse, N.Y.: Multi-State Consortium on Performance-Based Education, n.d.

Heilbroner, R. *An Inquiry into the Human Prospect.* New York: W.W. Norton, 1974.

Heim, J. and Perl, L. "The Educational Production Function: Implications for Educational Manpower Policy." *Institute of Public Employment Monograph 4,* June 1974.

Heiss, A. *An Inventory of Academic Innovation and Reform.* Berkeley, Calif.: The Carnegie Commission on Higher Education, 1973.

Henry, N.B., ed. *Education for the Professions: 61st Yearbook of the National Society for the Study of Education, Part II.* Chicago: University of Chicago Press, 1962.

Hilliard, F.L., ed. *Teaching the Teachers: Trends in Teacher Education.* London: George Allen and Unwin, 1971.

Hinton, L. *Engineer and Engineering.* London: Oxford University Press, 1970.

*Hodgkinson, H.L. *Lifelong Learners—A New Clientele for Higher Education.* San Francisco: Jossey-Bass, 1974.

Holbrook, C.A. "The Erosion of Humanitas." *World View* 17, no. 7 (July 1974): 36-37.

Holder, A.R. *Medical Malpractice Law.* New York: John Wiley and Sons, 1975.

Hopkins, J.O. *Basic Legal Issues in New York State on Teacher Certification.* Commissioned by the Study Commission on Undergraduate Education and the Education of Teachers—East Coast Network, University of Neberaska, Lincoln, Nebr. September 1973.

Horton, B.J. "Ten Criteria of a Genuine Profession." *Scientific Monthly* 58 (1944): 164.

Houseman, W. *Architectural Registration Handbook 1973.* Washington, D.C.: National Council of Architectural Registration Boards and Architectural Record, 1973.

Houser, H.W. *Objectives in American Medical Education: A National Survey of Medical Faculty Opinions.* Des Moines: University of Iowa Press, 1971.

*Houston, W.R., ed. *Competency, Assessment, Research, and Evaluation: A Report of a National Conference.* University of Houston, Houston, Texas, March 12-15, 1974.

Houston, W.R. and Howsam, R.B., eds. *Competency-based Teacher Education: Progress, Problems and Prospects.* Chicago: Science Research Associates, 1972.

*Howsam, R.B. *The Governance of Teacher Education.* Washington, D.C.: ERIC Clearinghouse on Teacher Education, 1972 (ERIC Document No. ED 062 270).

*Howsam, R.B. "Governance of Teacher Education by Consortium." In J.H. Hansen, ed., *Governance by Consortium,* undated. Monograph developed under the direction of the National Consortium of Competency-Based Education Centers funded by the U.S. Office of Education—National Center for the Improvement of Educational Systems, under Grant #OEG-071-1099, (72).

*Hughes, E.C. *The Professions in America.* Boston: Houghton Mifflin, 1965.

Hughes, E.C., et al. *Education for the Professions of Medicine, Law, Theology, and Social Welfare.* New York: McGraw-Hill, 1973.

Hughes, J.M. *Education in America.* Evanston, Ill.: Row, Peterson, 1960.

Hunt, W.D. *Comprehensive Architectural Services—General Principles and Practices.* New York: McGraw-Hill, 1965.

Hunter, W.A., ed. *Multicultural Education through Competency-Based Teacher Education.* Washington, D.C.: American Association of Colleges for Teacher Education, 1974.

145

Indiana State University Chart, "Selective Admission and Retention of Education Personnel." *Journal of Teacher Education,* 25 no. 3 (Fall 1974): 238.

"Interest of the Community in a Professional Education." *California Western Law Review* 10 (Spring 1974): 590-612.

Jake, D.G. "Who Killed Cock Robin? Or Does AMA Limit Physician Training?" *Arizona Medicine* 30 no. 12 (December 1975): 865-67.

*James, Lord of Rusholme. *Teacher Education and Training* (Known as the James Report). London: Her Majesty's Stationery Office, 1972.

James, Lord of Rusholme. *Time for Decision in Teacher Education.* The Fourteenth Charles W. Hunt Lecture. Presented at the twenty-fifth Annual Meeting of the American Association of Colleges for Teacher Education, February 21, 1973.

Jenkins, W.A., ed. *The Nature of Knowledge: Implications for the Education of Teachers.* Milwaukee, Wis.: The Edward A. Uhrig Foundation, 1961.

Johnson, J.A. *A National Survey of Student Teaching Progams.* July 1968. USOE Project No. 6-8182.

Johnson, J.A. "Government of the Professions: Setting Public Standards Through Private Organizations—Future Directions for Licensing, Certifying & Reviewing Performance." *American Journal of Occupational Therapy* 27 (July-August 1973): 257-58.

Johnstone, Q. and Hopson, D., Jr. *Lawyers and Their Work.* Indianapolis: Bobbs-Merrill, 1967.

Journal of Teacher Education. "Challenge of Change: America's Frontier" (Theme). Spring 1975.

Journal of Teacher Education. "Futurism in Education" (Theme). Summer 1974.

Journal of Teacher Education. "Protocol Materials" (Theme). Winter 1974.

*Joyce, B.R. "Teacher Innovator: A Program to Prepare Teachers" (Teachers College Columbia University). In *A Readers Guide to the Comprehensive Model for Preparing Elementary Teachers.* J. Burdin and K. Lanzillotti, eds. Washington, D.C.: American Association of Colleges for Teacher Education and ERIC Clearinghouse on Teacher Education, 1969.

Jules, F.A. "An Approach to Architectural Education." *Journal of Architectural Education* 26, no. 4, pp. 114-18.

Katz, M.C. *Bureaucracy, and Schools: The Illusion of Educational Change in America.* New York: Praeger, 1971.

Katz, M.S. "Teaching People to Think: A Philosphical and Futuristic Analysis." In D.R. Thomas, ed., *Futurism as an Approach to Decision-making in Teacher Education.* Washington, D.C.: ERIC Clearinghouse on Teacher Education, February 1975.

Kiel, F.W. "Government Medical Schools as Sources of Military Physicians." *Journal of Medical Education* 46 (June 1971): 485-94.

Kirkendall, L.A., et al. *Goals for American Education.* Written for the Commission on Educational Re-construction of the American Federation of Teachers, 1948.

Klatt, J. and LeBaron W. *A Short Summary of Ten Models: Teacher Education Programs.* Washington, D.C.: U.S. Government Printing Office, 1970.

Klein, R. *Complaints Against Doctors.* London: Charles Knight, 1973.

Koff, R.H. "Educational Policy and Professional Education." Speech delivered to the Illinois Association of Colleges for Teacher Education, Aurora, Ill., October 11, 1974.

Kolb, R. "This Is the AMA." *Journal of the Medical Association of Georgia* 62 (November 1973): 372-76.

Kuhli, R.C. "Accreditation: The AMA View." Speech given before the American Society of Allied Health Professions Institute, Atlanta, Ga., January 1974.

LaGrone, H.F. *A Proposal for the Revision of the Pre-service Professional Component of a Program of Teacher Education.* Washington, D.C.: American Association of Colleges for Teacher Education, 1964.

Larkin, P.G. "The Challenge to Higher Education of National Manpower Priorities." *Journal of Higher Education* 41 (March 1970): 195-203.

Larson, R.W. *Accreditation Problems and the Promise of PBTE.* Washington, D.C.: American Association of Colleges for Teacher Education and ERIC Clearinghouse on Teacher Education, 1974.

Levine, D.M. and Bonito, A.J. "Impact of Clinical Thinking on Attitudes of Medical Students: Self-perpetuating Barrier to Change in the System?" *British Journal of Medical Education* 8 (March 1974): 13-16.

*Lieberman, M. *Education as a Profession.* Englewood Cliffs, N.J.: Prentice-Hall, 1956.

Lierheimer, A.B. "Changing the Palace Guard." *Phi Delta Kappan* 52, no. 1 (1970): 20-25.

*Lindsey, M., ed. *New Horizons for the Teaching Profession.* Washington, D.C.: National Education Association, 1961.

Lindsey, M. *Accreditation in Teacher Education.* Reston, Va.: The Council for Exceptional Children, 1973 (ERIC Document No. ED 084 760).

Lortie, D.C. "Structure and Teacher Performance: A Prologue to Systematic Research." In *How Teachers Make a Difference.* Washington, D.C.: U.S. Government Printing Office, 1971, p. 56.

*Lortie, D.C. *Schoolteacher: A Sociological Study.* Chicago: University of Chicago Press, 1975.

Lortie, M. "The Balance of Control and Autonomy in Elementary School Teaching." In A. Etzioni, ed., *The Semi-professions and Their Organization: Teachers, Nurses, Social Workers.* New York: The Free Press, 1969.

Lynch, P.D. "American Indian Education: Separation, Amalgamation, or What?" Paper presented at the American Association of School Administrators Annual Convention, San Francisco, March 1973.

McFarland, M.C. "New Legislation Leverage for the Shaping of Growth." *ALA Journal,* December 1974.

McGlothlin, W.J. *Patterns of Professional Education.* New York: Putnam, 1960.

Malkemes, L.C. "Resocialization: A Model for Nurse Practitioner Preparation." *Nurses Outlook* 22 (Fall 1974): 90-94.

Manning, R.K. "A Socio-ethical Foundation for Meeting the Obligations of the Legal Profession." *Cumberland-Sanford Law Review* 5 (Fall 1974): 237.

Mantell, M.I. *Ethics and Professionalism in Engineering.* New York: MacMillan, 1964.

Markowitz, G.E. and Rosner, D.K. "Doctors in Crisis: A Case Study of the Use of Medical Education Reform to Establish Professional Elitism in Medicine." *American Quarterly* 25 (March 1973): 83-107.

Marshall, B. "Professional Responsibility and the Constitutional Doctrine." *Tulane Law Review* 48 (April 1974): 465.

"Mathews Reflects on Roles of HEW at Swearing-in" *Higher Education and National Affairs* 24, no. 32 (August 15, 1975): 1-2.

"Methods and Compensation for Architectural Services." AIA. Washington, D.C.: Case and Co. Management Consultants, June 1969.

Miller, J.W. "The Creditability of Nontraditional Education: A Conceptual Framework for Recognition" 1973 (ERIC Document No. ED 090 805).

*Miller, J.W. *Organizational Structure of Nongovernmental Postsecondary Accreditation: Relationship to Uses of Accreditation.* Washington, D.C.: National Commission on Accrediting, 1973 (ERIC Document No. ED 082 591).

Miller, S. and Hulsey, J. "Which Direction for Schools of Education?" 1971 (ERIC Document No. ED 087 763).

Mills, G.H. "Accreditation, Licensure, Certification and Public Accountability." Bibliography prepared for the Annual Meeting of the Education Commission of the States, Los Angeles, May 1972.

"Model Teacher Standards and Licensure Act." Washington, D.C.: National Education Association, 1971.

Mondale, Sen. W.F. Draft Bill on Teacher Centers. Not submitted to Senate, 1975.

Montoya, Sen. J.M. "Bilingual Education: Making Equal Educational Opportunities Available to National Origin Minority Students." *The Georgetown Law Journal* 62 (1973): 991-1007.

Moore, W.E. and Rosenblum, G.W. *The Professions: Role and Rules.* New York: Russell Sage Foundation, 1970.

Mortimer, K.P. *Accountability in Higher Education.* Washington, D.C.: American Association for Higher Education, 1972.

Mushkin, S.J. *Consumer Incentives for Health Care.* New York: Prodist for Milbank Memorial Fund, 1974.

Nash, R.J. "Humanistic Teacher Education: A Future Look." *AACTE Bulletin* 28, no. 6 (August 1975): 3.

Nash, R.J. and Agne, R.M. "The Ethos of Accountability—A Critique." *Teachers College Record* 73 (February 1972): 357-70.

Nash, R.J. and Ducharme, E. "A Futures Perspective on Preparing Educators for the Human Service Society: How to Restore a Sense of Social Purpose to Teacher Education." (Unpublished manuscript). Burlington, Vt.: College of Education and Social Services, University of Vermont, 1975.

Nash, R.J. and Ducharme, E.R. "The University Can Prepare Teachers: An Unfashionable View." *The Educational Forum* 39 (November 1974): 99-109.

National Advisory Commission on Health Manpower. *Report of the National Advisory Commission on Health Manpower.* Vol. I, II. Washington, D.C.: U.S. Government Printing Office. n.d.

National Advisory Council on Education Professions Development. *Gatekeepers in Education: A Report on Institutional Licensing.* Washington, D.C.: National Advisory Council on Education Professions Development, April 1975.

National Advisory Council on Education Professions Development. *Windows to the Bureaucracy.* Washington, D.C.: National Advisory Council on Education Professions Development, 1971.

National Education Association. *Education Adds Up.* Washington, D.C.: National Education Association, 1966.

National Education Association. *Commission on Professional Ethics.* Washington, D.C.: National Education Association, 1966.

National Education Association. "Some Inhibitors to Professionalization as Reported by Teachers." In *Negotiating for Professionalization.* Washington, D.C.: National Education Association, 1970, pp. 66-70.

National Education Association, Division of Instruction and Professional Development. "Licensure and Accreditation in Selected Professions." *Today's Education,* December 1971, pp. 18-19.

National Education Association, Division of Instruction and Professional Development. *National Professional Accrediting Agencies: How They Function.* Washington, D.C.: National Education Association, 1974.

National Education Association, Division of Instruction and Professional Development. "Special Feature on Governance of the Profession." *Today's Education,* December 1971, pp. 18-25.

National Education Association, Educational Policies Commission. *Professional Organizations in American Education.* Washington, D.C.: National Education Association, 1957.

National Educational Association, National Commission on Teacher Education and Professional Standards. *The Education of Teachers: Curriculum Programs, Report of the Kansas TEPS Conference, 1959.* Washington, D.C.: National Education Association, 1959.

National Education Association, Program for Professional Excellence. *Teachers Can Change Teacher Education.* Washington, D.C.: National Education Association, August 1975.

National School Boards Association. *Report '75: 35th Annual Convention.* Evanston, Ill.: National School Boards Association, 1975.

New York State Education Department, Division of Teacher Education and Certification. *State Education Departments' Policies and Practices in the Approved Program Approach to Teacher Certification.* n.d. (ERIC Document No. ED 029 852).

*Olson, P. "The Preparation of the Teacher: An Evaluation of the State of the Art." In P. Olson, L. Freeman and J. Bowman, eds. *Education for 1984 and After.* Schiller Park, Ill.: The Directorate of the Study Commission on Undergraduate Education and the Education of Teachers, 1971.

Olson, P.A. "Issues in Teacher Education as Perceived by a Liberal Arts Professor." In *A Conference on Teacher Education.* Lincoln: University of Nebraska, 1973.

Olson, P.A. ed. "Analysis of Carnegie Commission Survey Data Completed." *Study Commission Newsletter.* Lincoln: University of Nebraska, January 1975.

Olson, P.A. and Schadt, D. "Compared with Professors in Other Fields . . . ." In *Study Commission Newsletter,* January 1975, p. 15.

Orlosky, D. and Smith, B.O. "Educational Change: Its Origins and Characteristics." *Phi Delta Kappan,* March 1972, pp. 412-14.

Paltridge, J.G. *Organizational Forms Which Characterize Statewide Coordination of Public Higher Education.* Berkeley, Calif.: Berkeley Center for Research and Development in Higher Education, June 1965.

Patrick, M. and Tree, M. *A Career in Architecture.* London: Museum Press, 1961.

Patterson, L.R. and Cheatham, E.E. *The Profession of Law.* Mineola, N.Y.: The Foundation Press, 1971.

Petit, M.L. "The Need for Comparative Educational Research to Concentrate on the Culture Revolution Within the United States." Paper delivered at the annual meeting of Comparative and International Education Society, San Antonio, Tex., March 1973.

Pitman, J.C. *Competency-based Certification: What Are the Key Issues?* Durham, N.H.: New England Center for Continuing Education, 1973.

Pomeroy, E.C. "What's Going on in Teacher Education—The View from Washington." *Journal of Teacher Education* 26, no. 3 (Fall 1975): 196-201.

Popham, W.J. "Performance Tests of Teaching Proficiency: Rationale, Development and Validation." *American Educational Research Journal* 8 (1971): 105-18.

Postman, N. and Weingartner, C. *Teaching as a Subversive Activity.* New York: Delta, 1969.

"Preparing and Qualifying for Admission to Teaching." K. Goldhammer, issue ed. In *New Directions for Education* 1, no. 2 (Summer 1973).

Proffitt, J.R. "Professions and the Public: A Crossroads of Interest." *The American Journal of Medical Technology* 37 (January 1971): 3.

Program/cost study done by dean's office, College of Medicine, University of Vermont, 1973. Unpublished.

Raywid, M.A. *The Ax-Grinders.* New York: MacMillan, 1962.

Redfield, M.P. *The Social Uses of Social Science: The Papers of Robert Redfield.* Vol. 2. Chicago: University of Chicago Press, 1963.

Rhode, R.D. "Bilingual Education for Teachers." *Educational Forum* 38 (January 1974): 203-9.

Rivlin, H.N. *A Case Study in Changing the Governance of a Teacher Education Program.* Lincoln, Nebr.: Study Commission on Undergraduate Education and the Education of Teachers, n.d.

Rivlin, H.N. "If I Had My Way." *Theory Into Practice* 13, no. 3 (June 1974).

Rosenberg, Motley, and Rubenfeld. "Training Tomorrow's Lawyers: A Response to the Chief of Justice's Challenge." *Columbia Law Journal* 11 (1974): 72-98.

*Rosenstein, A.B. *A Study of a Profession and Professional Education.* Los Angeles: University of California, Los Angeles, 1968.

Roth, R.A. *The Role of the State in Performance-Based Teacher Education Certification.* Trenton: New Jersey State Department of Education, 1972 (ERIC Document No. ED 093 818).

Rousselot, L.M. "Federal Efforts to Influence Physician Education, Specialization Distribution Projections and Options." *American Journal of Medicine* 60 (August 1973): 123-30.

*Ryan, K., Kleine, P., and Krasno, R. *Realities and Revolution in Teacher Education.* Report #6 of the Commission on Public School Personnel Policy in Ohio. Cleveland: Greater Cleveland Associated Foundation, 1972.

*Ryan, K., ed. *Teacher Education. The 74th Yearbook of the National Society for the Study of Education, Part II.* Chicago: University of Chicago Press, 1975.

Sagan, E.L. and Smith, B.G. *Alternative Models for the Cooperative Governance of Teacher Education Programs.* Lincoln, Nebr.: Dean's Committee of the Study Commission on Undergraduate Education and the Education of Teachers, 1973.

Schaefer, R. *The School as a Center of Inquiry.* New York: Harper & Row, 1967.

Scheffler, I. *Conditions of Knowledge: An Introduction to Epistemology and Education.* Chicago: Scott Foresman, 1965.

*Schein, E.H. *Professional Education.* New York: McGraw-Hill, 1972.

Schein, E.H. "Professional Education: Some New Directions." In *Sponsored Research of the Carnegie Commission on Higher Education.* New York: McGraw-Hill, 1975, pp. 148-52.

Schiff, S.K. "Training the Professional." *University of Chicago Magazine,* Fall 1970, p. 10.

Schmidt, A. "The Role of Regulation." *Journal of Medical Education* 50, no. 2 (February 1975): 124-29.

Schnaufer, P. *The Uses of Teacher Power.* Chicago: American Federation of Teachers Research Department, 1966.

"School-University Partnership for Teacher Growth" (Thematic section). *Educational Leadership* 32, no. 5 (February 1975).

Selden, W.K. *Accreditation: A Struggle Over Standards in Higher Education.* New York: Harper and Brothers, 1960.

Selden, W.K. "Dilemmas of Accreditation of Health Education Programs." *Part II: Staff Working Papers, Accreditation of Health Education Programs.* Washington, D.C.: National Commission on Accrediting, 1971.

Selman, G.R. *Toward Cooperation: The Development of a Provincial Voice for Adult Education in British Columbia, 1953 to 1962.* November 1969 (ERIC Document No. ED 034 934).

Shroeder, O., Jr. *Lawyer Discipline: The Ohio Story.* Ohio: Ohio Legal Center Institute, 1967. (Final Draft, June 1970.)

*Silberman, C. *Crisis in the Classroom.* New York: Random House, 1970.

Simpson, M.A. *Medical Education: A Critical Approach.* New York: Appleton-Century-Crofts, 1972.

Skinner, F., et al. "Census Survey Shows Education Major Drop." *Higher Education and National Affairs* 23, no. 13 (March 29, 1974): 4.

Slade, G.R. "Governance—Annual Administrative Reviews." *Hospitals* 47, no. 7 (April 1973): 51-54.

Smith, B.O., et al. *A Study of the Logic of Teaching.* Urbana, Ill.: Bureau of Education Research, n.d.

*Smith, B.O., Cohen, S.B. and Pearl, A. *Teachers for the Real World.* Washington, D.C.: American Association of Colleges for Teacher Education, 1969.

*Smith, B.O. and Orlosky, D.C. *Socialization and Schooling.* Bloomington, Ind.: Phi Delta Kappa, 1975.

Sparks, R.K. "Are We Ready for National Certification of Professional Educators?" *Journal of Teacher Education* 21 (September 1970): 342-46.

The Spirit of 1975. Washington, D.C.: American Federation of Teachers, 1975.

Sprague, C.C. "Undergraduate Medical Education, Elements-Objectives-Cost." *Report of the Commission on the Financing of Medical Education.* Washington, D.C.: Association of American Medical Colleges, 1973.

Starr, P. "The Edge of Social Science." *Harvard Educational Review* 44, no. 4 (November 1974): 393-415.

Stearns, N., Getchell, M.E. and Gold, R.A. *Continuing Medical Education in Community Hospitals, A Manual for Program Development.* Boston: Massachusetts Medical Society.

Stevens, R. *American Medicine and the Public Interest.* New Haven, Conn.: Yale University Press, 1971.

Stewart, L.O. *Careers in Education,* 3d. ed. Ames, Iowa: Iowa State College Press, 1956.

Stinnett, T.M. and Pershing, G.E. *A Manual on Certification Requirements for School Personnel in the United States.* Washington, D.C.: National Association of State Directors of Teacher Education and Certification, and National Education Association, 1970.

Stone, J.C. *Breakthrough in Teacher Education.* San Francisco: Jossey-Bass, 1968.

Strauss, A.L. *Where Medicine Fails.* Chicago: Aldine Publishing Co., 1970.

Stuckman, J.A. *Statewide Coordination of Community Junior Colleges.* Gainesville, Fla.: Gainesville Institute of Higher Education, November, 1969.

Stuckman, J.A. and Wattenbarger, J.L. "Coordination Within the State System." *Junior College Journal* 41 (March 1971): 43-45.

Study Commission Newsletter. Lincoln, Nebr.: Study Commission on Undergraduate Education and the Education of Teachers, May 1974.

Study Commission Newsletter. Lincoln, Nebr.: Study Commission on Undergraduate Education and the Education of Teachers, December 1973.

Study Commission on Undergraduate Education and the Education of Teachers. "October Document." Unpublished Manuscript. University of Nebraska, Lincoln, Nebr., 1974.

*Study Commission on Undergraduate Education and the Education of Teachers. "Teacher Education in America" (Draft copy of final report). Lincoln: University of Nebraska, July 1975.

Sutton. "Code of Professional Responsibility and Delivery of Legal Service." *Pennsylvania Bar Association Quarterly* 45 (June 1974): 343-68.

Swick, K.J. and Lindberg, D.H. "An Approach to Educating Teachers to Work with the Culturally Different." 1972 (ERIC Document No. ED 090 153).

"Teacher Supply and Demand in Public Schools, 1974." *NEA Research Memo 1975-3.* Washington, D.C.: National Education Association, May 1975.

Teachers in the Seventies. Washington, D.C.: American Federation of Teachers, 1975.

Theory Into Practice. "A Workshop in the Analysis of Teaching" (complete issue) 7, no. 5 (December 1968).

Thiel, P. "Architecture and Beginning Student." *Journal of Architectural Education* 27, no. 1, pp. 13-20.

Thomfarde, F.H., Jr. "Public Opinion of the Legal Profession: A Necessary Response by the Bar and the Law School." *Tennessee Law Review* 41 (1974): 503-33.

Tomson, B. *Architectural & Engineering Law.* 2nd ed. New York: Reinhold, 1967.

152

Torrey, E. *Ethical Issues in Medicine.* Boston: Little, Brown, 1968.

*Travers, R.M.W., ed. *Second Handbook of Research on Teaching.* Chicago: Rand McNally, 1973.

Trivett, D. *Goals for Higher Education: Definitions and Directions.* Washington, D.C.: American Association of Colleges for Teacher Education, 1973.

Tunley, R. *The American Health Scandal.* New York: Harper & Row, 1966.

Turner, R.L. *A General Catalog of Teaching Skills.* Albany, N.Y.: State Education Department, Division of Teacher Education and Certification and Multi-State Consortium on Performance-Based Education, 1974.

UCLA Educator 16 (Spring 1974). Los Angeles, Calif.: Graduate School of Education.

U.S. Department of Health, Education, and Welfare. *Better Schools Through Better Partnerships: The Final Report and Recommendations of the Council of Chief State School Officers' National Field Task Force on the Improvement and Reform of American Education.* Washington, D.C.: U.S. Government Printing Office, 1974.

U.S. Department of Health, Education, and Welfare. *The Education Professions 1968.* Washington, D.C.: U.S. Government Printing Office, 1969.

U.S. Department of Health, Education, and Welfare. *The Final Report and Recommendations of the Summer Institute on the Improvement and Reform of American Education.* Washington, D.C.: U.S. Government Printing Office, 1974.

U.S. Department of Health, Education, and Welfare. *Inside-Out: The Final Report and Recommendations of the Teachers National Field Task Force on the Improvement and Reform of American Education.* Washington, D.C.: U.S. Government Printing Office, 1974.

U.S. Department of Health, Education, and Welfare. *Institutional Viability: The Final Report and Recommendations of the Administration and Supervision National Field Task Force on the Improvement and Reform of American Education.* Washington, D.C.: U.S. Government Printing Office, 1974.

U.S. Department of Health, Education, and Welfare. *Medical Malpractice.* Report of the Secretary's Commission on Medical Malpractice. Washington, D.C.: DHEW Publication, No. 1, 1973.

*U.S. Department of Health, Education, and Welfare. *Obligation for Reform: The Final Report and Recommendations of the Higher Education National Field Task Force on the Improvement and Reform of American Education.* Washington, D.C.: U.S. Government Printing Office, 1974. Also, American Association of Colleges for Teacher Education, 1974.

U.S. Department of Health, Education, and Welfare. *A Real Alternative: The Final Report and Recommendations of the Community National Field Task Force on the Improvement and Reform of American Education.* Washington, D.C.: U.S. Government Printing Office, 1974.

U.S. Department of Health, Education, and Welfare. *Working Together: The Final Report and Recommendations of the Basic Studies National Field Task Force on the Improvement and Reform of American Education,* Washington, D.C.: U.S. Government Printing Office, 1974.

U.S. Office of Education. *Report on Higher Education.* (The Newman Report). Washington, D.C.: U.S. Government Printing Office, March 1971.

Verduin, J.R., Jr. *Conceptual Models in Teacher Education: An Approach to Teaching and Learning.* Washington, D.C.: American Association of Colleges for Teacher Education, 1967.

Washington, E. "The Expert Teacher Action Study: A New Approach to Teaching." *Journal of Teacher Education* 21 (Summer 1970): 258-63.

Wedeen, S.U. "Screening for Teaching." *Improving College and University Teaching* 20 (Spring 1972): p. 124.

Weinberger, C.W. "The Role of the Federal Government in Education of the Public About Health." *Journal of Medical Education* 50, no. 2 (February 1975).

Weisor, C. and Phelps, J.R. "Lawyers and Accountants on Trial. Professional Responsibility." *American Bar Association Section of Litigation.* Montreal, Quebec: National Institute, 1974.

Wilensky, H.J. "The Professionalization of Everyone." *American Journal of Sociology* 70, no. 2 (1964): 143.

Woodring, P. *The Higher Learning in America: A Reassessment.* New York: McGraw-Hill, 1968.

Woods, B.G. "Designing Programs for Teacher Educators." *Theory Into Practice* 13, no. 3 (June 1974): 167-76.

Ylvisaker, P.N. "Memorandum to Members, ACSESULGC Legislative Liaison and Planning Committee." Boston: Harvard University Graduate Faculty of Education, June 9, 1975.

Young, K.B., et al. *Accreditation Issues in Teacher Education.* Special Current Issues Publication (SCIP) No. 1. Washington, D.C.: ERIC Clearinghouse on Teacher Education, July 1975.

Zephier, R. "American Indian Education: Separation, Amalgamation, or What?" Paper presented at the American Association of School Administrators Annual Convention, Atlantic City, N.J., February 1973.

Zerfoss, E. and Shapiro, L.J. *The Supply and Demand of Teachers and Teaching.* Lincoln, Nebr.: University of Nebraska Printing and Duplicating Service, 1972.

Zorn, R.L. "Co-op Buying: You Pool Your Power and Pocket Your Savings." *American School Board Journal* 160 (April 1973): 42-43.

A Conceptual Framework for Analysis of Collaborative Efforts in Governance

TEACHER CENTERS

In Chapter One, the governance characteristic of professions is stated as follows:

> 6. The profession is organized into one or more professional associations which, within broad limits of social accountability, are granted autonomy in control of the actual work of the profession and the conditions which surround it (admissions; educational standards; examination and licensing; career line; ethical and performance standards; professional discipline).

Chapter Two reported that the teaching profession falls far short of meeting the self-governance criterion. State government, through its educational branch, long has held control of important governance functions. Others are in the hands of college and university administration. For whatever reasons, these two major controllers have not succeeded in moving teacher education toward attainment of its potential and the profession toward maturity. Change in the governance system appears to be sorely needed.

An Analysis and a Model

In the following model, the simple notions of suprasystem, system, and subsystem are used. In systems terms, everything is composed of parts. If the

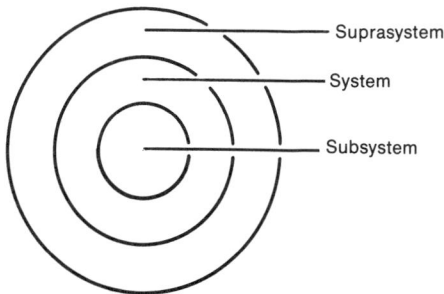

LEVELS OF SYSTEMS

155

object is called the system, then its parts are subsystems of it. The object, however, is a part of a larger system which is its suprasystem.

The model also makes use of a concept of accountability as it relates to systems. Two concepts are used, namely, *accountability* and *responsiveness*.

1. *Accountability* is to the suprasystem only. It is never to another element or subsystem of the same suprasystem. It is never to a subsystem. A child (subsystem) is accountable to his father and mother (larger system) but not to a brother or sister (other subsystems of the same larger system).

2. A system must be *responsive* to other systems in its environment to which it relates. Though the children in a family are not accountable to each other, they are expected to be considerate of or responsive to the others' situation or need.

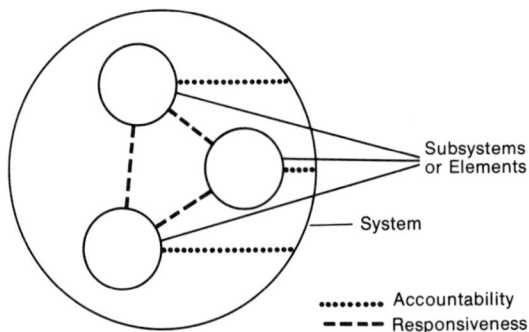

ACCOUNTABILITY—RESPONSIVENESS IN SYSTEMS

The Teacher Education System

Education is a complex system serving society by providing learning opportunities. The system is made up of many parts, each of which is itself a system.

Teacher education in this report is held to be the preparation arm of the teaching profession.

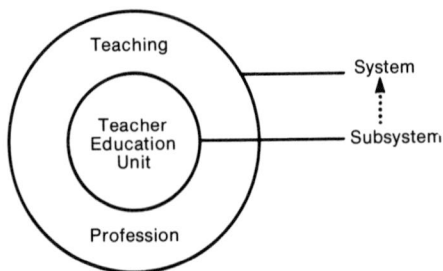

As such, it is a subsystem of the teaching profession, and so it is accountable to the profession for what it does. Additionally, it is subject to control by the profession. Systems can be simultaneously elements or subsystems of more than one suprasystem. A child is a member of a family social system but at the same time may play with a

156

group of other children, be in a
school class, and play ball with
a team.

Teacher education is a unit of
a college or university which is
also its suprasystem. By changing
the shape of the suprasystems the
drawings can be combined to
show the two suprasystems of
teacher education.

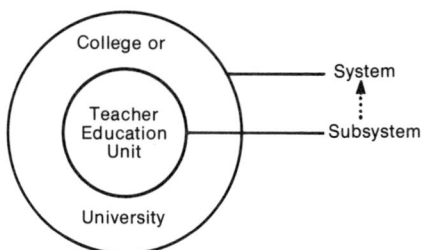

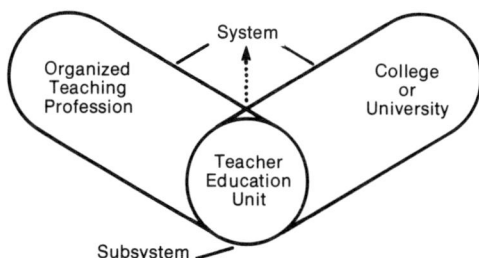

College or
Teacher Education Unit
University
System
Subsystem

System
Organized Teaching Profession
College or University
Teacher Education Unit
Subsystem

Here teacher education is shown as responsible for a teacher program and
accountable to both the university and the teaching profession. This is a representation of how the governance of teacher education ideally should be.
However, at the present time, the state unit of government exercises the
dominant role in controlling what goes on in teacher education.

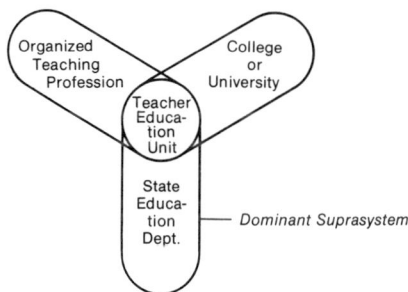

Organized Teaching Profession
College or University
Teacher Educa- tion Unit
State Educa- tion Dept.
Dominant Suprasystem

In accordance with principles of professionalization, every effort should
be made to decrease state dominance and increase college and professional
control of teacher education.

The Public School System

As was indicated earlier
in this discussion, education
is a function of the state;
and school systems are
created by and accountable
to the state.

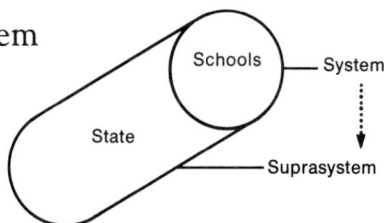

Schools
State
System
Suprasystem

States have, however, delegated substantial control of the schools to the local education authority.

Once again there are two major partners.

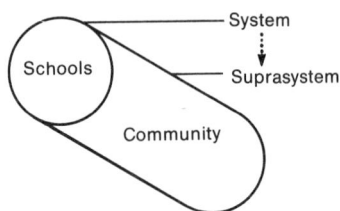

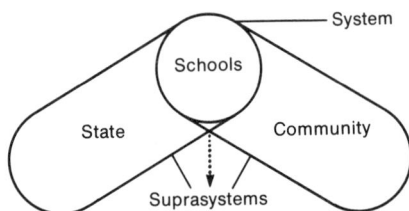

The Larger Education System

It will be observed that there now are two sets of system-suprasystem, both of which are part of the larger education system.

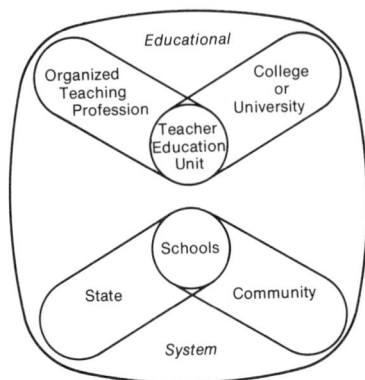

EDUCATIONAL SYSTEM

The teacher preparation system and the public school system, each with its own function, exist side by side within the larger educational system. Each is accountable to the larger system; they are not accountable to each other. Since they live together within a larger system and since they have necessary relationships with each other, they need to be *responsive*. This is to say that they must consider each other as they act. They will both do better if they act together. Thus a collaborative relationship is indicated.

158

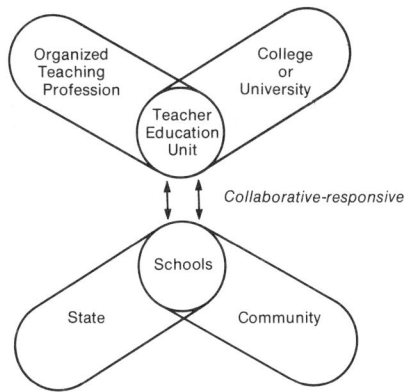

COLLABORATIVE-RESPONSIVE RELATIONSHIP

It should be observed that there are six partners in the operation of a teacher center:
1. Teacher education unit
2. The schools
3. The teacher organization(s)
4. The university outside the teacher education unit
5. The school board and the community
6. The state or intermediate agency of the state

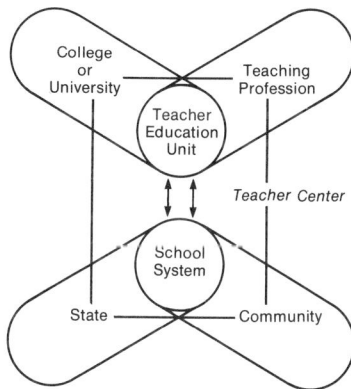

TEACHER CENTER PARTNERSHIP

Teacher centers are governance mechanisms; they are not places. They can, however, establish places where teacher education takes place. These too are called Teacher Centers or Teachers Centers (National Education Association). In such centers, an array of preservice, inservice, and continuing education can take place as each of the major partners assumes responsibilities that fall within its jurisdiction.

Teacher Competencies*

The following teacher competencies are stated at a subgoal level; that is, they include a behavioral statement, but not the criteria for successful demonstration of the competence nor the conditions under which it is to be demonstrated.

The Teacher and Students: Designing and Evaluating (Preactivity and Postactivity)

Diagnosis and Evaluation

1. Administers and interprets standardized tests.
2. Designs and uses teacher-made diagnostic tests.
3. Interviews pupils using Piagetian techniques.
4. Describes environment, values, and needs of students; is familiar with background and language of students.

Organizing Classroom

1. Groups students on basis of data.
2. Makes resources and materials accessible to students.
3. Plans for routine tasks.

Goals and Objectives

1. Identifies goals and objectives appropriate to student needs.
2. Organizes instruction around goals and objectives.
3. States criterion-referenced objectives correctly.

Planning

1. Plans daily to contribute to long-range goals.
2. Sequences activities and experiences logically and psychologically.

The Teacher and Students—Active Interaction

Communication

1. Counsels students with personal problems.

---

*College of Education, University of Houston (a preliminary, working document), Fall 1972.

2. Asks higher-order questions.
3. Presents instruction using inductive and deductive procedures.
4. Gives clear, explicit directions to students.
5. Responds to "coping" behavior of students.
6. Identifies clues to student misconception or confusion.

Instruction

1. Establishes sets (motivation, transitions, classroom environmental conditions) which are varied and appropriate.
2. Employs a variety of instructional strategies (programmed instruction, games, and simulation).
3. Utilizes instructional materials and resources.
4. Individualizes instruction.
5. Plans activities with children.

Management

1. Uses positive reinforcement patterns with students.
2. Manages classroom environment.
3. Manages deviant behavior.

Interpersonal Relations

1. Builds self-awareness and self-concepts in students.
2. Develops understanding of cultural pluralism concepts in students.
3. Demonstrates sensitivity to others.

Evaluation

1. Monitors classroom interaction and modifies plans on basis of feedback.

The Professional Teacher

Self-Improvement

1. Engages in a designed professional development program.
2. Evaluates teaching behavior using coded instruments (interaction analysis, check lists, etc.) and plans for change on basis of results.

Colleagues and Other Professionals

1. Works effectively in an educational team.
2. Evaluates effectiveness of school program and contributes to improvement efforts.

Costs and Life Space

Teacher education receives the lowest support per credit hour of instruction of any professional education program funded in universities. Data from the Carnegie Commission Study and the National Center for Higher Education management profiles show that in a comparison of full education programs for teachers and programs for students in other professional programs, the cost per full-time equivalent (FTE) in education programs is lower than that in other professional sequences; and more than 60 percent of teachers in preparation attend institutions of low quality according to the Gourman ratings and college ratio ratings. Furthermore, even in Carnegie-rated high quality institutions, support for teacher education is less than for other programs.

The Study Commission on Undergraduate Education and the Education of Teachers,* using the 1970 Carnegie Commission Study indices, examined the National Center for Higher Education Management Systems (NCHEMS) FTE reports on institutions supporting teacher education at the various levels. Carnegie indices rank colleges as "high quality," "middle quality," and "lower quality," using the Gourman indices (supported by several other "quality indices" which rate quality of academic departments in terms of quality of instruction, proportion of students receiving scholarships and fellowships, and quality of nondepartmental features (e.g., administration "commitment to excellence," level of financial aid, board of trustees, faculty morale). Another quality index which the Carnegie group found to support Gourman was the Gross-Grambsch index, which includes fiscal features. Carnegie "Quality I" institutions scored 580 on Gourman; "Quality II" scored 477-579; "low quality" had less than 477. According to Study Commission calculations, the average FTE cost per education major is about $1,500 at Carnegie I universities; $1,300 at Carnegie II universities; $2,100 at Carnegie I colleges, $1,200 at Carnegie II, and about $1,300 at Carnegie III. The lower the Carnegie rating of NCHEMS-analyzed institutions, the larger percentage of education undergraduates. Except for the Class I colleges, all Carnegie levels appear to spend about $1,300-$1,500 per FTE undergraduate in education ('72-'73). This is lower than the cost for other undergraduate professional or preprofessional areas. In the other areas (engineering, nursing, social work, audiology, etc.), lower division costs tend

---

*Study Commission on Undergraduate Education and the Education of Teachers, "Teacher Education in America," Draft copy of final report (Lincoln: University of Nebraska, July 1975).

to be around $1,300-$1,800 per FTE major and upper division aound $2,000-$2,800.

Average tuition at public colleges in '72-'73 was about $500, and in private colleges about $2,200; education students appear to have paid about $650 average tuition or about half their full annual FTE cost per major. On the average, American students at all levels pay 1/5 of their full FTE costs (5.9 billion out of 29.5 billion). Moreover, it seems highly unlikely that any other professional area educates 65 percent of its professionals at Carnegie Quality III colleges and universities. Most important, even the Carnegie I and II "quality" universities and the Carnegie II colleges do not spend much on educating teachers.

In 1969-70, about 30 percent of the undergraduates were in education or planned a teaching career. There were 6 million undergraduates in 1969-70, about 1,800,000 potential teachers or 450,000 for each college year. In 1970, about 880,000 degrees were conferred, and about 1.8 million students started college. Dropouts reduced the number of education graduates to around 300,000 of the 880,000, or well over 30 percent of the undergraduates graduating. Undergraduate education witnesses a drifting phenomenon—out of hard science and engineering areas into education. The total cost of undergraduate teacher education in 1970 at $1,300 per FTE and 1,800,000 students would have been about 2 billion, 340 million dollars. Total expenditure for higher education in the year was 24.7 billion dollars, of which the 2 billion plus dollars for teachers seems a remarkably small sum. Medical education and graduate education are included in the $24.7 billion figure.

When one puts this in "campus-by-campus" terms, comparing costs for courses in education-fieldwork courses with other fieldwork courses (i.e., elementary and secondary education with social work, nursing, or engineering), and when one compares education "clinical" courses with other field clinical courses (pathology, audiology, etc.), or education "liberal studies courses" (history, philosophy) in arts and sciences, education comes in short-changed 75 percent of the time. Costs per credit hour and per FTE are lower 75 percent of the time in fieldwork areas and 100 percent of the time in foundation areas; only in clinical areas—educational psychology and special education—are they equal, and these areas have had heavy federal support. The figures were obtained from the 40 NCHEMS model institutions (Cost Data and Descriptive Information booklets) and calculated by Gary Rex of the Study Commission staff. The National Center for Educational Statistics (NCES) has no statistics available in this area, but a recent calculation of "instructional program cost" in FTE majors in elementary education and special education using the most recent NCHEMS data shows basically the same pattern described here, with a few exceptions (Fisk; Shippensburg; State University of New York, College of Arts and Science at Plattsburgh; University of New Mexico "special ed."). This calculation was done by Lewin & Associates, "Design Study for a National Survey of the Preparation of Education Personnel" (Study Review Panel Book, June 3, 1975), pp. 13-16.

Process Skill Domains as Goals for the Helping Professions

Name	Description	Rationale
1. Achieving, exhibiting and maintaining competence in the academic content of one's disciplines or profession.	Being an expert in the organized knowledge and practice of one's field.	Essential to the self-esteem of the individual, his ability to serve well and inspire others, and the esteem which his clients and colleagues may exhibit toward him.
2. Cogent and accurate verbal communications (semantics).	Being able to recognize and construct precise and unambiguous statements which accurately describe some action, event, ideas, or situation.	Essential to efficient, clear communication with others as well as to logical, consistent "nonfuzzy" thinking.
3. Making observations, constructing inferences, and distinguishing between the two.	Describing objectively. Forming reasonable hypotheses about what course of action to take (decision making). Not confusing inference with observations (hypotheses with facts).	Essential to fair, rational, and impartial thought and evaluation. Essential to avoid stereotypic, judgmental thinking which can impose self-fulfilling prophecy situations on others and self.
4. Using multiple theoretic-conceptual frameworks to observe and infer.	Being able to explain a given situation, event, or instance in multiple ways with different accepted theories with differing assumptions, biases, and implications.	Essential to not becoming a "true believer" who dogmatically applies one set of constructs to all situations and becomes blind to many other interpretations and problem solutions.

5. Showing and maintaining respect and regard toward others, especially one's clients.	Being able to exhibit nurturant behavior toward others, establish esteem for others and recognize their competence and worth to whatever degree these qualities are present.	Essential to establishing a supportive environment where the helpee can profit from the nurturance and direction of the helper and will implement the action prescribed by the helper.
6. Value-clarification.	Recognizing what one values, likes, and dislikes. Questioning and clarifying one's own beliefs, values, and preferences. Evaluating and judging the effects of one's own beliefs, values, likes, dislikes, and habits on one's perceptions, biases, actions, and interactions with others. Being able to express what one values. Being able to judge which theories, techniques, or methods agree or conflict with one's values. Being able to comprehend and accept as different, but appropriate, habits and values different from one's own.	Essential to consistent and wise behavior in areas of personal integrity, ethics, and morals.
7. General fluency and flexibility of thought, perception, and response.	Being able to break set in one's ideas, observations, feelings, actions, and responses. Being able to see things from multiple perspectives.	Essential to adaptive behavior and problem solving in true problem situations, be they rational, emotional or social, personal or cooperative.

Source: H.P. Cole and W.E. Lacefield, Skill Domains for the Helping Professions (Lexington, Ky.: College of Education, University of Kentucky, 1975). Unpublished manuscript.

Selective Admission and Retention of Education Personnel

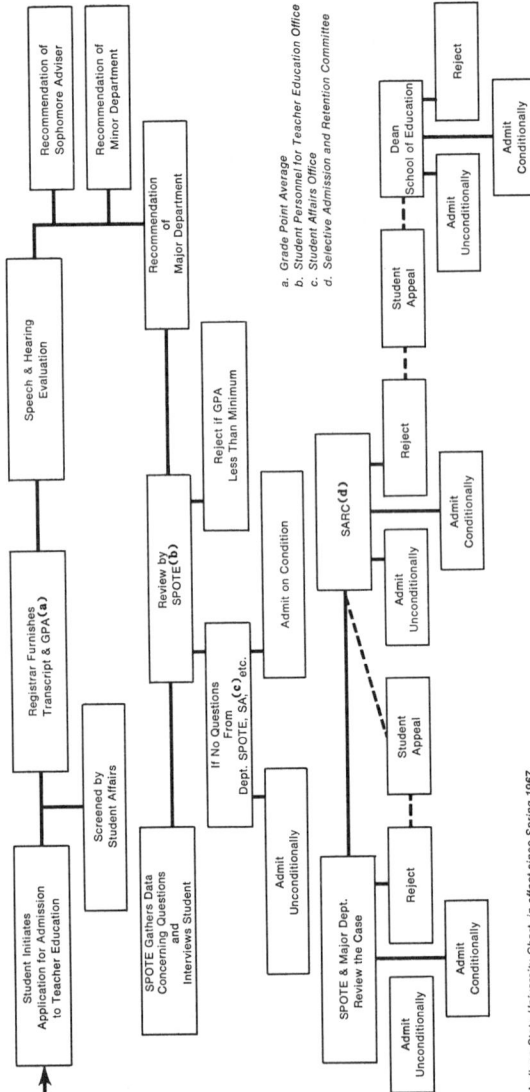

FLOWCHART OF PROCEDURE
FOR ADMISSION TO TEACHER EDUCATION

Student Initiates Application for Admission to Teacher Education

Registrar Furnishes Transcript & GPA(a)

Screened by Student Affairs

SPOTE Gathers Data Concerning Questions and Interviews Student

Speech & Hearing Evaluation

Recommendation of Sophomore Adviser

Recommendation of Minor Department

Recommendation of Major Department

Review by SPOTE(b)

Reject if GPA Less Than Minimum

Admit on Condition

If No Questions From Dept. SPOTE, SA(c) etc.

Admit Unconditionally

SPOTE & Major Dept. Review the Case

Student Appeal

Admit Unconditionally

Admit Conditionally

Reject

SARC(d)

Admit Unconditionally

Admit Conditionally

Reject

Student Appeal

Admit Unconditionally

Admit Conditionally

Dean School of Education

Reject

a. Grade Point Average
b. Student Personnel for Teacher Education Office
c. Student Affairs Office
d. Selective Admission and Retention Committee

Indiana State University Chart, in effect since Spring 1967.

Source: *Journal of Teacher Education* 25, no. 3 (Fall 1974): 238.

Selective admission and retention procedures are designed to get the desired kinds of education personnel into the schools. In view of the current concern regarding teacher oversupply in *some* fields, and the expressed need for quality teaching, more professional selection and retention criteria are needed in colleges of education.

The procedures shown on these flowcharts provide numerous chances for college personnel to determine strengths and weaknesses and design programs which are sensible for prospective education personnel. Another plus is that the processes help candidates determine whether the education profession is the right one for them. Ideally, no one enters the classroom without the commitment, characteristics, and competencies which collectively determine how well a person performs. (Charts provided by Indiana State University.)

FLOWCHART OF PROCEDURE FOR SELECTIVE RETENTION IN TEACHER EDUCATION

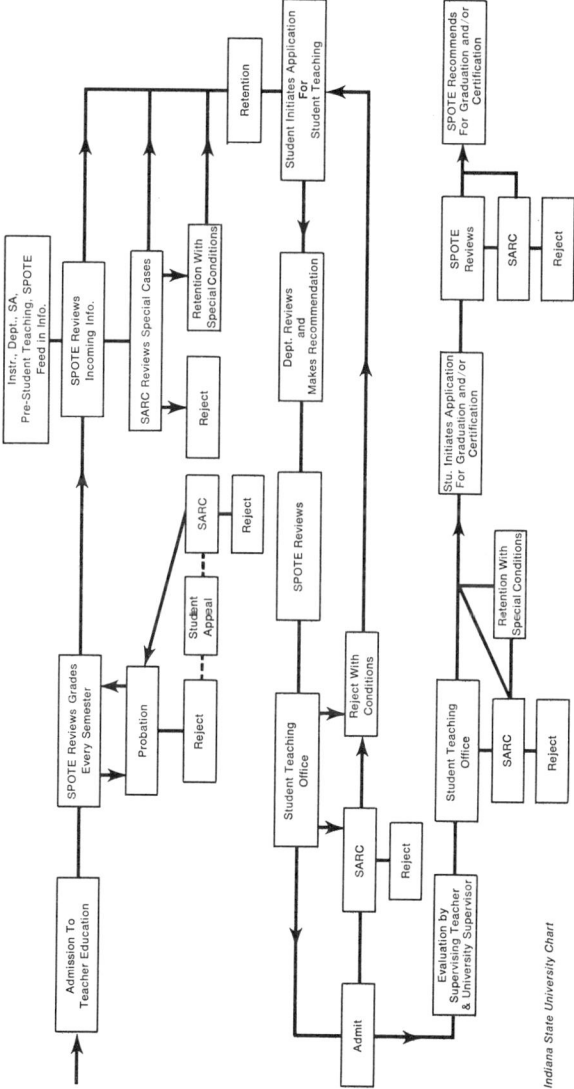

Admission To Teacher Education

SPOTE Reviews Grades Every Semester

Instr., Dept., SA, Pre-Student Teaching, SPOTE Feed in Info.

SPOTE Reviews Incoming Info.

SARC Reviews Special Cases

Retention With Special Conditions

Retention

Student Initiates Application For Student Teaching

Dept. Reviews and Makes Recommendation

Probation

Reject

SARC

Student Appeal

Reject

SPOTE Reviews

Student Teaching Office

Reject With Conditions

SARC

Reject

Admit

Evaluation by Supervising Teacher & University Supervisor

Stu. Initiates Application For Graduation and/or Certification

Student Teaching Office

Retention With Special Conditions

SARC

Reject

SPOTE Reviews

SARC

Reject

SPOTE Recommends For Graduation and/or Certification

Indiana State University Chart

Supply and Demand Data

Table 1.
Demand for New Teachers Based on the Quality Criterion, 1974

Source of demand	Estimated demand for new teachers		
	Elementary	Secondary	Total
1	2	3	4
Enrollment change and trends toward improved staffing	4,600	9,400	14,000
Teacher turnover	78,350	62,100	140,450
Replacement of teachers having substandard qualifications	13,800	4,750	18,550
Reduction in number of overcrowded classes	175,900	160,450	336,350
Enlarged numbers enrolled in special education	101,500	101,500	203,000
Enlarged numbers enrolled in kindergarten and nursery school	15,000	. . .	15,000
Reduction in number of teachers who are misassigned	35,200	24,700	59,900
Reinstatement of financially induced program cutbacks, and increased provision of at least minimally comprehensive school programs	1,000	11,000	12,000
Total	425,350	373,900	799,250

Source for Tables 1-3: "Teacher Supply and Demand in Public Schools, 1974," *NEA Research Memo 1975-3, May 1975,* pp. 8-10.

Table 2.
Summary of Estimates of the Supply and Demand for Public School Teachers, Fall 1974

Level and category of personnel	Supply	Demand to achieve minimum quality (Quality Criterion Estimate)			Actual demand Adjusted Trend (Criterion Estimate)		
		Demand	Supply minus demand	Supply as percent of demand	Demand	Supply minus demand	Supply as percent of demand
1	2	3	4	5	6	7	8
Elementary schools							
Beginning teachers	106,500	352,350	−245,850	30.2	57,600	48,900	184.9
Re-entering teachers	73,000	73,000	0	100.0	25,350	47,650	288.0
New teachers (total)	179,500	425,350	−245,850	42.2	82,950	96,550	216.4
Secondary schools							
Beginning teachers	116,950	337,600	−220,650	34.6	50,800	66,150	230.2
Re-entering teachers	36,300	36,300	0	100.0	20,700	15,600	175.4
New teachers (total)	153,250	373,900	−220,650	41.0	71,500	81,750	214.3
Total							
Beginning teachers	223,450	689,950	−466,500	32.4	108,400	115,050	206.1
Re-entering teachers	109,300	109,300	0	100.0	46,050	63,250	237.4
New teachers (total)	332,750	799,250	−466,500	41.6	154,450	178,300	215.4

Table 3.
Statistics About the Supply of and Demand for
Beginning Teachers in Public Schools, 1974

Number completing preparation to teach

Assignment area	1974	1973	Percent change, 1973 to 1974
1	2	3	4
ELEMENTARY			
Regular instruction	111,502	120,917	−7.8
Art	1,761	1,688	+4.3
Foreign language	285	316	−9.8
Music	1,550	1,540	+0.6
Phys. & health education	2,271	2,223	+2.2
Special education	11,432	10,804	+5.8
Total Elementary	128,801	137,488	−6.3
SECONDARY			
Agriculture	1,753	1,829	−4.2
Art	8,986	8,970	+0.2
Business education	8,753	9,514	−8.0
Distributive education	854	856	−0.2
English language arts (total) ...	(25,572)	(28,671)	(−10.8)
English	20,546	23,598	−12.9
Journalism	680	600	+13.3
Speech & dramatic arts	4,346	4,473	−2.8
Foreign languages (total)	(8,452)	(8,932)	(−5.4)
French	3,284	3,538	−7.2
German	928	995	−6.7
Latin	147	177	−16.9
Russian	82	106	−22.6
Spanish	3,669	3,844	−4.6
Other foreign language	342	272	+25.7
Home economics	7,628	8,156	−6.5
Industrial arts	5,847	5,809	+0.7
Junior high school (general) ...	569	806	−29.4
Mathematics	10,755	11,826	−9.1
Music	9,106	8,319	+9.5
Phys. & health ed. (total)	(24,952)	(25,016)	−(0.3)
Phys. & health ed.—boys	14,472	14,484	+0.1
Phys. & health ed.—girls	10,480	10,532	−0.5
Nat. & phys. sciences (total) ...	(10,633)	(11,092)	(−4.1)
Nat. & phys. sci. not spec. ...	1,976	2,084	−5.2
General science	1,293	1,367	−5.4
Biology	5,603	5,673	−1.2
Chemistry	1,123	1,260	−10.9
Physics....................	638	708	−9.9
Social sciences (total)	(29,651)	(32,136)	(−7.7)
Subject not specified	13,708	15,482	−11.5
Soc. studies (hist.-geog. etc.)	9,986	10,507	−5.0
Economics, sociol., psychol. .	3,790	3,745	+1.2
Other social studies	2,167	2,402	−9.8
Trade, indust., vocational, tech.	1,137	1,282	−11.3
Other secondary subjects	1,760	1,636	+7.6
Special education	11,431	10,803	+5.8
Total Secondary	167,839	175,653	−4.4
Total Elementary and Secondary	296,640	813,141	−5.3

| | Beginning teachers | | | Status November 1, 1973, of 1973 graduates prepared to teach | | |
| | | | | Percent employed | | |
Estimated supply, 1974	Estimated demand, 1974	Supply minus demand	Supply as percent of demand	In teaching	In other gainful employment	Percent seeking teaching position
5	6	7	8	9	10	11
92,900	47,406	45,494	196.0	54.9	6.8	10.4
1,467	1,267	200	115.8	47.4	8.7	12.1
237	230	7	103.0	67.6	2.9	4.0
1,291	1,843	−552	70.0	69.0	6.2	2.8
1,892	2,016	−124	93.8	53.6	5.3	6.5
8,713	4,838	3,875	180.1	60.0	4.0	5.7
106,500	57,600	48,900	184.9	55.0	6.8	10.3
1,213	711	502	170.6	51.4	16.3	0.7
6,218	1,575	4,643	394.8	42.7	11.2	11.7
6,057	2,692	3,365	225.0	41.9	21.2	6.4
591	356	235	166.0	51.8	16.6	6.7
17,697	8,534	(9,163)	(207.4)	(43.1)	10.7	11.0
14,219	8,022	6,197	177.3	44.7	10.3	11.1
471	85	386	554.1	39.2	12.2	9.2
3,007	427	2,580	704.2	34.9	12.8	10.6
5,849	1,778	(4,071)	(329.0)	(39.8)	10.8	12.9
2,273	530	1,743	428.9	...	...	...
642	293	349	219.1	...	...	...
102	75	27	136.0	...	...	...
57	11	46	518.2	...	...	...
2,539	841	1,698	301.9	...	...	...
236	28	208	842.9	...	...	...
5,279	2,692	2,587	196.1	47.6	13.7	8.2
4,046	2,235	1,811	181.0	60.4	13.2	3.5
...	...	...	...	57.2	7.5	4.3
7,443	5,283	2,160	140.9	58.3	10.0	6.1
6,301	2,235	4,066	281.9	56.7	8.3	6.1
17,269	4,674	(12,595)	(369.5)	(44.0)	12.4	11.7
10,016	2,337	7,679	428.6	41.9	13.9	10.9
7,253	2,337	4,916	310.4	46.8	10.5	12.8
7,358	4,572	(2,786)	(160.9)	(53.0)	9.8	5.9
...	...	...	...	54.5	9.8	6.8
...	...	...	...	56.9	8.2	4.5
...	...	...	...	52.4	10.0	6.6
...	...	...	...	51.2	10.6	3.4
...	...	...	...	49.7	10.1	4.7
20,519	5,182	(15,337)	(369.0)	(32.5)	14.4	12.7
...	...	...	...	...	...	...
...	...	...	...	...	...	...
...	...	...	...	...	...	...
...	...	...	...	...	...	...
787	2,032	−1,245	38.7	47.5	18.9	5.3
1,612	1,473	139	109.4	40.0	12.3	3.2
8,711	4,776	3,935	182.4	60.0	4.0	5.7
116,950	50,800	66,150	230.2	44.6	12.5	9.6
223,450	108,400	115,050	206.1	49.8	9.7	9.6

171

A PROFESSION AT RISK

Nine years have passed since the 1976 Bicentennial Report, *Educating a Profession*, was issued. The intervening years represent a period of both encouragement and frustration for those committed to strengthening the teaching profession and through it, our nation's schools. Recent events provide a new context for the report and the recommendations of AACTE's Bicentennial Commission on Education for the Profession of Teaching.

In 1976, the Bicentennial Commission's dominant interest was to stimulate recognition of teaching as a profession rather than an occupation. With its many subtleties and its unrealized potential, teaching seemed on the way to achieving full professional status. The following conditions seemed to ensure that professional recognition was imminent:

• Society's recognition of the importance of education was growing.
• The validated knowledge and skills base for the profession was growing and appeared likely to be incorporated into practice.
• The organized profession was growing in strength and influence.
• Teacher education was being more fully understood within the profession and throughout the academic community.
• Society was becoming more aware of the need for change in schools and for reconceptualizing the role and functions of teachers.
• The profession and responsible leaders throughout the nation seemed willing to work together toward common goals.

Frustrated by teaching's semiprofessional status, the commissioners believed that educators would take advantage of these conditions and mature as a profession. Nine years later, there are reasons for both satisfaction and discouragement.

First, the quality of education has become a major locus of attention and study. People are deeply concerned that American children and youth do not achieve as well in school as their age-mates in other developed nations. This concern has brought about intensive examination of education, as reflected in a host of reports and recommendations from different agencies and organizations.

Second, significant research and development progress has been made in expanding the knowledge and skills base of the teaching profession. No previous period has been as productive. Although the usual frustrating lag remains between knowledge generation and its implementation, impressive evidence shows some translation of this base into practice. These developments, however, have not been broadly incorporated into teacher education and school practice. As a result of an unfavorable economy and other conditions, teacher education has not yet achieved professional status.

Third, the organized profession has been slow to develop coalitions that generate action. However, some major efforts have been made and others are in prospect. The diversity of professional organizations engaging in narrow pursuits and working at cross purposes complicates the situation. Failure to act cooperatively threatens the ability of the profession to respond effectively to new challenges.

Fourth, little evidence can be found to show that teacher education is better accepted by the total education profession or by the academic community. The past nine years—the very time when progress seemed most likely to be made—have been characterized by economic difficulties for teacher education, with cutbacks, tight budgets, and declining enrollments. In the competition for scarce resources, teacher education has often been neglected.

Finally, those who direct teacher education in colleges and universities are not in accord regarding the changes needed to respond to the profession's challenges. This fact causes special concern. A survey, for example, of heads of schools, colleges, and departments of education (SCDEs) regarding their perceptions of methods for improving teacher education revealed a low level of support for some of the most important recommendations the Commission made. The report stated the following:

> No consensus emerged from department heads [deans] on methods to improve the teacher education curriculum. . . . "Increasing professional studies" was perceived as least important; only 15 percent of the department heads rated it highly important, while 41 percent said it was of low importance. . . .
>
> Another suggested method for improving teacher quality is extending teacher education beyond 4 years. SCDEs gave this method little support, a finding that contrasts sharply with the recommendations of many education authorities, both in testimony to the commission and in education literature. Only 5 percent had extended their teacher education programs, and only 15 percent expressed a high preference for doing so. Moreover, a majority (57 percent) gave this measure a low preference rating (not shown in table). It is not clear whether this lack of support represents the perception that such reform is undesirable, infeasible, or both.[1]

We have little reason to believe that this evidence misrepresents the level of acceptance for reforms in teacher education. Due to a lack of incentives, teacher educators and teachers are reluctant to assume the initiative for reform efforts.

A NATION AT RISK

In 1976, evidence was not as compelling as today that the educational system itself is in trouble. In the interim, significant evidence has accumulated

174

to indicate that the achievement levels of students in schools have deteriorated.[2] International data show that only the best of our students match those of other industrialized countries while the remainder fall far behind. This deterioration of standards is viewed as threatening our nation's position among developed nations, and it jeopardizes our ability to maintain the quality of life developed by previous generations. People are concerned not only about levels of learning, but also about violence, drug abuse, poor motivation, and lack of disciplined effort. Questions are raised about the basic ability of our schools to educate.

Public reactions to these findings have exceeded those of the post-Sputnik era in intensity. In response to the perceived problems in the schools, many organizations and agencies have established study groups to assess the situation and make recommendations. In April 1983 the National Commission on Excellence in Education released its report to "the nation and the Secretary of Education." Titled *A Nation At Risk: The Imperative for Educational Reform*, the report is "An Open Letter to the American People." Within the year more than 150 similar reports were released, each representing a serious effort by a responsible group. Though confusing in their multiplicity, the duplication provides a useful view of divergence as well as consensus. This need to give serious attention to schools is almost certain to persist. We hope the teaching profession will also be seen as worthy of reform efforts and will not be circumvented. The latter is likely to happen, however, if teacher educators remain aloof or downgrade their role.

A Nation At Risk reported:

> The teacher preparation curriculum is weighted heavily with courses in "educational methods" at the expense of courses in subjects to be taught. A survey of 1,350 institutions training teachers indicated that 41 percent of the time of elementary school teacher candidates is spent in education courses, which reduces the amount of time available for subject matter courses.[3]

Although this reference contains a serious statistical error, the sentiment is widespread. The National Center for Education Statistics' report for the National Commission on Excellence in Education clarified the 41 percent as 41.8 *semester credit hours*, which is only 32.65 percent of a 128-hour bachelor's degree program, or 34.83 percent of a 120-hour program. Apparently, hours were mistakenly cited as percentage. In fairness the report should have indicated that for students preparing to teach in secondary schools the corresponding credit hours are 28.8, or 24 percent of the total program. If teacher education is confined to the bachelor's program, neither the academic nor the professional needs can be fully satisfied. The allocation of course work to each component is inevitably an unfortunate compromise.

In addition, a national accreditation standard for all teacher education programs requires at least one-third of the curriculum for prospective teachers to be devoted to a sequence of studies in the symbolics of information, in natural and behavorial sciences, and in humanities. It should also be noted that state requirements for secondary teachers mandate an average of 38 percent of the baccalaureate program for general liberal studies and 33 percent for the academic teaching major. Only 29 percent is allotted for pedagogical study, of which a third or more is devoted to student teaching. Also ignored was a comparison with the credit hours devoted to professional course work in other professions; professional requirements in other fields far exceed those in teacher education.

Those who serve in the teaching profession, and particularly those who serve the profession in the education and training of teachers, might have anticipated that the reports would recommend an emphasis on upgrading the education of teachers. Specifically, they might have hoped for commitments that would implement the recommendations made nine years ago in *Educating a Profession*. However, such expectations were unfulfilled. Teacher education was largely ignored, but when mentioned was criticized and urged to improve by reducing the time devoted to pedagogical study.

A Nation At Risk paid little attention to the concept of equity inherent in Public Law 94-142, the Education for All Handicapped Children Act of 1975. This law mandates that every teacher must be prepared—by teacher education programs—to teach children with disabilities who are main-streamed from special classes into regular classes. All teachers are now expected to work with children who manifest the whole range of learning aptitudes and differences. No longer can teachers be protected from problems by excluding children with disabilities from their classrooms. Realization of the law's implications should sober those who believe that anyone can teach and that the solution to both quality and availability of teachers is to hire graduates who have no teacher preparation. It should also disabuse those who believe that teacher education can be improved by devoting *less* time and credit hours to professional education.

To the extent that the various reports discussed teacher education and the teaching profession, their approach was similar to *A Nation At Risk*. The reports contain general recommendations or exhortations to improve the preparation of teachers and the conditions under which they serve. Implicit throughout, however, are assumptions that excellence will be achieved by raising admission standards, imposing specific professional courses, increasing liberal studies, and including internships under highly qualified teachers.[4]

Most of the reports assume that the education of teachers occurs in traditional four-year college programs. Boyer, on the other hand, recommends eliminating the education major and requiring instead a "fifth year" of professional instruction and apprenticeship experience.[5] However, he is almost alone in this promotion of extended programs—a recommendation of the Bicentennial Commission nine years ago. The many reports continue to reflect a reluctance to commit resources to the professional preparation of teachers. Throughout the reports, the assumption is made that teaching effectiveness depends on academic subject matter, almost to the exclusion of pedagogical study. As long as this assumption predominates, both the teaching profession and the nation will remain at risk.

Another common theme is that "qualified outsiders" can and should be recruited to teach. This recommendation responds to the shortage of qualified teachers in mathematics, science, and technology, but its implications go far beyond these areas. Consider, for example, applying the recommendation to other professions: Imagine that because of the shortage of doctors in rural and minority areas "qualified outsiders" will be licensed to practice there. Use of inadequately trained personnel is a response to a crisis; as such it is a short-term response. Under normal conditions, qualified outsiders should be called upon only to enrich the classes of qualified, fully certified teachers. Teaching requires intensive and extensive preparation in general studies, the disciplines that undergird instruction, the academic subjects to be taught, and the generic and specialized knowledge and skills of pedagogy. As in the case of the other professions, the nation's interest in our educational system must be protected by uniform entry requirements based on rigorous and complete training.

The nation is at risk when any of its professions is severely weakened. Teaching is such a profession, and national study groups do the nation harm when they slight the sources of teaching expertise—the research and development that undergirds professional knowledge and skills, and the professional training that provides the basis for practice. The basis for the genuine, sound practice of pedagogy is substantial and growing dramatically. If the nation wants to reduce its risk, it must upgrade the teaching profession *and* the conditions under which teachers practice. The achievement of one goal is inextricably linked to the other.

PROFESSIONALISM REVISITED

The Bicentennial Commission was aware that the context in which a profession exists and serves markedly affects its development. A considerable part of its report is devoted to describing such conditions and making recommendations. It now seems evident that considerably greater attention should have been given to the conditions, forces, and influences that shape the profession and determine the quality of its practice.

Events in the broader society also have prevented professional development. Not foreseen in the upbeat mid-'70s were factors that would affect society in general and teaching and teacher education in particular. Circumstances brought about reductions in funding for education and other social sectors, efforts to move policy decisions from national to state and local control, and a psychological climate of conservatism, discouragement, and insularity. Although the relative strength and consequent impact of these factors upon teachers and teacher education are impossible to assess with accuracy, we believe there are still opportunities for realizing our aspirations.

Aspirations can condition reality. Too often, lack of vision becomes a

177

major obstacle to overcoming our problems. Dewey, referring to the power of an ideal, reminds us that just as aims and ideals are changed as they are applied to existent conditions, so too are existent conditions modified by interaction between the ideal and the real.

The position taken in *Educating a Profession* is that quality in schooling depends upon the effective interface of *two* institutions, each of which must be strong. One is the *school*, which delivers educational services; the other is the *profession*, which provides the educational services within the school. The Bicentennial Commission believed in 1976 that the United States had concentrated its energies and commitments on developing a strong system of delivery institutions—the schools—but had neglected or even suppressed the development of the teaching profession, which would provide the expertise necessary to accomplish school goals. The Commission's recommendations pointed out the need to reverse this tendency.

The logic of the Commission's position is straightforward. Society needs a multiplicity of services. All societies create organizations and institutions to deliver those services, and all organizations and institutions have people who perform the services. Work is specialized and categorized as occupations, trades, and professions; the latter require specialized knowledge, intensive academic preparation, and a high level of expertise. Medicine, law, and the university professoriate are widely recognized as established professions. In serving society, the professions develop, have custody of, and are responsible for their members' knowledge and skills. To provide a place where the services are rendered, public or private organizations are established. Courts, hospitals and clinics, university laboratories and classrooms are examples of such delivery institutions. Service is provided at the interface between *organized professions* and *delivery institutions*. Each is autonomous; neither controls nor is responsible to the other; and each is accountable to the society.

Educating a Profession stated that teaching is by its nature a profession, but it has been slow in developing a "professional culture of teaching," that is, an advanced body of specialized knowledge and an extensive repertoire of behaviors and skills needed in professional practice. Because teaching has long been perceived as a skill that can be learned within the general culture, few people recognize the need for preparation in pedagogy, the science of teaching. However, the public does recognize the need for preparation in the academic subjects that the teacher will teach and in general education. This view is continually reinforced by the academic units in universities where pedagogy is undervalued or actively disdained. The Bicentennial Commission maintained that teachers must have both academic and professional expertise. Knowing the subjects to be taught does not qualify a person to teach any more than knowing anatomy qualifies one to be a surgeon or knowing the law admits one to the bar.

Because of its belief in the teacher's need for increased professional expertise and stronger academic preparation (at least five years plus an internship), the Commission suggested that the profession consider a future in which fully prepared teachers would hold a Doctor of Teaching professional degree. The group also recommended a greater investment in research and development to support the professional base of teaching. In addition, it recognized the need for the practicing teacher and the teacher educator to work together for a stronger profession and more effective schools.

A PROFESSION AT RISK

Unless and until technical substitutes are developed for conventional instruction, live teaching will remain the dominant strategy of schooling. The great need for dedicated, professionally competent teachers will continue, as will the rationale that teachers are most effective when, in addition to personal qualities and academic knowledge, they possess professional knowledge and skills and interact with students in conducive conditions. Learning to teach in new, improved ways is no accident. It happens because of pedagogical instruction, supervised practice teaching, internships, and continuous inservice development. Why the teaching profession should be denied this process while it is demanded of other professions is difficult to understand or explain.

The National Commission on Excellence in Education concluded its report with this assertion:

> It is their America, and the America of all of us, that is at risk; it is to each of us that this imperative is addressed. It is by our willingness to take up the challenge, and our resolve to see it through, that America's place in the world will be either secured or forfeited. Americans have succeeded before and so we shall again.[6]

All would hope that such optimism is justified, but hope is not enough. Success will depend on identifying key elements in complex educational systems and dealing effectively with these elements as they interact.

The current reports on education, including *A Nation At Risk*, tend to follow the popular bias in undervaluing the importance and the status of the teaching profession. The authors have focused their studies on the crises in schooling and educational outcomes and their reports on the schools, the delivery institutions. They have addressed superficially or ignored the profession and the institutions that educate professional teachers. Had their charge been to study a crisis in the delivery of medical or legal services, the competence of professionals and the conditions of their preparation and practice would not likely have been slighted or ignored.

The conditions for professional practice called for in the Bicentennial report still do not exist. Further, it is now apparent that the educational system will not improve by merely changing programs of teacher education at colleges and universities. If we prepare teachers with the latest knowledge and skills and place them in work situations where they cannot use their knowledge and skills, we will just produce more candidates for the teacher resignation list. Unless we change the conditions for professional practice, teaching will not become a profession. Reforming teacher education will not be enough. We will not improve the professional status of teaching by merely expanding the knowledge and skills of teachers. These are essential but insufficient to achieve professionalism. Indeed, the *professional culture of teaching*, on which the Bicentennial Commission placed its hopes, may be a false hope given the dominance exercised by the system of schooling—state and university control. The system itself must also be challenged to improve.

ALTERNATIVE PERSPECTIVES ON PROFESSIONS

Johnson, an English sociologist, brought to the study of professions a different approach from the one used in *Educating a Profession*.[7] Rather than classifying professions on the basis of possession or nonpossession of given characteristics, he suggested that what happens to a professional occupation depends upon the conditions under which the profession is practiced. Of particular importance, according to Johnson, is control of the profession, i.e., the source and exercise of power.

A major theme in Johnson's work is the inherent tension or conflict between professionals and the clients who use their services. Professionals seek autonomy while consumers seek to retain control. "Power relationships will determine whether uncertainty is reduced at the expense of producer or consumer."[8] Further, "the social distance which is generated in the relationship between the practitioner and the client is partly the product of factors other than the expertise of one and the ignorance of the other."[9] He described three ways by which power relationships are resolved: Collegiate; Patronage; and Mediation.

Collegiate is the concept that the Bicentennial Commission used in *Educating a Profession*. The authority of the profession, rooted in expertise in the area of need, causes the clients to yield control to the organized profession and its practitioners. The profession develops toward the ideal condition with both society and the profession reaping the benefits.

Patronage is closely akin to practices of the Middle Ages when artists and musicians were maintained and supported by people of privilege, their patrons. In its modern counterpart, professionals are employed by organizations or corporations "where the dominant demand for occupational services comes from a small, powerful, unitary clientele."[10] Corporate accounting is cited as an example. The corporation sets its requirements for service and the profession accepts the corporate intrusion on professional autonomy.

Mediation occurs when "the state intervenes in the relationship between practitioner and client in order to define needs and/or the manner in which such needs are catered for," or "the state attempts to remove from the producer or the consumer the authority to determine the content and subjects of practice."[11]

180

Johnson's descriptions of these concepts open new avenues for examining the teaching profession and its conditions. Without abandoning the ideal of a profession in the *collegiate* sense, the teaching profession will need to develop new perceptions, new intermediate objectives, and new strategies. Clearly, it is futile for the profession to cling to the ideal of a profession without addressing the power relationships that are necessary to working out the tension between the profession and the client system.

The Teaching Profession as Patronage or Mediation

Both *patronage* and *mediation* as means of control can be applied to the present relationship of the teaching profession to public education. Whether one chooses patronage or mediation probably depends upon the definition of client, which can be student, parent, community, employer, or the state. Public schools throughout their history have been subject to local control, but this control has been eroding steadily in favor of increased centralization. Because school districts are creations of the state, they are subject to state discretion as to the scope of their authority. In this sense the state is the owner, and patronage is its form of control. Under such a condition, mediation is at best a tactic and at worst a ploy.

The failure of the teaching profession to mature may be a result of the paradox in which it finds itself: The mediator is also the patron. In such a case, relatively futile confrontation, political action, or supplication are the available resources for teachers. State boards of education and legislatures have the option of acting as mediators between the profession—which they control—and the local communities—which they invest with power; or they can revert to the role of patron whenever it is to their advantage. A subtle tyranny is inherent in this arrangement, a tyranny that is felt, if not identified, by the teaching profession and that may account for the accepting, submissive behavior so typically displayed among teachers.

It is not unique to education that professional practitioners experience mediation of their role and interference with their professional authority and responsibility. The phenomenon is present wherever professionals are employed by institutions or organizations. The needs of the organization and those of the profession and the professionals often come into some degree of conflict. In Johnson's sense, tension is generated. Except when the group of employed professionals has organized to protect itself, the tension is likely to be resolved in favor of the organization. When the organization is the state or its local educational subdivision, the power of law is behind it and the processes of redress or change are difficult.

The difficulty of achieving any reasonable measure of control over their destiny and condition seems in part to explain the behaviors and attitudes of teachers. Living at or near the bottom of a vast bureaucratic hierarchy, which takes unto itself control of all aspects of the system and which pays slight deference to the professional aspects of teaching, results in teachers' passive acceptance. In this way the school system tends to suppress talent and initiative, and to sacrifice the creative energies and contributions of the people on whom it depends.

The Extent of Patronage

Quite different from other professions, the teaching profession emerged long after its delivery system (schools) was in place. States began mandating public schools almost 200 years before they introduced normal schools as separate training institutions for teachers, with graduation from these as the basis for certification. From this origin the teaching profession *in both its preparation and its practice* became a part of the state and local system of schools. Efforts to win a reasonable measure of control over its destiny or to gain the conditions necessary to its practice have failed.

Characteristic of semiprofessions, an administrative and supervisory superstructure in education has emerged and assumed many of the functions usually performed within a profession. Teachers have become a subtly rule-directed work force. The states continue to control not only the schools, their clientele, the curriculum, textbooks, testing, resource allocation, in-service education, management, and supervision, but also the preparation and licensure of all who serve in professional capacities in the schools. Thus, the system is mediated to the point of patronage. The profession has little to say and little power in matters that concern it. A recent observer commissioned by the Ford Foundation to study schools of education wrote:

> Teachers in the United States have long (perhaps always) been severely limited in the exercise of anything that might be considered professional autonomy. School boards, directly and through appointed superintendents, expect to resolve all important questions related to educational policy and practice. Teachers are made to feel that they are no more than the hired servants of volatile bodies for which they often have little respect. Teachers have no clients; they only have patrons.[12]

One of the more serious impediments to the professionalization of teaching is the nature of the administrative hierarchy within the school system and the way it chooses to exercise its responsibility. Unlike the management systems common in other organizations staffed by professionals, educational managers have both professional (former teachers) and management (school administration) sources of authority. They have been delegated responsibility for policy making, management, and supervision, including the direct supervision of teachers. In addition, because they have teaching certificates, teaching experience, and advanced degrees in education, they are viewed and tend to view themselves as having knowledge, expertise, and wisdom that transcends that of teachers. Teachers, because of their position in the hierarchical structure, are subordinate to principals and superintendents in matters of administration, instruction, curricula, and educational leadership.

It is not that administrators have had more preparation in pedagogy and curriculum or more experience in classroom teaching. Often their experience as teachers is relatively short and their pedagogical training is typically neglected in graduate studies in favor of preparation for administration. Appointment as an administrator or supervisor in a school system inevitably carries an assumption of the professional expertise necessary to perform the functions. This is an affront to legitimate expertise and to teachers who strive to continue their own professional education and enlarge their own repertoire. Their professional role and function have been preempted, leaving them as subordinates. Small wonder that so many prepare for administration and seek release from the classroom.

In all mature professions the practitioner's authority to act derives from the profession, is legitimized by the license, and is paramount. In these professions administrators facilitate practice but neither control nor supervise it. The practitioner is accountable to the profession, not to the managers, for performance. For these reasons managers in other professions seldom are drawn from members of the profession.

In Pursuit of Professional Autonomy

Little legal or constitutional basis exists for challenging the exercise of state control of the teaching profession or the subordination of the teaching profession to the institutions that deliver educational services. Responsibility for education under the Constitution is a residual power of the states. Control of professions through accreditation and licensure also is a state function. Whatever basis there is for challenging this system must lie in public recognition of the consequences and the perceived advantages that an alternative system might offer. To achieve a desirable level of professional autonomy, teachers will have to convince themselves and the public, the legislatures, and state boards that policy with respect to the teaching profession is seriously in error and that the consequences of such error undermine and threaten the public schools.

Reaching this level of understanding has been made more difficult by the long, and understandably adversarial posture of teacher organizations regarding salaries, benefits, conditions of work, and appropriate professional status. The difficulty is further confounded by the reality that teachers would be confronting an administrative hierarchy over the source of its authority to preside over the *professional* process of the workplace. From its position of advantage, the management position would be both dangerous and difficult to assault.

A problem with the present system of control is that almost everyone accepts it or takes it for granted. Rarely are the assumptions upon which it is based questioned deeply enough to prompt new insights. In contrast, management theory and practice as they apply in corporate and organizational life are being questioned.

Progress has been made, and in some respects the stage has been set for developing the conditions of a profession. Some 20 states already have passed professional practices acts. In Texas, for example, legislation ordered that "Teaching is hereby declared to be and is recognized as a profession. The members of such profession shall accept responsibilities incumbent upon them to serve and improve the teaching profession in the state."[13] In implementing the bill, the Texas State Board of Education undertook to grant to the Professional Practices Commission the sole right to initiate provisions, practices, and standards respecting the teaching profession and teacher education. The board still mediates, but from a position of enhanced recognition of the profession.

Productivity is today a major concern in a wide variety of production and service organizations, and reports indicate that new kinds of control and power relationships—such as quality control groups—increase worker satisfaction and output. It seems reasonable to anticipate that schools also could profit from such changes. One solution that has reappeared in the current rhetoric over quality in schools is differentiated status and roles of teachers (e.g., master teacher, teacher, apprentice teacher). Such a development is consistent, for example, with the medical profession (e.g., specialist, doctor, intern) and is sound in principle, provided there is a genuine differentiation of status, role, and responsibility. Such differentiation is not likely if schools continue to use the single teacher, self-contained classroom model. A highly desirable transfer of some function now reserved to administration to a professional teaching team could provide a basis for differentiation. Functions that would lend themselves to such transfer or sharing include consultation, supervision, evaluation, staff development, resource allocation, continuing education, and involvement in preservice and inservice teacher education. Such a change in policy and practice could be expected to contribute to a shift from the mediated toward the collegiate mode, and simultaneously improve the effectiveness of schools.

Master teachers are central to this development. However, the rhetoric of the national reports on education indicates that the master teacher recommendations are based upon a preoccupation with finding a way to introduce merit pay for teachers. For master teachers, higher pay schedules must be subordinate to role definition and to a reorganization and reallocation of functions. Otherwise, such efforts will fail.

From a long-term perspective, the loss to the nation of its ability to educate would be more serious than the loss of its ability to compete in world markets with quality goods at favorable prices. The improved education of its teachers and the provision of conditions that satisfy, reward, and motivate them should be high on the national agenda. Solutions will not be reached by mandates, tighter control, or even tangible rewards. Teachers already possess the desire to assume professional responsibility; what they need is the freedom to implement this commitment.

Explicit Role for the Profession

As the teaching profession seeks the conditions under which it can more effectively serve the schools and the public, it should itself be clear and it should make clear to the public that *the schools belong to the people* and not to professional educators. The role of the profession is to provide expert pedagogical services that implement the public curriculum in achieving the goals and objectives set for the schools. In doing so, it bears and exercises the professional responsibility of advising the public on matters of curriculum and instructional conditions within the schools. Obversely, the public retains the right, through its legislatures, to exercise the necessary control over the profession.

The principle of dual sources of authority is common to all professions in society. The public interest is best served when the public decides *the what*, and the profession, *the how* and *the when*. Each must respect the role of the other. If this principle cannot be applied to teaching, the schools are deprived of the services of a mature profession and remain in jeopardy.

INCLUSIONARY SCHOOLING: IMPACT ON THE PROFESSION

In the two years while the Bicentennial Commission was preparing its report, there was reason for optimism that public policy would embrace a genuine profession of teaching. Education was moving up on the nation's agenda. Congress and the Courts were taking the final steps in a long process of ending the *exclusionary* practices of schools and making them *inclusionary*.

Because inclusionary schools make much greater demands on the professional skills of teachers than do exclusionary schools, it seemed logical to expect that upgrading the preparation and professionalism of teachers would also be placed high on the agenda. Once again, however, such logic did not predict reality. In our society, rigorous education and high level expertise seem to be important for all professionals except professional teachers.

Exclusion is the practice of removing from a population of students those who are sufficiently different from the other students to require an undue amount of special attention or to cause disruption of the teaching/learning process. Its purpose is to reduce "the range of pupil profiles (educational, social, and behavioral characteristics)" in a class to a level that can be handled effectively.[14] Within limits, exclusion is a sound educational principle for teaching; but it lends itself to discrimination and socially unacceptable consequences.

Inclusion, on the other hand, achieves the purposes and benefits of interaction and provides social justice; but it increases the problems teachers face with diverse groups having widely divergent needs. Educators have a relatively small number of alternative instructional strategies with which to

185

address the increasing range of pupil profiles. Smaller classes, special and more advanced training for teachers, assistance from teacher aides and specialists, teams of teachers, technology, and instructional materials all have potential. *However, the most promising, most economically feasible approach is to ensure that the central actor—the teacher—possesses a level of knowledge and skill necessary to effectiveness in any teaching situation, and particularly where a broad range of profiles is present.*

Exclusion was common practice in American schools for the first 300 years of their existence. Before compulsory attendance, students who proved to be problems for the teacher could be allowed, encouraged, or required to stay away. Later they could be placed in special education, and often learning-reluctant and behavior-problem students with no diagnosed handicapping condition were so assigned. Tracking permitted students to be sorted into slow, middle, and fast groupings and placed in separate classes. Vocational education was used in the higher grades for those deemed to lack academic interest or aptitude. Many failed or repeated grades. In a different form, exclusion was also practiced through housing patterns coupled with neighborhood schools.

The exclusionary school was, in considerable part, a reflection of the inadequacy of the schools and the teaching profession of the time. Inadequate facilities and resources, large classes, minimally prepared and educated teachers, and the needs and value systems of the times all combined to limit what the schools could undertake. Also the belief that the individual was responsible for his or her destiny prevailed. Sociological considerations did not join psychological and philosophical ones in influencing educational policy until the middle of the 20th century. Increasingly, students demonstrated that people are fashioned in considerable part by an environment over which many have no control. To change their destinies requires active intervention, which is a public responsibility. This recognition became part of the Great Society, and out of it ultimately came the inclusionary commitment in education.

Reversal of exclusionary practices began in 1954 with the *Brown* decision, which ruled that separate schools for black students were inherently unequal and hence illegal. The desegregation-integration inclusionary process, driven by the civil rights and equal opportunity movements, progressed steadily through the 1960s and '70s. Multicultural education, bilingual education, and equal rights for women were mandated. At the same time, the inclusion of students was sought through redistricting, mandatory busing across district boundaries, and more recently, magnet schools. Thus, social and educational policies were made to conform to constitutional rights.

Perhaps the most significant event in the process was the passage in 1975 of P.L. 94-142, the Education for All Handicapped Children Act. Under its provisions, students with disabilities were to be mainstreamed into regular school settings to the extent to which they could profit. Needed special services were mandated and each student was to have a contractually arranged

Individual Education Plan (IEP). Thus, the inclusionary school was finally achieved on a public policy level.

By the late 1970s, however, as the economy weakened, the cost of social programs mounted, and the complexity of problems became more apparent, privileged groups lost much of their enthusiasm for inclusionary reforms. Retreats from commitments began to occur. Retreats have been evident in the legislative repeal of court-ordered busing, the withholding of resources to public schools (particularly in the aftermath of Serrano v. Priest), the imposition of spending and tax limitations, the controversy related to educating the children of illegal aliens, the disagreements over bilingual education, and in widespread disputes over textbook selection and curriculum determination. Public groups also are exercising censorship in the name of morality and religion. A return to forms of exclusion was introduced in many states and school systems as basic skills assessment programs were mandated and as progress through the grades was made dependent on meeting minimum test scores. Such moves were not necessarily backward nor more than intermediate correctives. In overall perspective, however, a retreat is evident. Further retreats may occur as a result of inclination of state education departments and boards of education to restrict local initiatives and impose more restrictive regulations and controls.

The Reagan Administration established a new federal agenda for education. This called for the dismantling of the recently established U.S. Department of Education, the consolidation of existing programs through block grants and their reallocation to the states, the reduction and refocusing of various inclusionary school program efforts, and the diminution or elimination of many of the equity programs. The recasting of programs to emphasize efficiency and the establishment of the New Federalism as an overall agenda were particularly damaging to the aspirations of the teaching profession. The Education Consolidation Act of 1981 (P.L. 97-35) reinforced the occupational control efforts of the states and undermined the efforts of teachers to achieve a degree of professional autonomy.

The ultimate success of inclusionary schools as a social commitment and experiment depends upon the resources that can be made available. If schools cannot cope with the range of profiles and provide and maintain quality education for all, public education will fail to meet its obligation. A most tragic reaction would be to abandon our commitment to the inclusionary school, yet ample evidence is showing sentiment in this direction. More probable, however, are selective exemptions. In keeping with the concerns of A Nation At Risk and other studies, one exception could be separation (reverse exclusion) of the most academically talented for enriched schooling and a continuation of inclusionary schooling for the remainder. There is already a widespread trend toward private schooling, which by its nature is exclusionary and which in its practices restricts the range of pupil profiles. Also evident is continuing pressure in support of assistance to those who resort to the private option via tax relief or tuition vouchers—rationalized on grounds of relief to the public system by removing students from its responsibility.

Overlooked in such arguments is the probability—perhaps certainty—that the problems of inclusionary schools will increase in intensity as the privileged depart and the less privileged remain. Educability and socioeconomic status are closely related. The inclusionary school was designed to spread the burdens of equal access over the whole population. Voluntary exclusion, however much a matter of constitutional right, returns the problems to the people that inclusion was designed to help. Paying people with public funds to facilitate the exclusionary process undermines the fundamental purpose of public education. Parental concern for their children's education cannot be permitted to cause educational inequities for other children.

In the interests of the schools and their effectiveness, classes must continue to be "teachable groups." The incidence of widely atypical and problem students in one setting has to be kept within manageable limits. Voluntary exclusion ultimately could diminish the capacity of the schools to maintain the wholesome balance of profiles necessary to the pursuit of learning. Inclusionary schooling is public risk-taking in pursuit of equity and social justice. The privileged owe it to the nation to share in the risk-taking in pursuit of higher social goals. They also demonstrate their support to teachers by sending their children to and actively participating in public schools.

Providing public assistance to those who resort to private schools could, for schooling purposes, expand the privileged group so that it includes much of the middle class. It is unlikely that the public schools as we have known them can survive such change, because the middle class has long been the backbone of the public school system. Removal of the middle class not only would directly damage the schools, but also would undermine the political support that schools have enjoyed at all levels of government. A direct vested interest through their children has kept most of the public involved and supportive.

In the context of the inclusionary school, it would seem impossible to overstate the case for strengthening the work force on which the human services school must rely. It is unthinkable that the schools, which served earlier generations so well, would be unable to continue because they cannot compete for teacher talent.

As the current national reports have clearly revealed, there is an educational crisis, but accuracy in identifying the problem does not necessarily validate the explanations offered for its causes or the prescriptions proposed for its solution. The studies have generally not grasped either the needs of a teaching profession, or the conditions of making it a vital force in improving schools.

Education's challenge can best be realized by starting with the assumptions that every class is inclusionary: Each has a range of pupil profiles, including mainstreamed special education students, immigrant children with different languages and cultures, and minority students such as blacks and Hispanics;

188

and that among the pupils is a wide range of aptitudes, interests, and motivation. In the presence of such assumptions, the notion that teaching is a relatively simple task becomes unthinkable and subversive of schools and the teaching profession. Inclusive schools demand the highest level of professional preparation for teachers and the most favorable conditions of service. Those who would help the schools should start by examining the present state of the long ignored and neglected profession of teaching. It is neglected at our nation's risk.

BALANCE AND BREADTH IN TEACHERS' PROFESSIONAL REPERTOIRE

Educating a Profession affirmed that teaching is an emerging profession and that, in common with other professions, it possesses "a professional culture of teaching." That culture, consisting of "a body of knowledge and repertoire of behaviors and skills needed in the practice of the profession," was viewed in 1976 as seriously deficient but rapidly emerging. It was portrayed as needing systematic expansion through research and development.

In the intervening years, progress has met or exceeded the most optimistic expectations or predictions, and the pace continues. Ethnographic studies of schooling and teaching have been useful. These have revealed the essential importance of *time on task* and closely related strategies of *direct teaching*, *classroom management*, and *reinforcement*. Effective school studies have provided further evidence on the conditions of teaching, evidence that emphasizes leadership. A comprehensive study in Florida has provided teacher education with a careful compilation of research applications to teaching practices that are effective and ineffective.[15] The March 1983 issue of the *Elementary School Journal* reported extensive research findings on teaching effectiveness. Other journals also have increased their reporting of such research. This condition is markedly different from the situation a few years ago when research was limited and fragmentary.

The enthusiasm of the profession for these developments should not be allowed to narrow the concept of "repertoire." The teacher presides over many kinds of learning activities in many settings, and no one strategy of instruction can prevail. The new emphasis on direct teaching must be tempered with indirect teaching that addresses other learning objectives and responds to the learning needs of different children. Tomlinson implied that the common thread of meaning found in research on academically effective schools is that they are organized on behalf of consistent and undeviating pursuit of learning.[16] The common energies of all the parties to the enterprise—principals, teachers, parents, and students—are spent on teaching and learning in a systematic fashion. However, Peck and Veldman cautioned that

> beyond some moderate point, . . . those who get children to learn by mechanical, atomized knowledge and skills tapped by standardized

achievement tests might unwittingly deter other kinds of learning, creating a subtly depressing, low risk-taking atmosphere that could conceivably keep children from learning to cope vigorously, self-reliantly and happily with problems of learning and living.[17]

Brophy and Evertson concluded that

effective teaching is not simply a matter of implementing a small number of "basic" teaching skills. Instead, effective teaching requires the ability to implement a very large number of diagnostic, instructional, managerial, and therapeutic skills, tailoring behavior in specific contexts and specific situations to the specific needs of the moment.[18]

These passages remind us again of the unique, complex nature of the profession of teaching. No other profession serves a clientele that attends *in groups* under *in loco parentis* conditions on a *compulsory basis* in a *custodial setting* for *developmental purposes* over *sustained periods* of time. Individuals, the group and ever-changing subgroups must be managed attentively. As a result, detailed prescriptions for each specific situation elude the professional teacher; a wide array of instructional approaches is needed.

Constructs for Understanding the Profession

It is difficult to completely rationalize the complex process of how the teaching profession inducts and socializes its members. Much of the process continues to be inscrutable despite rapid progress in research and conceptual development.

Two widely accepted constructs are useful for understanding the concepts of teaching repertoire and effectiveness; each is worthy of elaboration. These are *linkage or coupling* and *interaction and emergence*. The first construct refers to the looseness or tightness of association among events (i.e., What is the probability that one event will be accompanied by another?). The second construct describes a systemic process by which behaviors, such as teaching, gradually "emerge" from interactions over time (see Figure 1).

Researchers and teachers are aware of the loose coupling between specific teaching practices and pupil behaviors or outcomes, and of the difficulty of controlling the many variables in research to identify whether couplings are tight or loose. Despite much progress, the profession faces a continuance of this problem and challenge. Recognition of the limitations of research should be accompanied by an impatient search for more powerful methodologies.

It is hoped that the public and those involved in public policy making can also become more enlightened regarding the sophisticated nature of teaching. Such understanding might increase public and private funding for educational research.

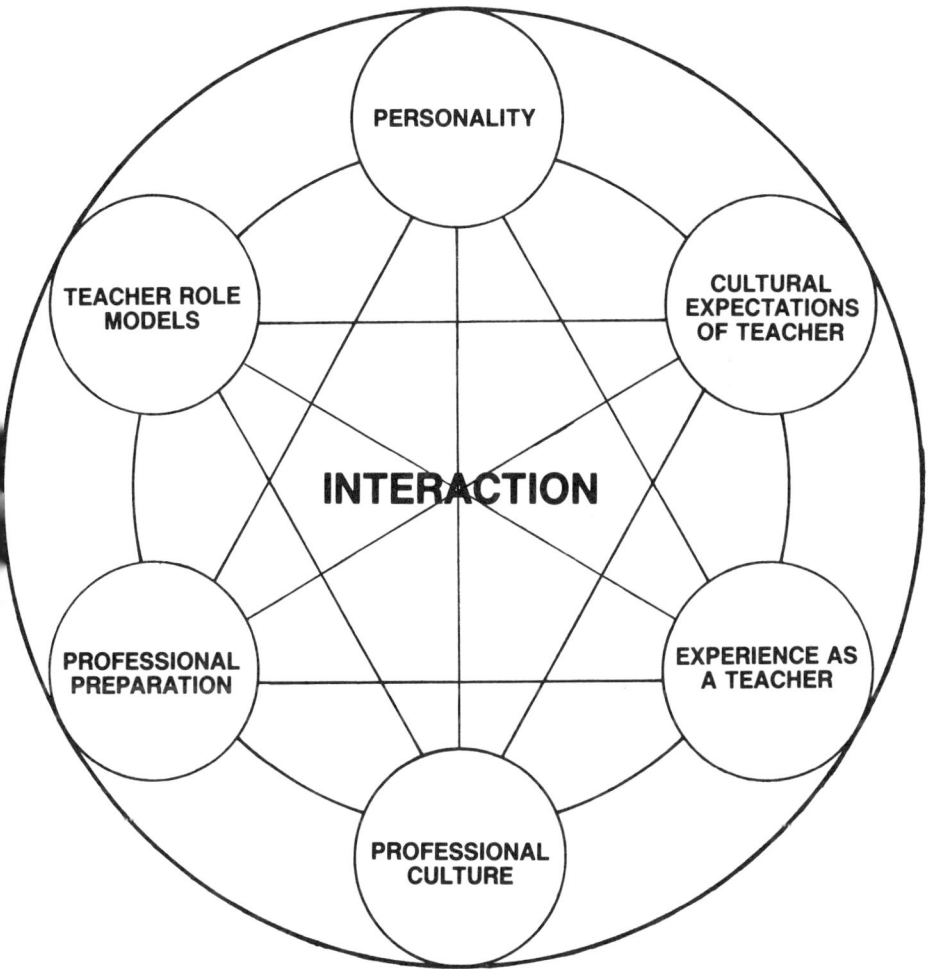

FIGURE 1
TEACHER DEVELOPMENT, INTERACTION, AND EMERGENCE
A SYSTEMIC PROCESS

In the meantime, it may be well to remind ourselves that universal agreement on precisely "the best" modes of teaching might facilitate mind and behavior controls that would be abhorrent. The public might be the first to reject the idea that teachers—by rule prescription, close control, and supervision—would be serving the public interest. A more tightly coupled, broad range of knowledge and skills, which teachers would use in accordance with professional judgment, is a more acceptable goal. Broadening rather than narrowing the repertoire should be the objective. At present, we are far from achieving it, and not all seem to recognize the need, or want it. Their hesitance and doubt are confirmed by the lack of research on teaching and learning in schools and in teacher education in general. The challenges to the teaching profession and to the educational system are to increase the pace of development efforts and to keep teachers abreast of new knowledge and skills as they emerge.

In living systems theory, the construct of interaction and emergence describes how living organisms interact with other elements in their environment and emerge changed but stable and more able to cope with their environment.[19] The construct should be declared a guiding principle of the teaching profession and teacher education. Students enter preparation programs as living systems already fashioned by individuality, personal experience, culture, teacher role models, and a host of other related influences extending over two decades of life; they emerge as potential teachers. After a dozen years of going to school for a thousand hours per year, students entering teacher preparation know much about schools and the way teachers perform. They do not know why teachers do what they do or understand the theoretical basis for decisions. They have little understanding of how the knowledge, philosophy, and skills of pedagogy have guided their teachers those many years. Without pedagogical study, they are victims of the accidents of prior experience.

In no other profession are clients subject to such prolonged exposure to professionals. The result is that many are misled into believing they can practice the profession with little or no formal training. As a consequence, no other profession has the same problem of having to justify the need for extended preparation to its own students, to academic colleagues in colleges and universities, to the public, and even to employers.

A graduate of the school system with a satisfactory record of achievement may enroll in a teacher education program. Unlike the other professions, the teacher education student is not naive and helpless in the absence of training. For better or worse, the teacher has been trained by culture and experience. That imprinting cannot be erased, but it must *interact* with the teacher preparation experience and from that experience a *professional teacher* must emerge. Further, the interaction will continue as the teacher experiences and learns on a career-long basis. The teacher is shaped by the conditions of the community, the school system, the teaching profession, and other forces.

The nature of teacher education and school practice demands of teachers a lifelong commitment to interaction and emergence. In place of a prescribed list of behaviors for each situation, there is an evolving repertoire that leads to teacher growth.

Whether the teacher wholeheartedly interacts and emerges depends on many factors, including conditions in the workplace. Most favorable to growth is a collegial situation; least favorable is a mediation condition where control is emphasized. Much current rhetoric, including that in the latest national studies, has strong control implications for the work of teaching and the role of the school. The consequences that result from interaction with outside controls are quite different from collegial interaction occurring in a professional environment. If we change without reflecting, the cure may be worse than the malady.

The newly re-inspired interest in education will result, we hope, in a new climate for the teaching profession. In it the teacher will continue in both the workplace and the profession to seek inputs from the emerging profession, continuing education, personal experience, experimentation, and colleagues. The personal repertoire of teachers will grow and improve. *Conscious interaction and emergence by its practitioners is the best hope of creating a profession.*

Balance Among Program Components

The concepts of balance and breadth in a teacher's repertoire extend to the needs of teachers to have strength both in one or more academic disciplines and in professional pedagogy. In 1976, the Bicentennial Commission identified the following essential components of a preparation program for teachers: (1) general or liberal studies; (2) the undergirding disciplines of the teaching profession; (3) academic teaching field(s); (4) the foundations of education; (5) pedagogy; and (6) supervised experience in schools. Each is essential, and none may be neglected or deemphasized. These six areas inevitably compete for adequate shares in the traditional four-year life space. Such limited life space cannot accommodate high quality preparation of teachers. Professional components suffer most in four-year programs, because students have no opportunity to make use of the most necessary and effective strategies of instruction. "Learning about" substitutes for "learning to" in clinical and real settings. Such training deficiencies force the beginning teacher to draw heavily on role models from early school days and personal experience. It simply is impossible to achieve the purposes of both teacher education and academic preparation in 120 to 130 semester credit hours. It was this realization that led the Bicentennial Commission to insist that the preparation period be expanded to at least five years as an interim step, with the professional school six-year model as the ultimate goal.

With the exception of a small number of developmental efforts, expanding the length of programs has failed to be realized. Teaching is so deeply imbedded in culture and custom that even crises do not readily lead to change. Teacher educators themselves do not adequately make the case for the time and resources needed to prepare beginning teachers to a reasonable level of professionalism. The authors of the prestigious national studies also ignored this need. Instead, the reports simply overlooked teacher education or called for its improvement with a few simplistic suggestions for change. Just as Flexner clearly saw that the quality of health services depended on rigorous preparation in quality professional medical schools, teacher educators now know that effective schools in our democratic society require substantial new commitments to the process of teacher education.

REAFFIRMATION AND CHALLENGE

Despite a decrease in confidence in public education, some evidence shows that many of the conditions the Bicentennial Commission believed important nine years ago are closer to being realized. Governors in 20 states have announced their intention to support public education as one of their priorities. Both political parties included education on their agenda for the 1984 national elections. A host of state legislative and regional initiatives designed to strengthen education have been mounted. The shortage of math and science teachers is receiving national attention. The public's ratings of the schools has stopped declining and Gallup Poll data show that the nation holds the schools in relatively high regard when compared with other public institutions.[20] These developments, when combined with the significant achievements made in expanding the professional knowledge base and the seriousness with which teachers and teacher educators are attempting to make use of that knowledge base, provide some basis for cautious optimism.

Mission and Role of Schools, Colleges, and Departments of Education

Only if the best institutions care about schools and their own schools of education will the public think they are worth caring about; and nothing could be more clearly the business of America's academic leaders.[21]

The time may never be more right for schools, colleges, and departments of education to enhance their missions and upgrade their images and aspirations. There may have been no time in their history when so many conditions were favorable, even though other prospects may seem dismal. In the quotation above, President Donald Kennedy of Stanford University reminds academic leaders not only of their responsibilities to schools, which is not unusual, but also to schools of education, which is most unusual. He is joined by President Derek Bok of Harvard[22] and by Chancellor Ira M. Heyman of

Berkeley[23] who independently have made similar commitments. Given such leadership, administrators in many other colleges and universities might well do likewise.

These institutional commitments, in combination with the thrust of the national studies, suggest that the door is ajar; it is time for education units on campuses and the organized profession to pursue new missions. It is not a time for caution or delay; the door of opportunity is not permanently open.

As SCDEs include improving teaching and schools in their missions, the prospects for teacher education brighten. To the extent that they fail to do so, the prospects diminish. An institution that does not have or cannot develop such an objective should be ineligible to serve the profession as a teacher preparing institution. Current evidence indicates that teacher education in many institutions neglects or ignores this function.

In their studies of knowledge production and utilization (KPU), Clark and Guba[24] found that only about 25 percent of some 1,340 SCDEs then engaged in teacher preparation were contributing to knowledge production. The researchers defined KPU broadly to include research and scholarly activity; development, dissemination, and demonstration; *ad hoc* services to schools; and effecting change in schools and other educational agencies.

Their findings, which have been confirmed by Judge,[25] lead to the discouraging conclusion that only about one in four of the institutions preparing teachers is engaged in significant KPU activities and that some of the most prestigious institutions so engaged are involved in activities peripheral to the task of preparing teachers and improving schools. Many of the institutions responsible for graduating the most teachers are doing little to contribute to the knowledge and skills base of the teaching profession. This means that many of the teacher education students are missing the opportunity to experience an inquiry/research environment as they prepare for teaching.

Differentiation of emphasis is to be expected from institution to institution. However, considering the range of functions included in the definition of KPU, the lack of attention to all of these is disturbing when it is found in three out of four institutions.

Professional schools, regardless of which profession, customarily include three major functions in their mission statements: teaching, research, and service. All three of these functions are essential in SCDEs, although variations occur in the relative emphasis of each area from institution to institution.

It is also characteristic of professional schools that they are located on university campuses or in organizational relationships with universities. Because of their specialized nature and the need for universitywide support, professional schools are generally located in relatively large, comprehensive universities, both public and private. Education—as are some other emerging professions such as nursing—is a notable exception. Teacher education is located on the campuses of small as well as large institutions. The demand for teachers and the interest of arts and sciences colleges in teacher education account for the existence of the large number of teacher education programs,

195

for its presence on campuses that do not include other professional schools, and for the difficulty in getting a commitment to extended programs of teacher education.

University Conditions

Since 1976 little progress has been made in improving the situation of teacher education on college or university campuses. However, substantial contributions have been made to the data documenting the conditions previously reported. It appears likely that further studies, especially at the state level, spawned by the national studies will focus more specifically on teacher education.

The Bicentennial Commission called for a longer, more effective teacher education program and for the resources necessary for improving quality. Evidence indicates that teacher education remains the slum of higher education in terms of both resources and status. It is challenged to do much with little and it is perceived as low status regardless of its efforts. It is another instance of blaming the victim.

In their investigation of resources, Peseau and Orr revealed that more is spent each year educating the typical third grader ($1,400) than is spent on a teacher education student who might become the child's fourth grade teacher ($927 average; low of $578). At the same time universities spend a yearly average of $2,363 on their students in undergraduate studies.[26] States continue through their allocation formulas to fund teacher education at the lowest levels. A university funded by a formula system may receive more per credit hour for a teacher education student enrolled in an academic course than it receives for the same student taking an education course; likewise, the university receives less for students in education courses than for students in all the other professional schools.[27] The national studies have not reported these conditions and their possible relation to quality education.

Other data from the 1977 report show that, despite the low level of funding provided teacher education, the programs generated 11 percent of the university's total credit-hour production, but received less than three percent back. Universities allocated from 16 percent to 62 percent less to teacher education programs than those programs generated. This is the continuation of a pattern. Teacher education has long generated funds which are reallocated for use by other university programs.[28]

Such evidence contributes to the perception that decision-making bodies in higher education have little respect for teacher education and a low regard for its importance to the public schools. The national agenda for improving the effectiveness of public schools and for improving the conditions of teaching in them will be frustrated if the administrators who control universities continue to be unwilling to create the circumstances necessary for improved teacher preparation. Almost certainly such improvements will require increased control by state boards of education and the school systems over which they preside.

Failure to adequately finance teacher education also frustrates SCDEs in their efforts to become genuine partners with the practicing profession and the school systems. Failure to fund teacher education for offering inservice and continuing education activities for teachers, or for providing high quality field-based experiences for student teachers, prevents teacher education from fulfilling its mission as a partner of the practicing profession. As a result states are moving increasingly into the areas of helping beginning teachers and providing other inservice programs without the cooperation or involvement of teacher educators in colleges and universities.

Teacher education continues in its perpetual dilemma. Held in low esteem because of its alleged low quality, it cannot gain the necessary allocation of time and resources; without such resources it cannot make the improvements necessary to quality and esteem. It is a you-cannot-get-there-from-here situation, a self-fulfilling prophecy causing everyone to suffer unacceptable consequences.

One of the persistent myths regarding teacher education is that its students spend all or most of their program of studies and time in teacher education courses. The reality is that teacher education students customarily do not even enter teacher education until their junior or third year of study. As indicated earlier, education courses on the average constitute 35 percent of the total four-year program for elementary teachers and 24 percent for secondary teachers.[29]

In principle, teacher educators are not inclined to quarrel over the proportion of arts and sciences courses and education courses in most teacher education programs. Professional educators not only recognize but insist upon the importance of general education and teaching-field arts and sciences courses for teachers. At the same time, professional educators are committed to professional knowledge and skills for classroom teachers. An open dialog between the two college areas will lead to the inevitable conclusion that four years is simply not enough time to learn enough in the necessary content areas. The total program should be increased. Teacher education must work for extended programs of preparation.

We believe no less strongly than we did nine years ago that an extended period offers the best hope for the future.

Data are not readily available regarding the quality of instruction in SCDEs. It is frequently argued that there is superior instruction and more attention to individual students in smaller institutions. This may be true if compared to larger institutions which offer only traditional forms of lecture, discussion, and student teaching. Future teachers, however, will have to be prepared much more extensively and intensively. For extensive purposes the period of preparation will be extended to at least five years plus an internship. For intensive purposes the lecture-discussion-student teaching simplicity will be replaced by a wide variety of higher order instructional strategies and with

197

professional interventions (see Figure 1). Strategies such as the following will be included: large group; seminar; small group; individual; peer; learning resources (including computers); laboratory-simulation; clinical studies; field experiences; internships. In using these strategies teacher education will serve as a *model* for its students and practitioners. Since modeling is a potent instructional strategy, it is essential that it be an integral part of the teacher education process.

The kind of instruction outlined here will undoubtedly require capital outlays, highly qualified teachers with specializations, lower teacher-student ratios, and continuous research and developmental activities. Institutions that cannot provide such facilities and services will have difficulty with accreditation. Affiliations between large and small institutions and linkages with institutions able to provide the technological support may become a necessity for smaller institutions to continue in teacher education. Unless the best interests of the profession take precedence over the preferences of individual institutions, the interest of the public will suffer.

Quality Controls

In the description of the "mediated" condition of the teaching profession, the states were represented as having control over the teaching profession and the schools and of arranging the operation of both for their perceived advantage. This circumstance was viewed as detrimental to the profession and the schools. External control of a profession has the effect of placing the authority of public policy and government ahead of the authority of knowledge and expertise. In the case of the teaching profession, the preparation of teachers is limited and, as a consequence, of low quality. While this provides a supply of inexpensive labor, it also makes it easier to subordinate the teacher to state curricula, testing programs, salary systems, policies, and systems of administration and supervision. Most significantly, it keeps teachers under control and subordinate.

There have been efforts to develop professional control systems for those matters that appropriately belong to the profession. In the early 1970s, the National Education Association (NEA) developed a model professional practices bill. It was designed to assist state affiliates to draft and pass their own bills. The essence of the bill was to declare teaching a profession, to establish a professional practices commission composed of professionals, and to assign to the commission control of teacher education, teacher licensure, and teacher standards and ethics. Although some states passed versions of the bill, the early optimism seems to have faded. Some states seem unready for a high level of professional control, influence, and accountability. It may be that teachers are themselves unready. Long years of having the states and school systems dominate them may have created a deep-seated dependence among teachers. While both major teacher organizations have resisted this dependency, a recent NEA publication, *Excellence in Our Schools: Teacher Education*[30], and resolutions of the American Federation of Teachers reaffirm the interest of the organized profession in governance and direction for teacher education. There has been little change in the basic system of quality control for the teaching profession during the past nine years. The states continue to control teacher education through the use of standards and a process of periodic review. Certificates to teach are issued by a state on recommendation of the teacher preparing institutions. In most states, committees of appointed educators advise the state board and state education agency on matters of policy and practice. Some states have two boards—one of which is responsible for professional practices, while the other is concerned with teacher education and certification. Some states have no advisory boards. The autonomy of these boards varies greatly. It is clear that current practice does not reflect the vision of the original NEA model bill proposed more than a decade ago. Current conditions are also far below the level of autonomy granted to other professions.

At present, except for a major effort by the National Council for Accreditation of Teacher Education (NCATE) and its constituent organizations to revise national accreditation standards and procedures for teacher education, little attention is being given to the development of a comprehensive system of quality controls for teacher education. Most of the effort from other quarters focuses on effects rather than causes. States have turned to mandatory entry-level tests for beginning teachers; at least 34 states have initiated such measures and an additional 10 are considering them. A 1983 Gallup Poll[31] revealed that a majority of parents favor licensure examinations which correspond to state board examinations. A few states are seeking to combine exit examinations administered for initial certification with performance evaluation of the beginning teacher during an internship year.

Folk wisdom holds that "desperate situations require desperate measures." Before taking such steps, however, there should be reason to believe that the measures taken will address the problems. For example, it is important to ensure that entering students have the basic abilities to become quality teachers, and to some extent this can be tested. It is essential also that new teachers have the expected professional knowledge and skills, and to a considerable extent this can be tested or otherwise assessed. The problem is that the common teacher education curricula upon which to base a teacher education board exam do not yet exist. These could be developed, and it is toward this task that a national effort should be directed.

If such efforts were successful, it would be possible to then reconstruct teacher education to deliver the common curriculum with reasonable fidelity and quality. At the same time, it will be necessary for teacher education programs to have a pool of high quality applicants to ensure sufficient numbers of competent teachers for the schools. As the national studies indicate, this requires raising teacher salaries and improving conditions in the schools to attract and retain teachers. No gimmicks and gadgets will get us out of the present crisis—though a little creativity might help. Competitive salaries, supportive working conditions, and preparation programs that are demanding and relevant to classrooms are all needed if our schools are to improve.

Teacher education should exemplify what it explicates. Its processes and procedures must conform to the principles that it espouses. Specifically, the Bicentennial Commission believed that institutional evaluation of potential and performance should occur at the following points: (a) admission to the university, (b) matriculation into the teacher education program, (c) before student teaching, and (d) before entry to the profession but after a period of demonstrated competence in an internship under the supervision of a mentor or a local review board of professional peers in a cooperating teacher center. A license should be awarded only after this period of demonstrated competence.

Each program should have integrity while conforming to national and state standards. Ideally, it should be assessed in terms of the outcomes it generates in those completing the training. In practice, however, the profession will find it necessary to establish program expectations and examine them during accreditation reviews that consider program rationale, resources, and other indicators of quality. In the same way, accreditation can ensure that only capable students have been admitted to the program. Periodic reports and audits may be used for this purpose. Most examinations and other assessments should be adjuncts to instruction and under the control of the institution. The only professional examinations should be those at the state level taken after completion of a program and before continuing licensure. Once admitted to the profession, only due process hearings before a state professional standards or ethics committee should be used to suspend or revoke a teaching license or certificate.

If states want to have professional teachers, they must establish a carefully designed professional system with characteristics similar to those that have proved successful in other professions. To develop the public trust that the profession can be accountable and responsible for its own testing and other forms of quality control, more rigor will have to be introduced into accreditation standards. Further, the use of emergency and transcript review certificates will have to cease. Loopholes that bypass professional program evaluation will continue to undermine the profession. State boards of education and school superintendents should be held accountable, along with teachers and teacher educators, for supporting rigorous, professional entry criteria.

Using the shortage of teachers in certain subject areas as a rationale, state and national groups, task forces on higher education, regional educational boards, state legislatures (e.g., Virginia), and even education departments (e.g., New Jersey) have been advocating that graduates without professional preparation be hired as beginning teachers. More recently a number of the national task forces also have urged such action. It is worth repeating that there is nothing to prevent such persons from serving as resource personnel to regular teachers, but just as other professionals would not tolerate unqualified persons practicing their professions, teachers must not be willing to permit unqualified persons entry into the teaching profession. Such recommendations not only are inconsistent with a professed commitment to quality control but also display an alarming lack of understanding of the knowledge and skills needed by elementary and secondary school teachers. They demean the teaching profession by assuming that, except for knowledge of the subject to be taught, there is nothing to learn about teaching.

Shortages of Qualified Teachers

The shortage of qualified teachers may well be the major educational crisis to emerge since the Bicentennial report was published. Many teachers are leaving the profession. The number of students entering teacher education programs declined precipitously and is just now turning around. A severe teacher shortage is imminent. Projected pupil enrollment increases will exacerbate the problem.

There is some uncertainty about the size and potential impact of the reserve pool of trained but unplaced teachers on this shortage. A *Condition of Education* report[32] projects that in 1985 the supply of new teachers nationwide will fall short of demand. By the late 1980s the shortage may be quite serious. Whether the reserve pool will significantly alleviate this shortage is uncertain.

At the same time, there is substantial evidence that we have fallen short in attracting the best and most capable students into teacher education. Among others, Timothy Weaver noted the persistent and prolonged decline in the quality of the applicant pool for teacher education.[33] He reported that SAT scores of 1980 high school seniors who planned to major in education were 37 points below the national average in math and 34 points below the national average in the verbal component. In the same year (1976), college seniors majoring in education ranked 14th out of the 16 college specialties on verbal measures and next to last on math scores. His subsequent studies show the pattern cited in the 1976 report to be continuing.

The situation is of crisis proportions. Teacher flight and decline in able students preparing to become teachers, combined with a dramatic increase in the number of emergency teacher certificates being issued to unqualified personnel, continue to create a situation that may be disastrous—one sufficiently serious to threaten the intellectual future of the United States. This conclusion is strongly supported in *A Nation At Risk*.

It is clear that low salaries for teachers, coupled with much higher salaries in readily available alternatives to teaching, are major factors that contribute to the crisis in recruitment. Conditions of teaching in schools and teacher stress also prevent successful recruitment of high potential students. The problem cannot be resolved by reverting to the simplistic remedies of earlier periods. Professionalization of teaching on all levels and in all its dimensions is still the basic need and the best hope.

Professional School Status for SCDEs

Closely linked to the necessity of achieving full professional status for teachers is the need for full professional school status for the teacher education units on college and university campuses. This involves recognizing teacher education as the preparation and development arm of the teaching profession. It also involves equating it organizationally with the other professional schools and according to it rights, privileges, responsibilities, and processes that the institution grants to its other professional units. Little progress has been made in this direction since the Bicentennial Commission made its recommendations, despite the positive statements by administrators of several prestigious universities.

The logic of achieving professional school status for teacher education is compelling. Universities have two distinct populations of professors and students: the faculty and students engaged in the studies organized into colleges of arts and sciences and the faculty and students of the professional schools. The academic disciplines are charged to search for truth and to disseminate it through teaching, research, publications, artistic performance, and public service. The primary concern is for the use of knowledge as generator of subsequent knowledge. The professions, on the other hand, share a common commitment to the improvement of practices that serve essential societal needs. Toward these ends, professions seek to find both useful applications of existing knowledge and new forms of knowledge, which may be useful in the future and enhance their capacity to serve society. Students in academic disciplines are urged to continue the search for knowledge as researchers, while students in professional schools are prepared to practice their knowledge and skills in the service of others. *Educating a Profession* stated that these two categories are mutually exclusive only in theory; in practice they overlap. Nevertheless, the academic disciplines and the professional schools do emphasize different values and behavior systems in their respective colleges.

A complication for the members of the teaching profession is that, unlike other professions, they study and practice in both areas. Teachers teach subjects derived from the respective disciplines and study those disciplines in some depth. Teachers also study about teaching and learning *and* how to teach. In the area of pedagogy the teacher is a professional. The knowledge and skills needed for *professional practice* may have some bases in selected academic disciplines.

These are not distinctions without differences. The differences are fundamental and functional. The two kinds of units—one housing academic disciplines, the other professional disciplines—have both developed on university campuses for reasons of mutual advantage and support. Each knows its role and bounds and each allows the other its development. Policy making and governance procedures must take these differences into account.

What is the appropriate place for teacher education, the preparation and development arm of the teaching profession? On many campuses, it is governed and managed according to what it has in common with the traditional academic disciplines rather than to what its role is in relation to the teaching profession. This is, for the teaching profession and for teacher education, a destructive departure from the principle and practice on which both universities and professions operate.

A common criticism of teacher education is that the validated knowledge base of pedagogy is weak. Not just critics and disparagers of professional education have proclaimed such views. At times, teacher education is also discounted by practitioners and education professors. Relationships between teacher behavior and changes in children and youth are, of necessity, loose and hard to document. Weak coupling is a general characteristic of attempts to tie the behavioral sciences to improved practices in all human service areas. Failure to establish such linkages through research, however, should not be cause for premature rejection. Hypotheses should not be discarded because they have not been proven in scientific terms; their use also depends on professional judgment. Laws are better than principles, but principles are not without utility in choosing among practices. Indeed, it is only unpracticed academic disciplines that have the luxury of such unequivocal choices. Professionals have to serve. They cannot withhold their services because they lack absolute certainty. They must do the best that their profession and their judgment allow.

Those who are concerned about the adequacy of the knowledge base for teaching are right in their concerns but often wrong in their conclusions. If professionals withhold their services on the grounds of imperfect knowledge and skill, they might inhibit the very process out of which professionals' knowledge develops.

The past decade has shown great progress in the research validation of teaching practices. The process continues with increasing vigor. It is safe to predict that by the end of this decade skeptics will have difficulty asserting that teaching is not a profession, at least when assessing the substance of its valid knowledge base.

When universities demonstrate their belief that teacher education is an equal partner among the professional schools, it will confirm the profession's faith in itself and its promise. It would also quicken the pace of research and hasten the process of professionalization.

It is a challenge that a nation at risk must accept.

RECOMMENDATIONS

1. **Those who speak for the profession should clarify and emphasize that teachers ask only for the right to control their own profession for the purpose of providing better professional services to the schools and community. The profession remains committed to the principle that the schools and their curricula belong to the public. The profession seeks the improved conditions needed to provide high quality professional**

services in order to help the people realize the aspirations they hold for their children.

2. The teaching profession should renew and strengthen its efforts to markedly improve the quality of teacher preparation and ensure an adequate supply of qualified teachers. In the future, inductees into the profession must know and demonstrate that they have been prepared in programs utilizing the knowledge bases related to effective teaching and effective schools.

3. The teaching profession should continue to make every effort to bring control of the profession under the aegis of professional educators who, as a group, accept responsibility and accountability for its quality.

4. Toward this end, a viable coalition of practicing professional and teacher education organizations should be achieved and enhanced.

5. This coalition should conduct, commission, and encourage studies of the political, bureaucratic, and other controls and influences on the teaching profession and use resulting reports to inform the public and influence public and professional policy making.

6. This coalition should conduct, commission, and encourage studies of the impact of administrative systems that now control teacher education and the teaching profession and make recommendations for improvement.

7. This coalition should conduct, commission, and encourage studies of programs preparing school administrators and make recommendations for ensuring that what administrators learn is consistent with the needs of a professional system.

CATALOG OF SPARE PARTS

James Grier Miller in *Living Systems* quoted George Miller's descriptions of scientific journals as "catalogs of spare parts for machines they never build."[34] The quotation is a remarkably apt description of the status of teacher education and the teaching profession in the 1980s. Scholars, researchers, and creative practitioners have built in a crescendo of effort the catalog or the encyclopedia of knowledge, insights, behaviors, and skills sufficient for a substantial profession of teaching—the machine we never build.

It is tempting to excuse ourselves on the grounds that we all are victims of the mediated system that the states have fashioned and imposed on both the schools and the profession. However, explanations are not excuses. Insights should provide new avenues to action. They also place new responsibilities for renewal of effort and rededication to the cause.

The researchers and developers of our profession do not bear the responsibility for change in practice or in the conditions under which professionals practice. This function resides in the administrators and teacher practitioners in the school workplace, in the teacher preparation workplace, and in the professional organizations. Those who lead teacher education units and professional organizations have major responsibility for change and improvement.

In the years immediately ahead, it will be especially difficult to excuse those who wear the mantle of leadership and responsibility without performing the functions; that is, those who facilitate the production of spare parts but who do not dedicate themselves to building the machine. A fleeting moment of new opportunity seems to be at hand. Following A Nation At Risk and the other national studies will be a relatively short opportunity to be heard and to have teacher education and professionalization agenda considered. It is not a time for endless pondering or for internal quibbling. It is a time for moving forward into whatever breeches are being created. There will be ample time later to improve and refine the changes that have been so long in the making.

COALITIONS

The sheer size and complexity of the teaching profession are both its strength and its weakness. There is power in numbers, but only if the numbers can act together in common cause. Size, combined with the diversity which results from education being a state function, make unified action on educational problems and issues difficult for the teaching profession to achieve. A plethora of organizations exists. The two major teacher organizations— National Education Association and American Federation of Teachers— compete for teacher membership at the national, state, and local levels. AACTE includes the majority of institutions that prepare teachers, but the deans and directors also have formed special-interest organizations on the basis of kind and size of institution. A number of organizations of teacher educators also operate at national, state, and local levels. The list can be expanded almost endlessly. With such a multitude of organizations, the profession and teacher education should be well represented. Unfortunately, differences—probably often unworthy of separate representation—stand in the way of common action. This fractionization reduces the capacity of the profession to effectively address the power relationship problems that stymie professional action. Too many voices carry neither power nor persuasion.

The agenda for the '80s and beyond must be to create the capacity to turn the progress of recent years into achievements. Such progress can be achieved either through unity or through effective coalitions; the latter is a more realistic hope.

A model already exists that can foster interaction and expression. At the instigation of Terrel Bell, then U.S. Commissioner of Education, representatives of 11 educational organizations came together on a regular basis to discuss educational problems and issues. The Forum of Education Organization Leaders works to promote discussion, communication, and understanding within the education community. It has sought to develop common strategies for action at the national level and to prevent inadvertent working at cross purposes and needless confrontation. Representatives of the 11 organizations seek to raise public awareness and engender enlightened public support for solving critical problems confronting elementary and secondary schools. If leaders of the American Federation of Teachers, National Education Association, National Congress of Parents and Teachers, American Association of Colleges for Teacher Education, National Association of State Boards of Education, Council of Chief State School Officers, National School Boards Association, American Association of School Administrators, Education Commission of the States, National Association of Elementary School Principals, and National Association of Secondary School Principals can meet together at the national level in order to explore areas of cooperation, it should be possible for local and state groups to do the same.

Also needed at this time is an extension of these collaborative practices in the area of policy making and active intervention in influencing public opinion and public policy. Only in this way can the growing collection of spare parts be turned into the effective profession that educators and our society so desperately need.

It is time for intolerance of inaction. If we fail to act, we deserve the consequences, but the society does not. We owe the profession and those we serve our best efforts.

FOOTNOTES

1. "Survey of Teacher Education: Perceptions of Methods for Improvement," *Bulletin of the National Center for Education Statistics* (October 1983), pp. 1-2,4.
2. National Commission on Excellence in Education, *A Nation At Risk: The Imperative for Educational Reform* (Washington, D.C.: U.S. Government Printing Office, April 1983), p. 5.
3. Ibid., p. 22.
4. *Educating Americans for the 21st Century: A plan of action for improving mathematics, science, and technology education for all American elementary and secondary students so that their achievement is the best in the world by 1995*, A Report to the American People and the National Science Board (Washington, D.C.: National Science Foundation, 1983), p. 31.
5. Ernest L. Boyer, *High School: A Report on Secondary Education in America*, The Carnegie Foundation for the Advancement of Teaching (New York: Harper & Row, 1983), p. 175.
6. National Commission on Excellence, *A Nation At Risk*, p. 36.
7. Terence J. Johnson, *Professions and Power* (London: Macmillan Press Ltd.), 1972.
8. Ibid., p. 41.
9. Ibid., p. 35.
10. Ibid., p. 65.
11. Ibid., p. 77.
12. Harry Judge, *American Graduate Schools of Education: A View from Abroad*, A Report to the Ford Foundation (New York: The Ford Foundation, 1982), p. 30.

13. Senate Bill 903, 66th Texas Legislature, 1979.

14. Arthur Kratzmann, Timothy C. Byrne, and Walter H. Worth, *A System in Conflict: A Report to the Minister of Labour by the Fact Finding Commission* (Edmonton, Alberta, Canada: Province of Alberta, 1980), p. 96.

15. *Handbook of the Florida Performance Measurement System* (Tallahassee: Florida Beginning Teacher Program, Office of Teacher Education, Certification, and Inservice Staff Development, 1982).

16. Tommy M. Tomlinson, "Effective Schools: Mirror or Mirage," *Today's Education* 70, No. 2 (April/May 1981): 60-3.

17. Robert F. Peck and Donald J. Veldman, "Personal Characteristics Associated with Effective Teaching" (Austin, Tex., The Research and Development Center for Teacher Education, The University of Texas at Austin, 1973), pp. 7-8.

18. Jere E. Brophy and Carolyn M. Evertson, *Learning from Teachers: A Developmental Perspective* (Boston: Allyn and Bacon, 1976), p. 139.

19. Gary E. Schwartz, "Behavioral Medicine and Systems Theory: A New Synthesis," *National Forum*, Winter 1980, pp. 25-30. Draws on James Grier Miller, *Living Systems* (New York: McGraw-Hill, 1978).

20. Stanley M. Elam, "The Gallup Education Surveys: Impressions of a Poll Watcher," *Phi Delta Kappan* 65, No. 1 (September 1983): 32.

21. Donald Kennedy, President, Stanford University, "Advancing Knowledge," Paper presented to the 75th Anniversary Colloquium of the Carnegie Foundation for the Advancement of Teaching, 23 November 1981, pp. 11-14.

22. Derek Bok, President, Harvard University, Commencement Address, Cambridge, Mass., 9 June 1983.

23. Ira M. Heyman, Chancellor, University of California-Berkeley, Memorandum re: School of Education, 13 January 1982.

24. David L. Clark and Egon G. Guba, *The Role of Higher Education in Educational Knowledge Production and Utilization*, The Deans' Network Issue Paper No. 1 (Evanston, Ill.: School of Education, Northwestern University, 1977).

25. Judge, *American Graduate Schools of Education*, p. 30.

26. Bruce Peseau and Paul Orr, "The Outrageous Underfunding of Teacher Education," *Phi Delta Kappan* 62, No. 2 (October 1980): 102.

27. Bruce Peseau and Paul Orr, "An Academic and Financial Study of Teacher Education Programs Through the Doctoral Level in Public State Universities and Land-Grant Colleges" (University, Ala.: College of Education, University of Alabama, 1979), Appendix C.

28. Ibid., p. 44.

29. "Survey of Teacher Education," *Bulletin of the National Center for Education Statistics*, p. 5.

30. *Excellence in Our Schools: Teacher Education, An Action Plan* (Washington, D.C.: National Education Association, 1982).

31. Elam, "The Gallup Education Surveys," p. 27.

32. Valena White Plisko, ed., *The Condition of Education, 1983 Edition, Statistical Report*, National Center for Education Statistics (Washington, D.C.: U.S. Government Printing Office, 1983).

33. W. Timothy Weaver, "Demography, Quality and Decline: The Challenge for Schools of Education in the 1980s," *Policy for the Education of Educators: Issues and Implications*, ed. Georgiana Appignani (Washington, D.C.: AACTE, 1981), pp. 50-65.

34. Schwartz, "Behavioral Medicine and Systems Theory," p. 5.

BIBLIOGRAPHY

Bok, D. President, Harvard University, Commencement Address, Cambridge, Mass., 9 June 1983. (mimeographed)

Boyer, E.L. *High School: A Report on Secondary Education in America*, The Carnegie Foundation for the Advancement of Teaching. New York: Harper & Row, 1983.

Brophy, J. E., and Evertson, C. M. *Learning from Teaching: A Developmental Perspective*. Boston: Allyn and Bacon, 1976.

Clark, D.L., and Guba, E.G. *The Role of Higher Education in Educational Knowledge Production and Utilization*, The Deans' Network, Issue Paper No. 1. Evanston, Ill.: School of Education, Northwestern University, 1977.

Educating Americans for the 21st Century: A plan of action for improving mathematics, science, and technology education for all American elementary and secondary students so that their achievement is the best in the world by 1995, A Report to the American People and the National Science Board. Washington, D.C.: National Science Foundation, 1983.

Elam, S.M. "The Gallup Education Surveys: Impressions of a Poll Watcher." *Phi Delta Kappan* 65, No. 1 (September 1983): 26-32.

Excellence in Our Schools: Teacher Education, An Action Plan. Washington, D.C.: National Education Association, 1982.

Handbook of the Florida Performance Measurement System. Tallahassee: Florida Beginning Teacher Program, Office of Teacher Education, Certification, and Inservice Staff Development, 1982.

Heyman, I.M. Chancellor, University of California-Berkeley. Memorandum re: School of Education. 13 January 1982.

Johnson, T.J. *Professions and Power*. London: Macmillan Press Ltd., 1972.

Judge, H. *American Graduate Schools of Education: A View from Abroad*, A Report to the Ford Foundation. New York: The Ford Foundation, 1982.

Kennedy, D. President, Stanford University, *Advancing Knowledge*. Paper presented to the 75th Anniversary Colloquium of the Carnegie Foundation for the Advancement of Teaching, 23 November 1981.

Kratzmann, A., Byrne, T.C., and Worth, W.H. *A System in Conflict*: A Report to the Minister of Labour by the Fact Finding Commission. Edmonton, Alberta, Canada: Province of Alberta, 1980.

National Commission on Excellence in Education. *A Nation At Risk: The Imperative for Educational Reform*. Washington, D.C.: U.S. Government Printing Office, April 1983.

Peck, R.F., and Veldman, D.J. "Personal Characteristics Associated with Effective Teaching." Austin, Texas: The Research and Development Center for Teacher Education, The University of Texas at Austin, 1973.

Peseau, B., and Orr, P. "An Academic and Financial Study of Teacher Education Programs Through the Doctoral Level in Public State Universities and Land-Grant Colleges." University, Ala.: University of Alabama, College of Education, 1979.

Peseau, B., and Orr, P. "The Outrageous Underfunding of Teacher Education." *Phi Delta Kappan* 62, No. 2 (October 1980): 100-02.

Plisko, V.W. *The Condition of Education, 1983 Edition, Statistical Report*, National Center for Education Statistics. Washington, D.C.: U.S. Government Printing Office, 1983.

Schwartz, G.E. "Behavioral Medicine and Systems Theory: A New Synthesis." *National Forum* (Winter 1980): 25-30. Draws on James Grier Miller, *Living Systems*. New York: McGraw-Hill, 1978.

Senate Bill 903, 66th Texas Legislature, 1979.

"Survey of Teacher Education: Perceptions of Methods for Improvement." *Bulletin of the National Center for Education Statistics*, October 1983.

Tomlinson, T.M. "Effective Schools: Mirror or Mirage." *Today's Education* 70, No. 2 (April-May 1981): 60-3.

Weaver, W.T. "Demography, Quality and Decline: The Challenge for Schools of Education in the 1980s." In *Policies for the Education of Educators: Issues and Implications*, edited by G. Appignani. Washington, D.C.: American Association of Colleges for Teacher Education, 1981.